EARTH*flight*

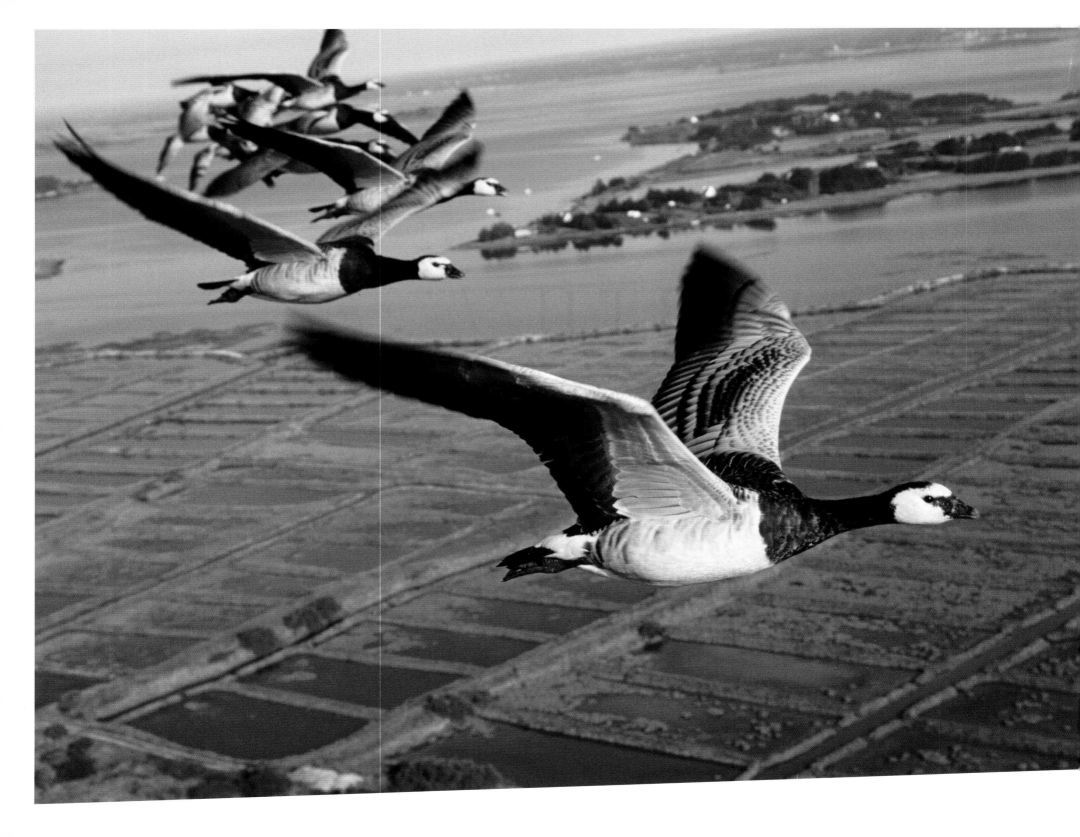

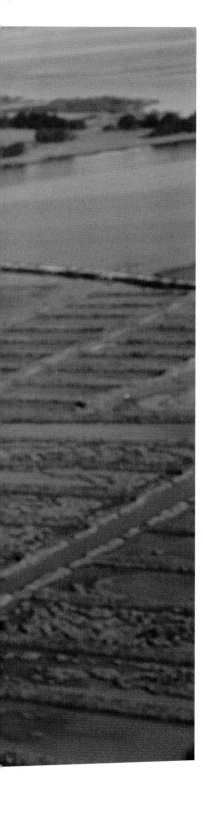

EARTH*flight*

John Downer

BOOKS

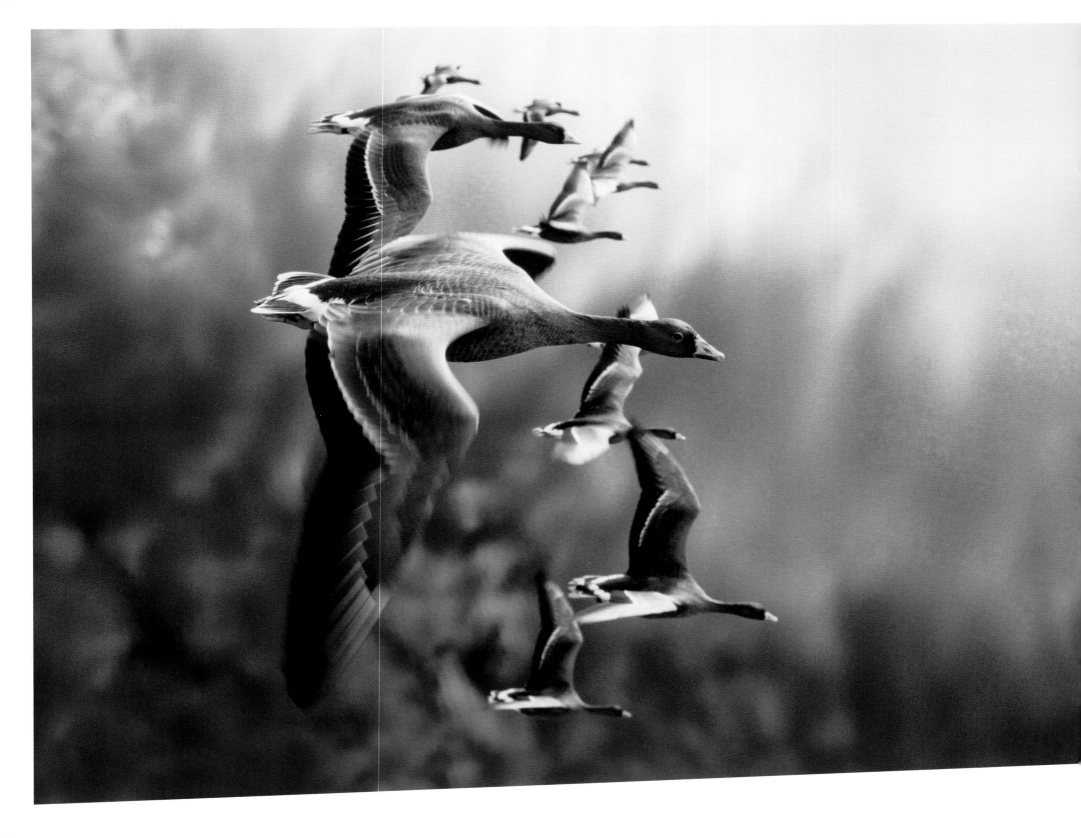

Contents

Introduction

ONE OF THE MOST COMMON of all dreams is to fly like a bird; the thought is both exhilarating and liberating. In fact, the whole idea has come to symbolise freedom, such is the admiration we have for a creature that is not bound by gravity, walls, country borders or even continents. For me, flight has been a personal obsession for as long as I can remember, and I have been fortunate enough to come close to fulfilling this dream through the BBC series *Earthflight*.

Earthflight is a journey like no other – a guided tour of the world through the eyes of birds. Whether sailing high above the Serengeti on the backs of vultures or skimming the surface of San Francisco Bay with a flock of pelicans, filming the series allowed me to take part in the miracle of flight, and capture a view of the world in a new and unique way. This book showcases many of the most spectacular images taken in the course of making the programmes.

But the realisation of this dream didn't take place overnight, and before we were able to film a single frame we had a major challenge to face – how to find ways of entering the birds' world. As it turned out, the solution to this problem lay with one of the earliest films I ever made.

Over twenty-five years ago, I started working for the BBC Natural History Unit as a rookie director on a series called *Wildlife on One*. To my great excitement, I was commissioned to make a programme called *In-flight Movie* about the wonders of bird flight. My immediate aspiration was to make the programme different from films of flying birds that had been shot before. I started to investigate how that could be achieved.

At that time, as it still is today, the most important piece of equipment in a wildlife cameraman's armoury was the long lens. This allows stunning close-ups of subjects to be shot from a great distance but it has one big disadvantage: although the images fill the frame they still feel distant. This is because they have a narrow depth of focus and show little of the animal's surroundings. These effects are totally alien to the way our eyes perceive the world, as we are used to experiencing a wide-angle view with everything in sharp focus. By the time I was ready to make my first film on flying birds, I had become intrigued by a new visual style based on breaking the dominance of the long lens.

In making other films, I had already experimented with using remote-controlled cameras equipped with wide-angle lenses that enabled me to capture footage from closer to wild animals than ever before. I loved the sense they gave of 'being in the animal's world'. I was surprised, however, to discover that something I considered so wonderful seemed somewhat contentious. Many well-established wildlife filmmakers of the day thought that these images were inappropriate and distracting, even unnatural. What I sensed from the shots was the complete opposite – a breathtaking feeling of immersion in the animal world. I soon became fixated with capturing that viewpoint. But now I was about to

Red-breasted goose, Romania
These geese set out from wintering sites in southeast Europe and migrate through Kazakhstan and Russia to their Siberian Arctic breeding grounds, where they often nest near birds of prey as protection from Arctic foxes.

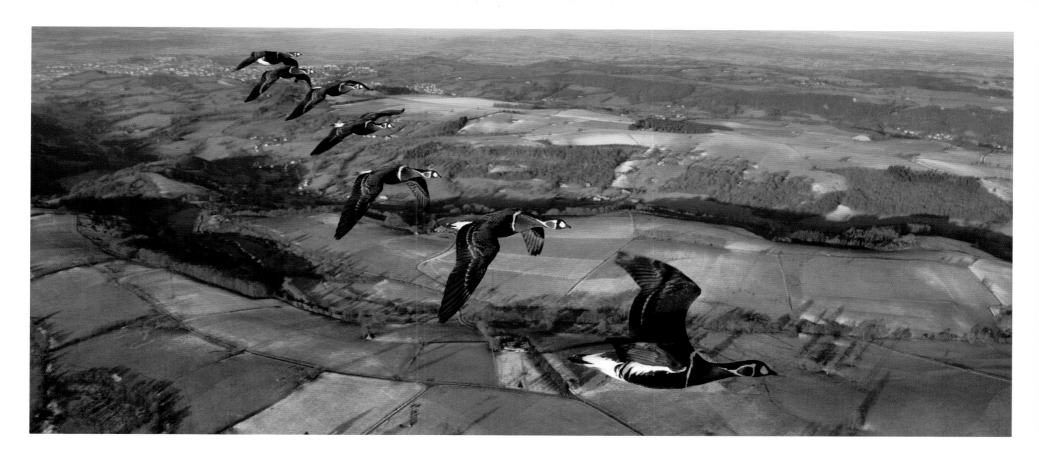

make a film on flying birds, had I shot myself in the foot? How could I get the kind of immersive images I liked so much on a subject that was not only elusive but inhabited a very different world than ours – the skies?

The techniques I developed in the 1980s to solve that challenge were to form the basis of *Earthflight* many years later. Since those early days, a revolution in camera technology has allowed far more possibilities than I could have dreamed of then. However, in many ways, the fundamentals of successfully entering the avian world remain the same – an empathy with the birds and an intimate understanding of their behaviour.

One of the most important techniques used in *Earthflight* is 'imprinting'. This is the phenomenon where, on hatching, certain species of bird regard the first moving thing they see as their mother. Once the bond has been forged, they will follow their surrogate parent anywhere, a behaviour that continues long after the young have fledged. This means that the chosen parent must be present the moment the eggs hatch. Filming is then relatively easy – the birds' foster parent simply needs to climb aboard a filming vehicle and the birds will fly alongside as though following their natural parent into the air. In this way it becomes possible to capture shots that give the sensation of being part of the flock.

This idea was in its infancy when I made my first film on bird flight and until then it had only been tried on geese. No one had attempted to use any other species and no one had ever filmed them from the air. This was all to change when I acquired a type of duck known as a green-winged teal.

My original plan was to have the bird reared by a willing and dedicated cameraman but, on the journey to his home, the egg hatched prematurely in my lap. Soon the duckling was chirruping merrily away at me and by the time I reached my destination the duckling had become firmly imprinted – on me! If she were placed on the floor she would run up to my feet. If I moved away she followed behind like a clockwork toy. In fact, I could not go anywhere without this animated ball of fluff running behind me. There was no possibility of transferring parental responsibility to another person so for the next six months I became her surrogate mother. Wherever I went and whatever I did the duck kept me company. In the car, she would sit beside me in the passenger seat. In the office, she would sit on my head while I tried to make telephone calls. In the evening, as I relaxed in front of the television, she would snuggle up to my feet. We would even go out to dinner parties together. By the time she was fledged and ready to be filmed, she was an integral part of my family. Most importantly, from the point of view of filming her in flight, she would come to me whenever I called.

My dream was to film her from the air, but in those days a lack of suitable technology meant that the options were limited. I had no qualifications to fly a microlight or similar craft and two-seater versions were simply too fast for a bird to fly alongside, but I had heard about a new invention called a 'parascender' and could see a potential solution. The basic idea was simple but utterly terrifying: a parachute would be strapped to my back and I would be towed into the air by a vehicle travelling along the ground at high speed. My job was to keep running until the moment of liftoff.

It was with some trepidation that my duck and I found ourselves in a field in the Brecon Beacons in Wales ready for our maiden flight. I solved the problem of taking the duck up with me by placing her in a shoebox fastened to my belt but for everything else I had to put my complete trust in the experts running the show. The parachute was soon stretched out behind me and the towing car quickly accelerated away. Sure enough, before I knew it, both my duck and I were 60 metres (200 feet) in the air. With no time to consider the consequences, I took my duck from the shoebox and carefully released her into the freedom of the open skies.

The plan was for her to fly alongside me but, unfortunately, she hadn't read the script. To my horror, she plummeted like a stone towards the ground. Then thankfully, at an altitude of 15 metres (50 feet), she suddenly remembered she had wings and began to flap like mad. Any momentary elation soon turned to despair as the duck made a beeline for the far horizon. I called after this rapidly vanishing speck but it seemed as if I was whistling in the wind. Six months of preparation seemed to have gone to waste until, suddenly, a miracle – the speck started to get bigger and bigger. In no time at all she was flying beside me as though it was the most natural thing in the world. I flicked the camera switch and captured the wonderful moment on film. The footage was priceless, all shot with a wide-angle lens just inches from the flying bird.

The experience has lived with me forever and was at the forefront of my mind when I decided to embark on *Earthflight*. Fortunately, since those early days, the techniques I experimented with then have also been developed and used by others, so it was possible to get off to a very good start.

My encounter with one of these contemporary bird-flying aeronauts could hardly have been more extraordinary. By chance, I was visiting the Bath and West agricultural show when my 8-year-old son, Rory, implored me to take him on a giant fairground ride – an instrument of torture consisting of some flimsy seats attached to a 15-metre (50-foot) rotor that whirred around at terrifying speed. Predictably, the next five minutes were to be among the most vomit-inducing of my life but, at the height of my nausea and while in full 360-degree rotation, I glimpsed what I thought was an apparition – a microlight flying over the

showground with several common cranes flying in close formation beside it. The pilot was Christian Moullec, an extraordinary Frenchman who had literally taken the idea of flying with birds to new heights. At various public events like this he occasionally put on shows that featured birds flying alongside his microlight. By pure chance this was one of those special occasions.

Christian and other dedicated individuals like him were to make an important contribution to *Earthflight*. They took their imprinted birds into the air over landscapes in a way that I could previously only dream of. They flew their flocks of geese and cranes over some of the most iconic cities and spectacular natural locations in the world and were responsible for many of the air-to-air shots seen in the series and in this book. Having had such an early experience with the intensive process of imprinting birds I fully understand and marvel at the dedication of these remarkable individuals.

Bird-imprinting was not the only technique developed for *In-flight Movie* and used in *Earthflight*. Another early dream was for the birds themselves to become part of the production team and carry a camera into the air to capture their unique viewpoint of the world. This required a tiny camera and a specially designed harness. At that time, the only movie camera small enough to consider was something called Super 8. This amateur camera, found in homes up and down the country, used a plastic cartridge containing a strip of film hardly wider than a bootlace. With the help of a bemused BBC technician, I stripped the camera down to the point that it was little more than a lens, a motor and the film cartridge. By then, it weighed just a few grams and could conceivably be carried by a large bird with no ill effects on its ability to fly.

A buzzard was nominated to become the world's first avian cinematographer, and to avoid causing any stress to the bird I chose a falconry buzzard that was used to being handled. The camera was placed on a harness on its back ready to capture a viewpoint that would take in not only the bird's head but also the landscape stretching out below. The first shoot was over the rolling hills of the Devonshire countryside, and I watched nervously as the bird was cast into the air carrying the added load of its precious cargo. I need not have worried – wind hitting the hillside gave the bird enough uplift to allow it to soar effortlessly upwards.

Although the flight looked promising, it would be a long time before I could confirm that the idea had actually worked. In those days, Super 8 cartridges had to be sent away for development along with thousands of holidaymakers' films. There was no special treatment, no rushed delivery for my in-flight experiment, so it was a full two weeks later that I was able to lace up a home projector. I watched in astonishment as the first moving pictures taken by a bird flickered on the screen in front of me. It was a seminal moment and one I've never forgotten – mesmeric and exhilarating, like the view from a fighter pilot's cockpit.

When I started making *Earthflight*, I knew that 'birdcams', as they came to be called, had to be one of the techniques we should return to. The contemporary challenge was to create footage in High Definition (HD), instead of the grainy images of my early endeavours, and to capture sustained shots that allowed the viewer to relish the unique experience. Fortunately, several new tiny cameras had been developed that could be modified for the purpose. It even became possible to use a tiny pan-and-tilt system on some of the larger birds,

allowing us to change the viewpoint in the air. Besides giving us an astonishing new viewpoint, this technique also proved a fascinating insight into the minute details of winged flight – the subtle way the birds' wings moved as they moved through the air, for example, was mesmerising to see in such detail.

In-flight Movie was also my first foray into the use of remote flying devices. It was the first time anyone had tried to put a movie camera into a model helicopter but in those early days it was really a work in progress and a risky one at that. For every successful test flight a spectacular crash seemed to follow, with rotor blades spinning in every direction. But the possibilities it offered made me persevere and I've used some kind of remote helicopter on almost every production since, though I can't count the number of model aircraft lost in the process. However, the ones we used in *Earthflight* were of a different breed altogether. They were totally reliable and capable of an uncanny ability to fly themselves, just like military drones.

In-flight Movie also pioneered the use of remote-controlled gliders and I even used one shaped like a bird to film storks migrating over Istanbul. The shots from inside the flock were so spectacular I was determined to repeat the idea in *Earthflight*. This time we used a remote-controlled glider built to resemble a vulture in order to film live vultures from the air. Technological developments even allowed this version of a flying bird to have an adjustable tail, just like a real bird's tail, allowing a far more convincing model to be made, and getting us closer to the action than ever before.

It is by harnessing the potential of such new technology that *Earthflight* was able to take us on a journey across

the world, exploring the natural events and physical features that define each continent. Central to this concept is the idea of specific birds that act as personalised 'guides' to each area that we filmed – charismatic species that are associated with each continent as a whole. So, for example, we are guided across the African landscape by the flamingo and the vulture, or are taken over the sights of Europe by the common crane and the barnacle goose. Using their local expertise, honed over thousands of years, we see the world through their eyes and on the way discover the greatest spectacles that exist in nature.

Thus we are able to witness how vultures track the great wildebeest migration in the Serengeti as they watch the life-and-death dramas that play out below, ready to swoop down to share in the spoils. In a similar way, we see Andean condors soar over the breeding beaches of sea lions, waiting for any casualties caught in the crossfire as fighting bulls collide.

At times, we followed more localised bird guides – species that have a particular connection to a certain area, and offer us a more detailed view of life in that region. So, on the Great Plains of North America, we watch as cowbirds shadow bison herds to feed on the insects disturbed by their hooves. In India, pigeons enter a rat temple to steal offerings left for the revered rodent inhabitants and in Peru, parrots arrive at muddy mineral-rich pools to compete for health supplements with the jungle mammals that gather there for the same reason.

As well as being a part of local ecosystems like this, birds can, of course, take us on much wider journeys – they are not neatly constrained by human boundaries, and

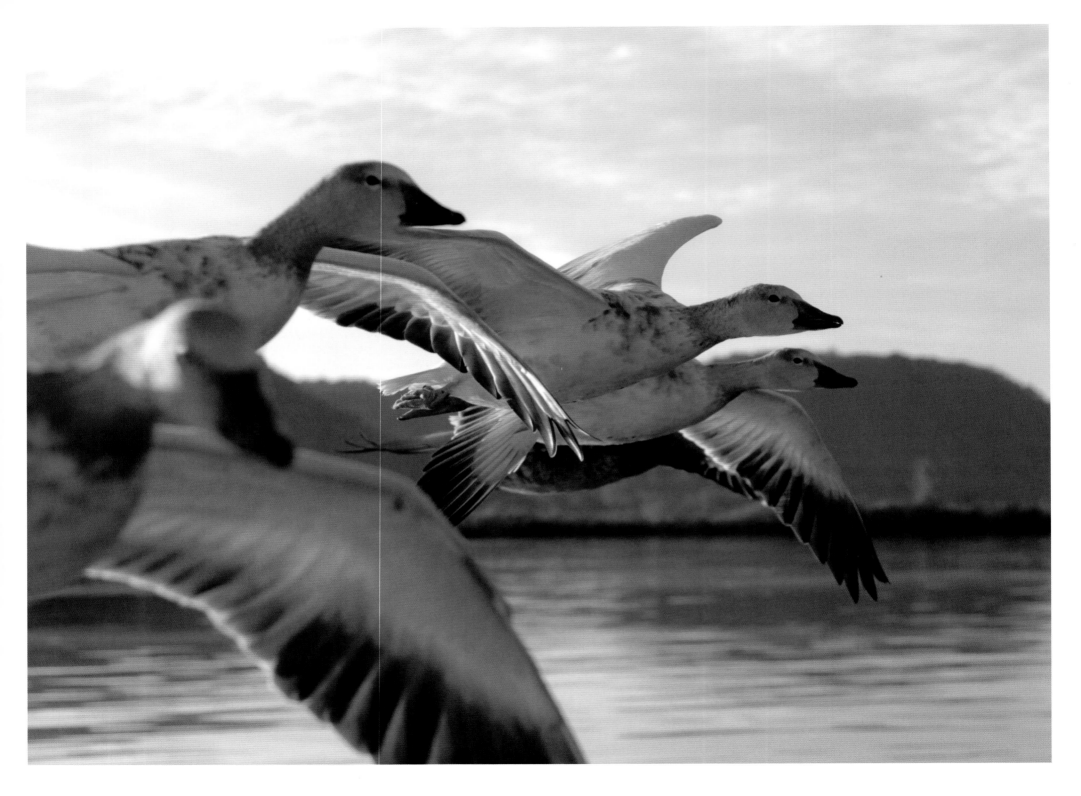

many travel from one continent to another in the course of their migrations. Swallows that overwinter in huge concentrations in South Africa are soon flitting over the barns and farmyards of the English countryside – a journey of nearly 10,000 km (6,200 miles) accomplished in just four weeks. But the greatest avian traveller, the Arctic tern, is even more extraordinary; its journey takes it from the high Arctic, where it breeds in the summer, to Antarctica where it overwinters later in the year. Furthermore, it does not even make this incredible journey directly. Scientists have discovered that, as it travels south, the Arctic tern takes a different route to the one it travels on its return trip. In fact, its flight takes in five continents and in all it travels 80,000 km (50,000 miles) in the course of a single year. Through incredible flights like these, birds unite the world.

I firmly believe that all the best wildlife films are written by their subjects, and the job of a director is to unravel the story that is there for the telling. It is vital to set off with a clear idea of what you are trying to achieve, but at every stage in the process you must be alert to the true story that lies beneath any preconceived notions and be prepared to adapt your ideas to fit the natural dramas that unfold. More than any other film, the *Earthflight* series grew out of this philosophy, and the finished films have become something I could not have fully envisaged at the beginning.

In every area, pioneering new technology allowed the series to explore the world of flying birds in a way that was not possible in the early days. But because *Earthflight* allowed us to enter the bird's world so spectacularly, it also suggested a shift in the way we told our story. As anticipated, our subjects soon began to guide the storytelling.

Once we started to consider how the birds themselves experienced the world around them, they began to show us another view of natural events. It rapidly became clear that the birds attending different wildlife spectacles often knew more about animal behaviour than any human expert. It was apparent that the birds had to understand the actions and habits of other animals to capitalise on the opportunities that these actions created. It seemed, in fact, that the birds were expert animal behaviouralists.

We first began to understand the significance of the birds' extraordinary knowledge when, in Mexico, we set out to film brown pelicans feasting on fish known as grunion. These unusual fish exhibit bizarre behaviour where, on the high spring tides, they deliberately strand themselves ashore to mate and lay their eggs at the high water mark. This bizarre strategy has a purpose – it keeps their developing eggs safe from the predatory jaws of fish. On the next wave they disappear back in the ocean before another battalion of breeding fish arrives to repeat the process. We knew that pelicans were one of their main predators, but had yet to discover that they held the key to finding the event's secret location. The spectacle was over in a flash and could take place in any spot along miles of featureless beach – a real nightmare to film. But it soon became apparent from the hundreds of pelicans streaming purposely along the shoreline that they knew exactly where the grunion were massing. Finding the location involved us in a madcap chase along the beach following the birds but they unerringly guided the crew to the heart of the action.

Likewise, in South Carolina, dolphins that use an ingenious technique of driving fish ashore in order to scoop them up with ease had an attendant posse of opportunist egrets and herons. These birds survive by stealing fish from under the dolphins' noses and, as a consequence, they can predict the behaviour of their specialist subject more reliably than any human.

We soon discovered that insights like these, that came directly from the knowledge of the birds themselves, were a feature of almost every event we covered. In South Africa, kelp gulls follow seals as they swim out to sea knowing that great white sharks are waiting to toss these hapless victims into the air like beach balls. Likewise, gannets are experts on the famous South African sardine run, studying and following the whales, dolphins and sharks that feed on this huge migration of fish. By following the animals and anticipating their behaviour in this way, the birds are able to share in the spoils of the hunt – and also to guide the film team right to the heart of the action.

As we started to discover these relationships the series became something that I could never have foreseen. Along with the technological capability to enter the birds' world came the ability to view familiar wildlife events from an entirely new perspective. We had gained a way of understanding nature by seeing it as birds do. This thought was tremendously exciting as it seemed so natural and ultimately so obvious: nothing in nature happens on its own, all life is entwined and animals have to understand each other in order to survive. The birds, whose world we set out to enter, were now not simply guiding the script, they were showing us a way of seeing nature with fresh eyes. It has been our aim to depict this unique viewpoint, not only within the series but also with this book.

JOHN DOWNER

EUROPE

Europe is like a great railway junction, where bird migration routes converge from all points of the compass. From the long northward flight path of the common crane to the transatlantic migration of brent geese, the skies over Europe are alive with activity.

Travelling vast distances, birds descend on Europe from across the world – some coming to see out the winter on the continent, others simply completing one leg of a much longer journey. Covering such distances, though, can be a struggle. Larger birds such as common cranes and white storks aren't built to simply flap their way across the globe and so they soar on rising columns of hot air, known as thermals. They spiral upwards and then glide, losing height as they go, until they reach the next thermal and then do it all over again. Thermals do not form over the sea, so storks and buzzards find the shortest routes across the Mediterranean, such as the Strait of Gibraltar. They rise on thermals in Morocco and then glide to the Mediterranean's northern shore.

This isn't to say that all large birds employ exactly the same techniques when riding these thermals; while storks gather in large groups at Mediterranean crossing points, common cranes from North Africa tend to fly on a broader front, often in family parties. They like to soar, but over water they struggle and many perish in bad weather, unable to find a column of hot air that will give them the altitude that they need. However, a single, small island is sufficient to provide the thermals that will help them gain height, and so many birds simply hop from island to island until they successfully reach the safety of the mainland.

Some cranes remain in Europe throughout the winter, but they still cross the entire continent each spring and autumn. One population winters in Spain, but travels to Scandinavia in a series of hops that takes it from one wetland to the next through France and Germany.

Although these larger birds glide their way across the continent, this soaring technique doesn't work for smaller species of bird, which must rely on wing power alone. For one such species, the journey starts half a world away at Mount Moreland in South Africa, where up to five million swallows gather in huge roosts before their long journey to Europe. The birds travel 300 km (185 miles) during the day, keeping low to the ground – unlike the many songbirds that travel at night and at high altitudes, where there's less turbulence to throw them off course. Trips such as this can take up to three weeks, meaning that small birds need frequent refuelling stops in order to sustain their exhausting flight.

This story of migration is the same all over Europe. In spring, birds are on the move in a frantic rush to be the earliest arrivals at often remote breeding sites scattered across the continent. In the British Isles, gannets arrive in Scotland from West Africa, gathering en masse at Bass Rock to feed. At the same time, swans and geese are leaving for the Arctic. Unlike soaring birds such as cranes and storks, which have a free ride on hot currents of air, swans and geese must use powered flight to reach their destinations, and so they stock up on food to put on fat before their journey. Brent geese, for example, travelling between winter sites in Ireland and breeding sites in the Canadian Arctic, increase their weight by 40 per cent before embarking on their flight.

All these transcontinental travellers are also accomplished navigators, and use many cues to find their way – the position of the sun, moon and stars, polarised light from the setting sun, low-frequency sounds, local landmarks and the Earth's geomagnetic field. Recent research indicates they actually 'see' the magnetic field and their path through it.

It means birds like the barnacle goose can navigate accurately from their winter quarters in the Solway Firth on Scotland's east coast to remote islands in the Svalbard Archipelago, far north of Norway. Here, global warming is having an unexpected impact. More ice-free days in summer mean that hungry polar bears are searching for new sources of food. Now, they raid geese nests and eat the eggs, threatening the very existence of the Solway Firth population – just one example of how changing conditions in one area of the world can greatly affect the lives of birds thousands of miles away.

FLIGHT PATHS / LOCATIONS
FEATURED IN THE BOOK

COMMON CRANE
Camargue, France to Wieringerwerf, the Netherlands

BARNACLE GOOSE
Edinburgh, Scotland to Svalbard, Norway

STARLING
Rome, Italy

GREYLAG GOOSE
Millau, France

BRENT GOOSE
Normandy, France

BARN SWALLOW
Somerset, England

SAND MARTIN
Tisza River, Hungary

ARCTIC TERN
Svalbard, Norway

Svalbard

Bass Rock

Edinburgh

Wieringerwerf

Somerset

Normandy

Tisza River

Millau

Camargue

Rome

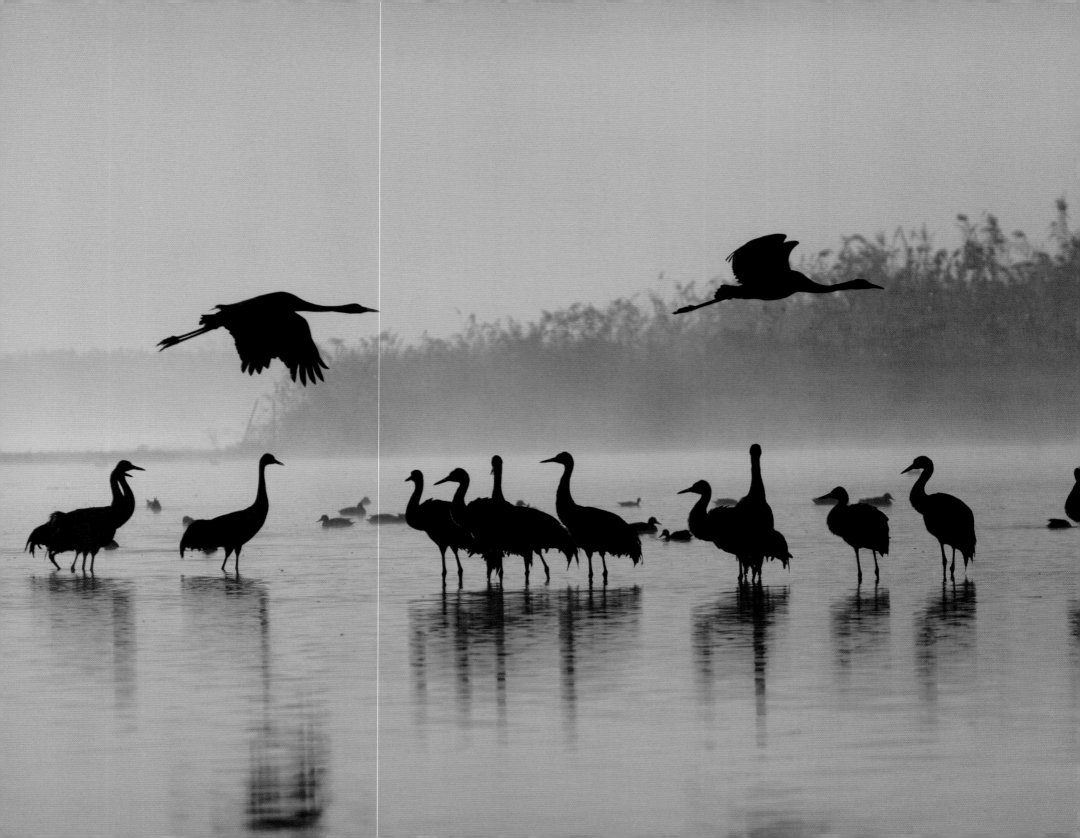

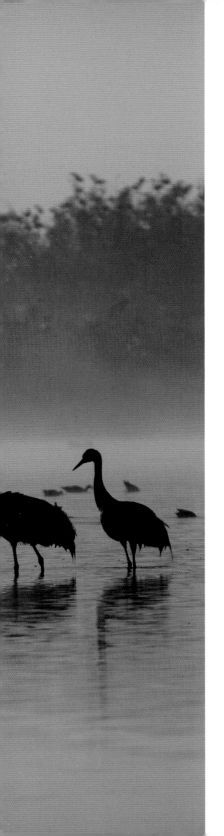

COMMON CRANE, southern marshlands, France
Each spring, cranes pause on their epic migration to
nesting sites in northern Europe and gather in wetlands
to refuel. The next leg of the journey will take them north
over central Europe.

COMMON CRANE, Auvergne, France
Flying at 40–80 kph (25–50 mph) and at an altitude
of 200–1,500 m (650–5,000 ft), a flock can cross France
in a day if wind and weather conditions are right, but
more usually they stop off at traditional staging sites
along the route.

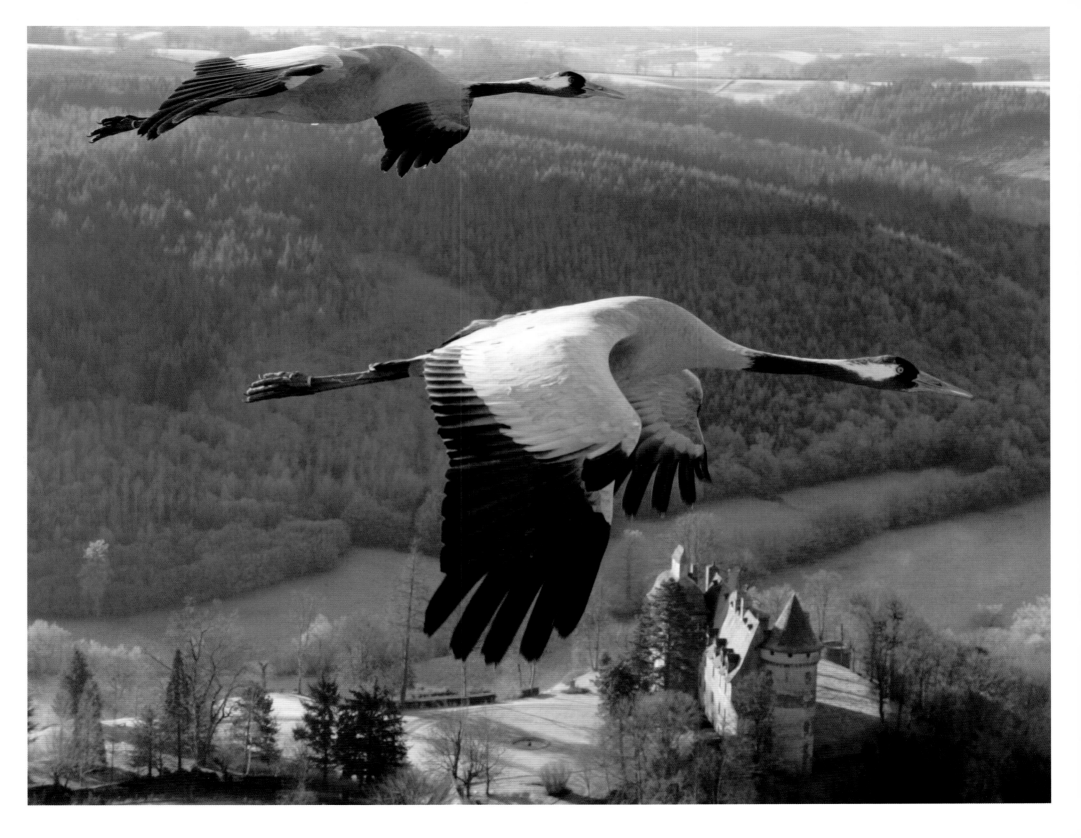

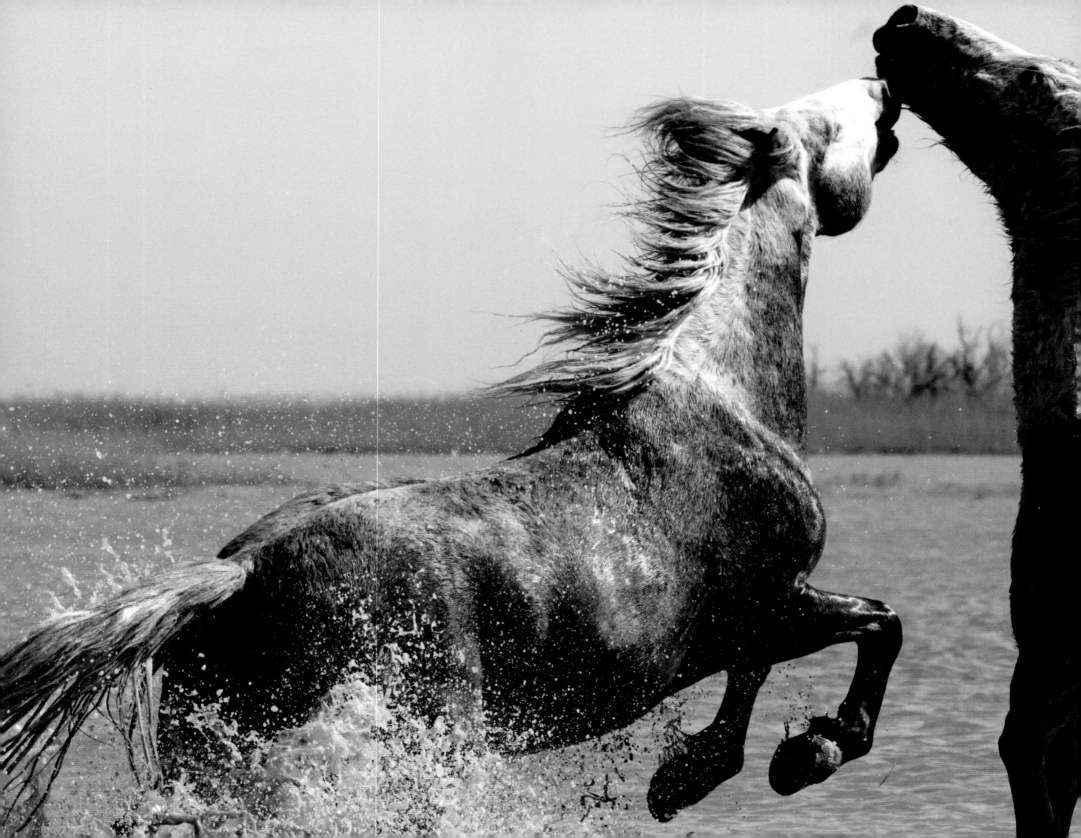

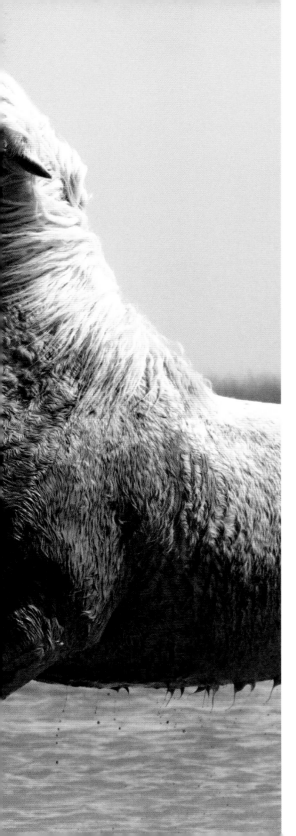

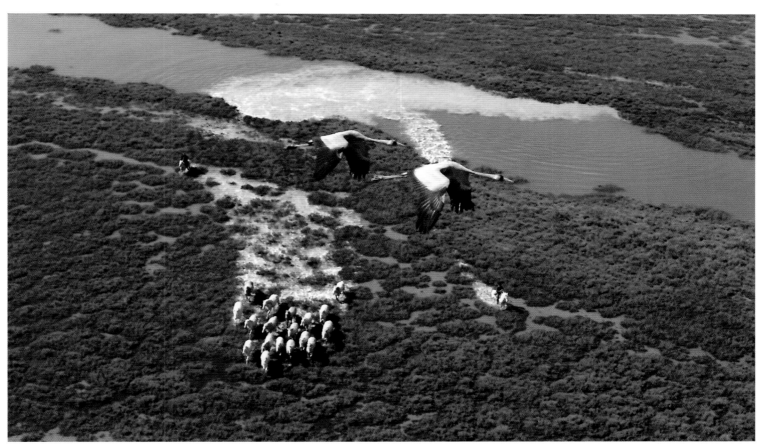

COMMON CRANE, Camargue, France
Some cranes overwinter here, sharing the wetland
with the region's famous semi-wild white horses,
while others journey further northwards.

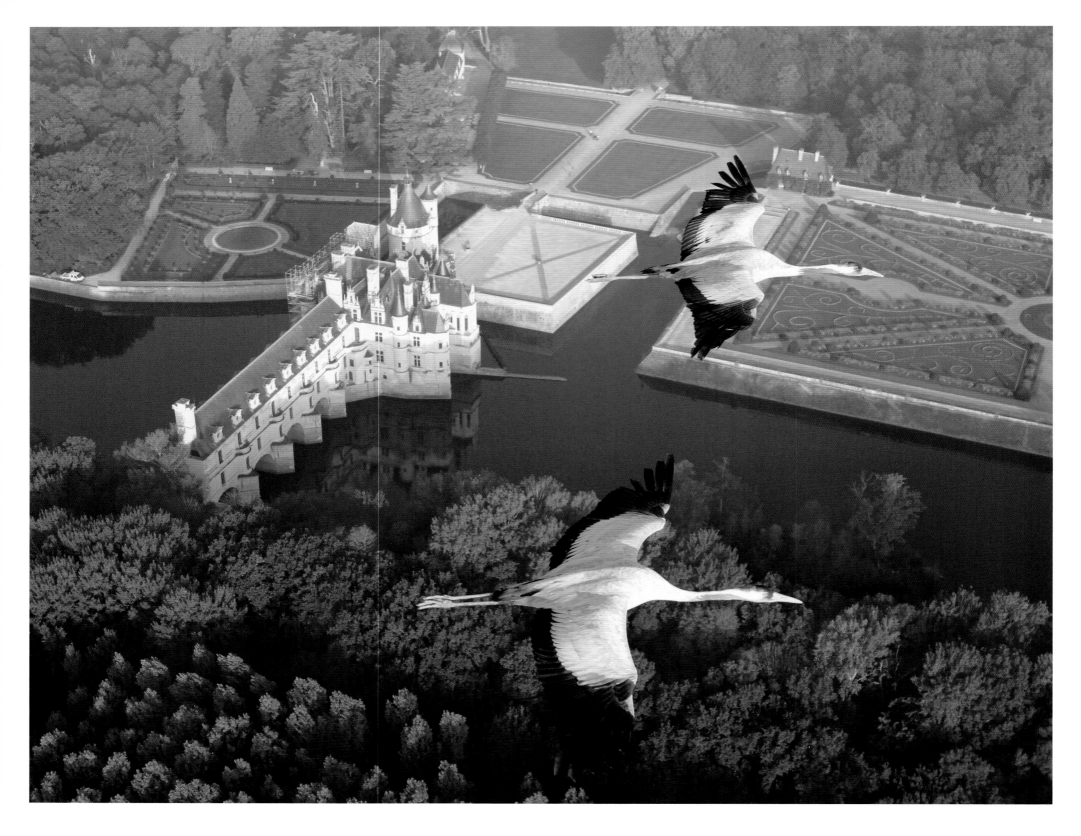

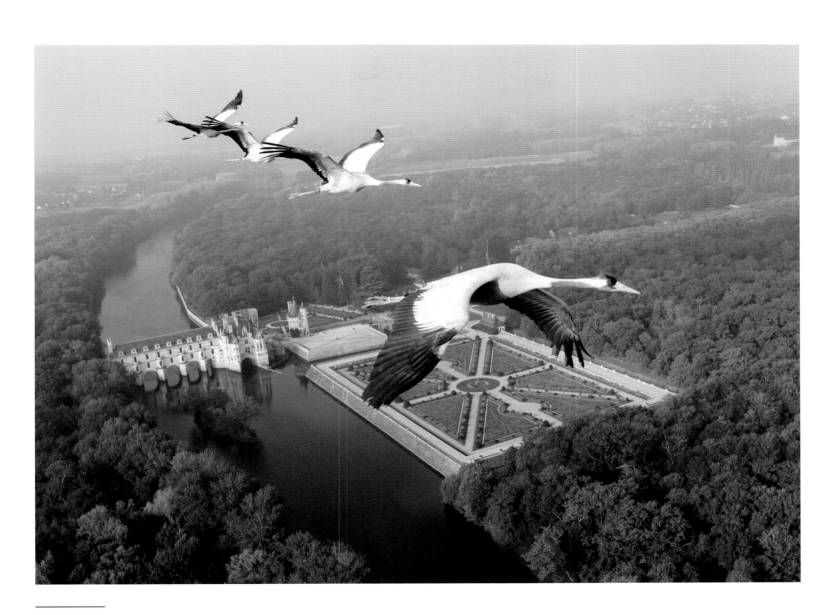

COMMON CRANE, Loire Valley, France
In March, birds fly over the châteaux of the Loire, here the
Château de Chenonceau, during the spring migration of the
western European population of cranes. Some birds now
spend the entire winter in the Loire region.

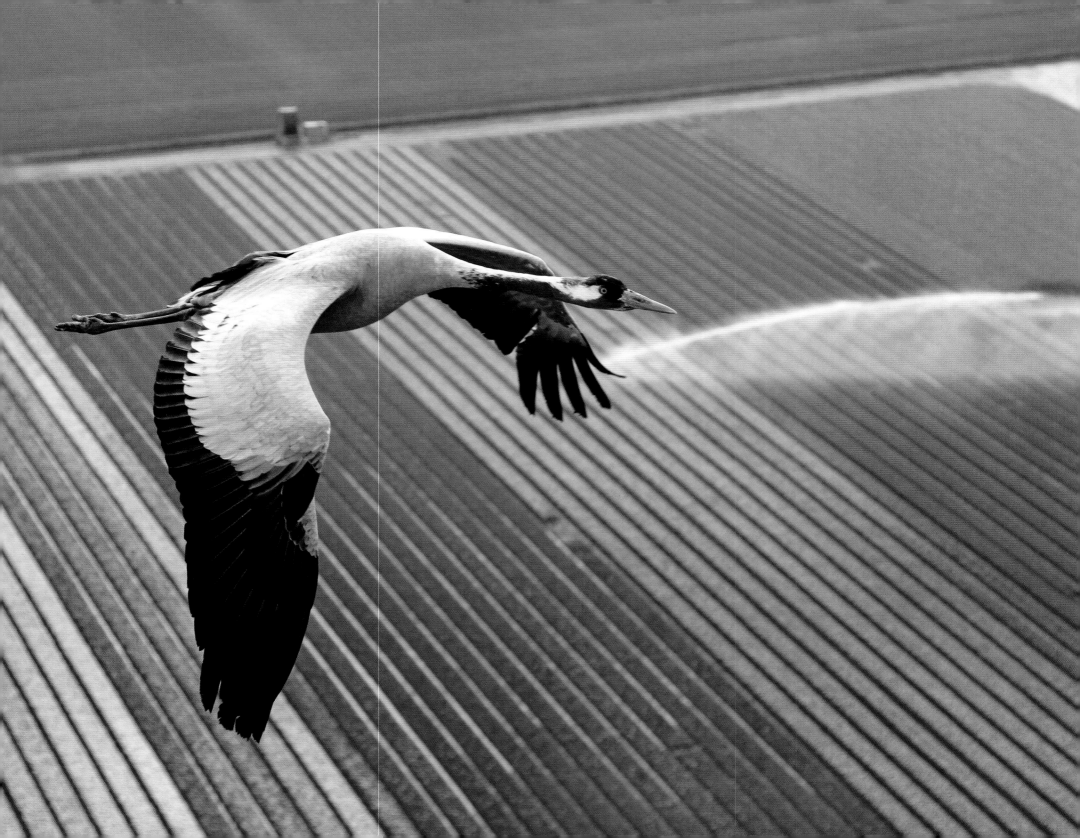

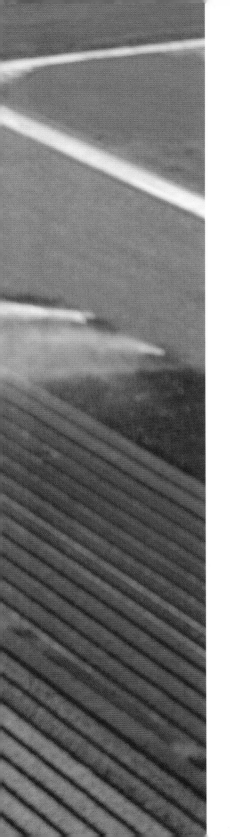

COMMON CRANE, Wieringerwerf, the Netherlands
While most cranes fly over the tulip fields and
on to Sweden to the north, in 2001 one pair nested
in the Netherlands – believed to be the first to do so
for 250 years.

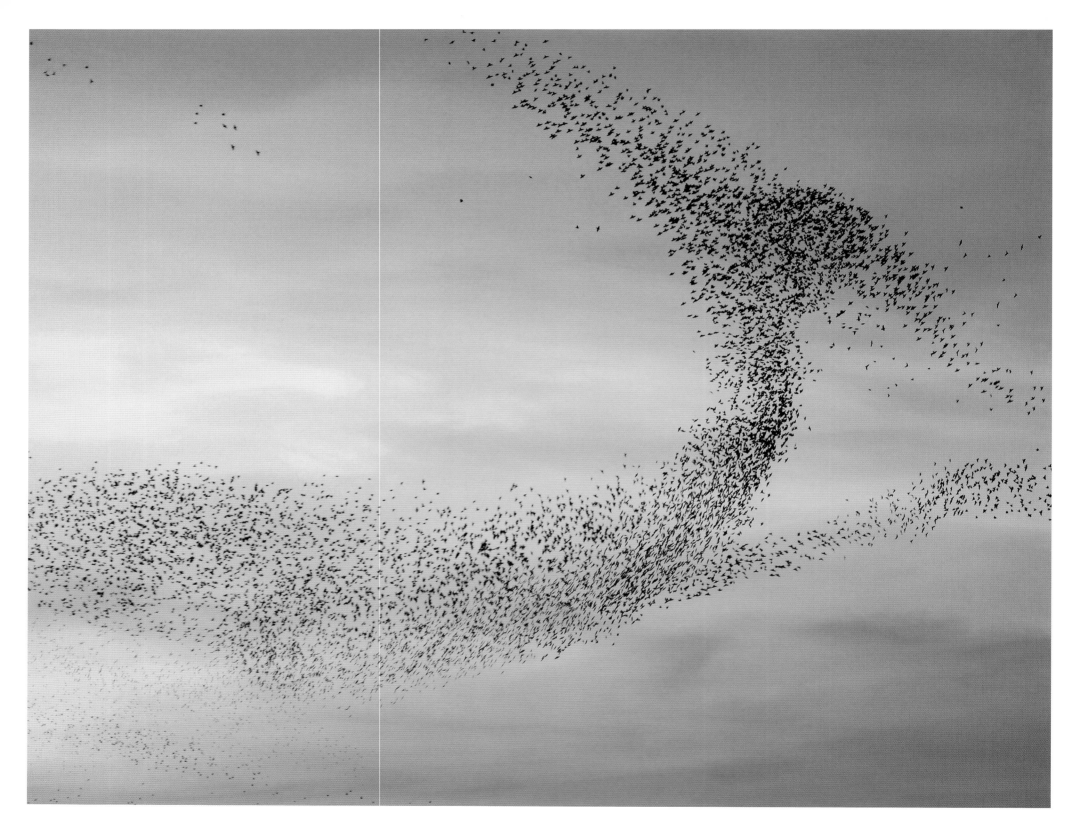

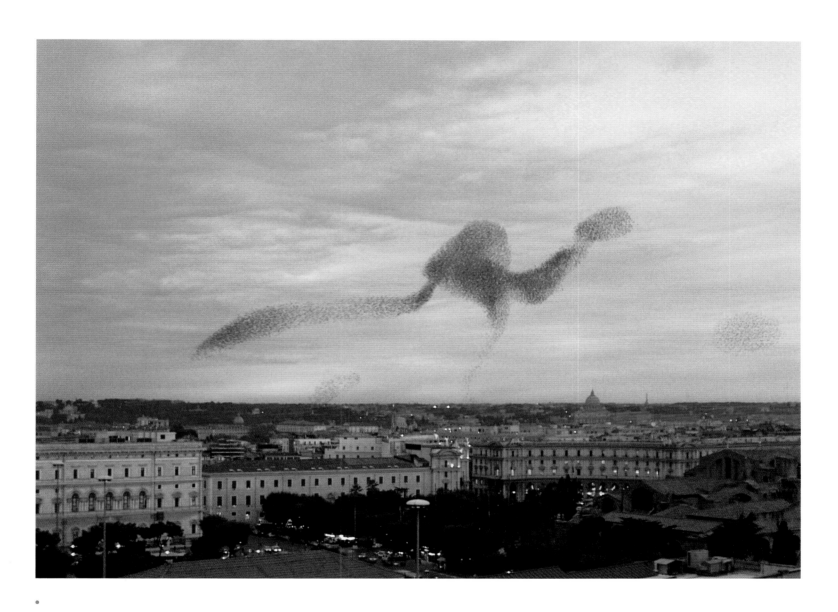

COMMON OR EUROPEAN STARLING, Rome, Italy
Arriving in mid-September, huge clouds of starlings whirl
over Rome's rooftops before settling into their nightly winter
roost. The birds leave the Eternal City in mid-March.

GREYLAG GOOSE, southern coast, France
The greylag was traditionally the last species of goose to embark on its spring migration, hence 'lag' in its name, although its departure date from wintering sites along the Mediterranean is becoming increasingly earlier – possibly due to climate change.

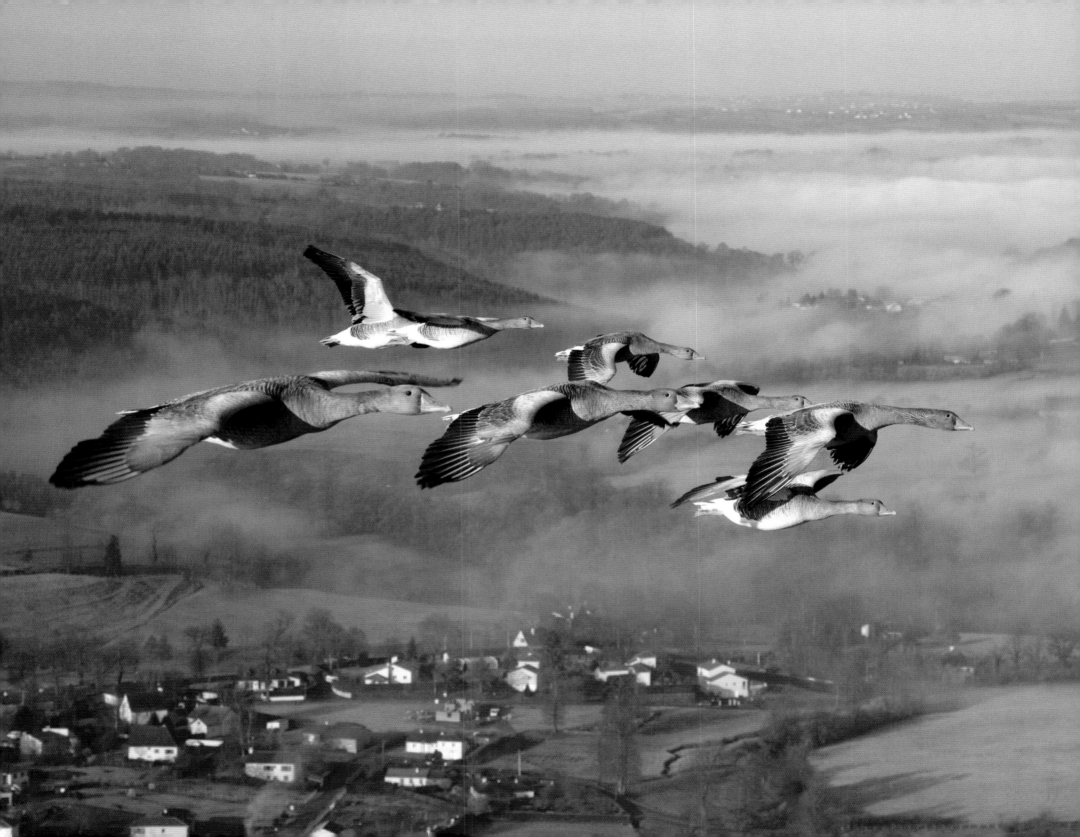

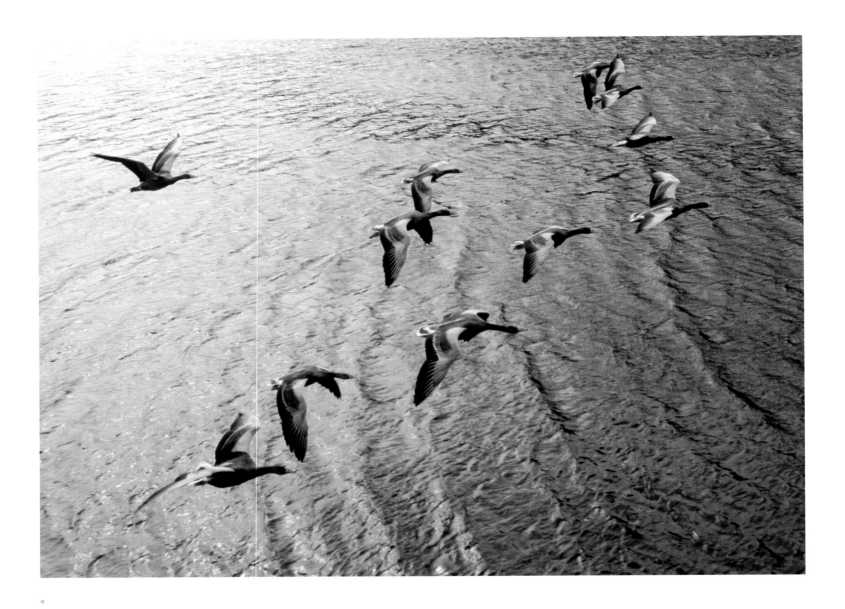

GREYLAG GOOSE, Millau Viaduct, France
Geese that overwinter in Spain follow the European Atlantic
Flyway through southwest France on their journey north to
breed in Norway and Sweden.

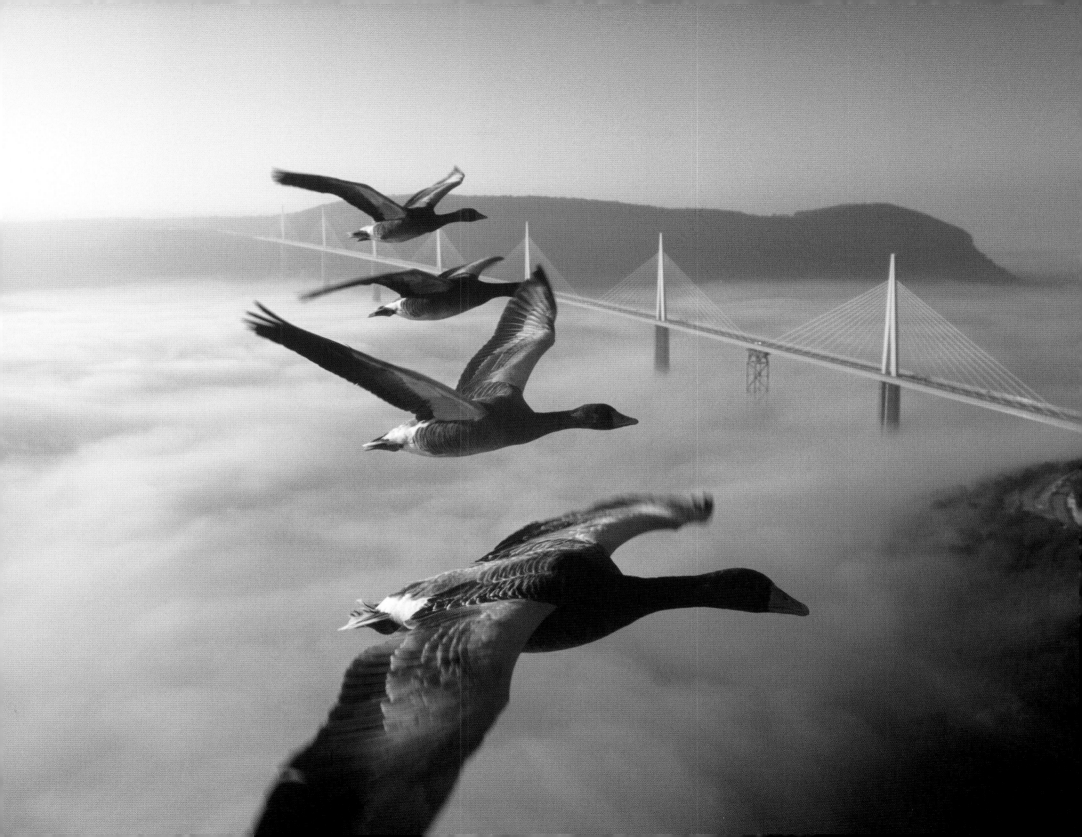

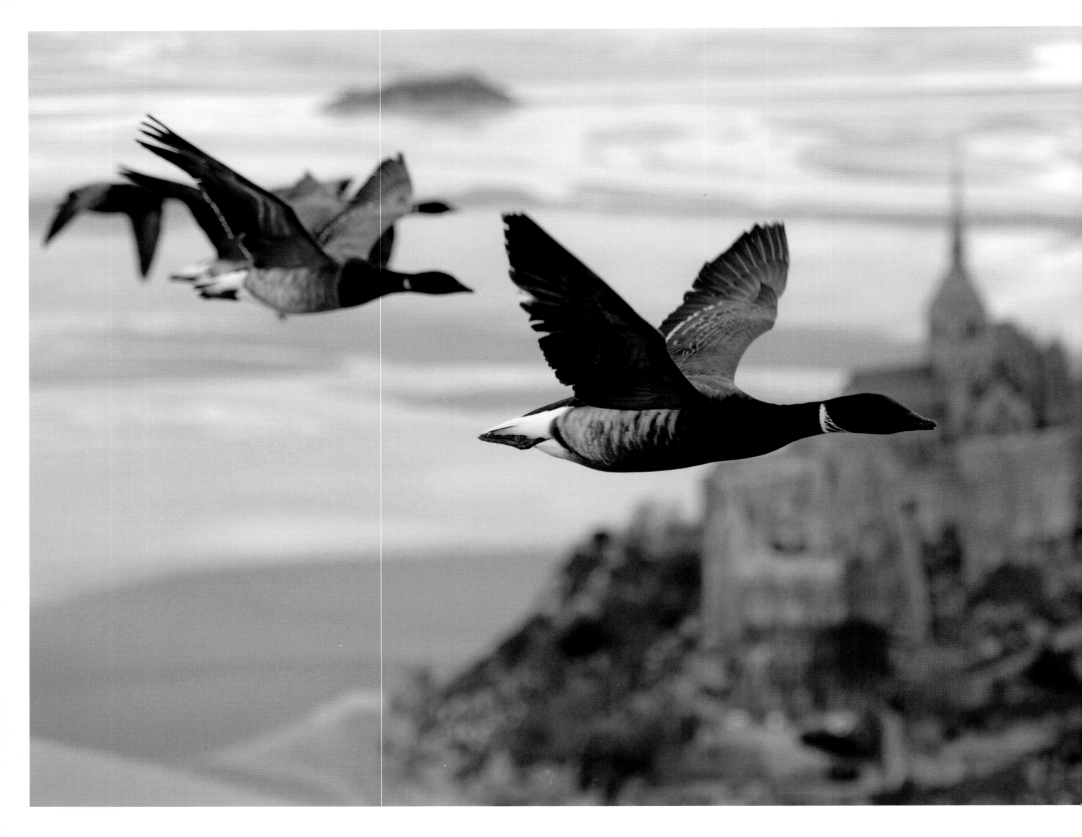

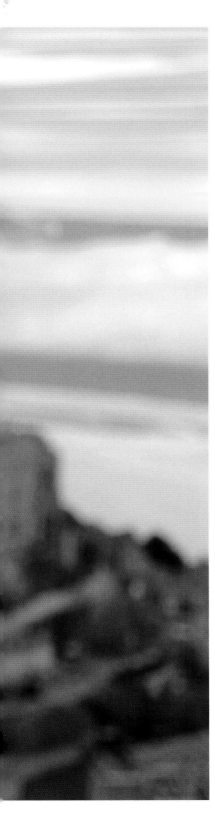

BRENT GOOSE, Mont-Saint-Michel, Normandy, France
Part of the dark-bellied population of this species winters in northern France and travels over this famous monastery on the way to the Arctic coasts of western Siberia to breed.

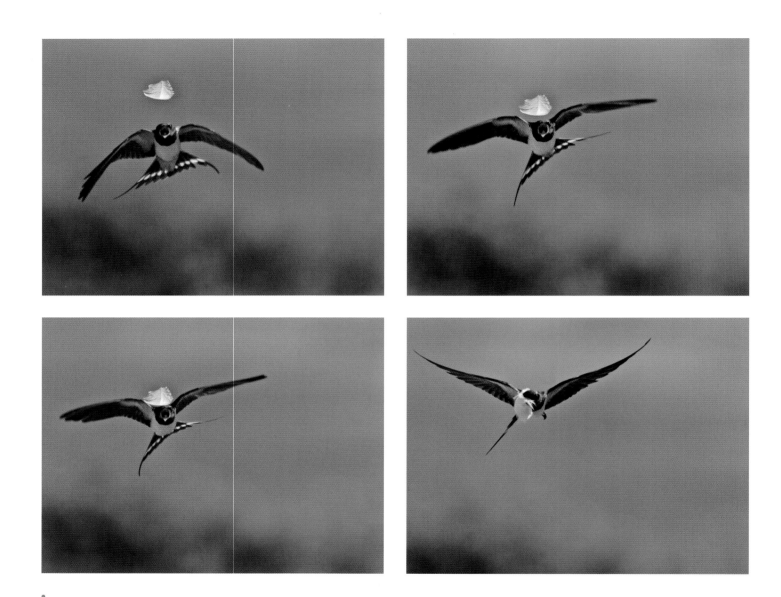

BARN SWALLOW, Somerset, England
Swallows demonstrate some astonishing aerobatics when
collecting feathers and other materials to line their mud
nests. Some nests are refurbished and have been in use
for nearly 50 years.

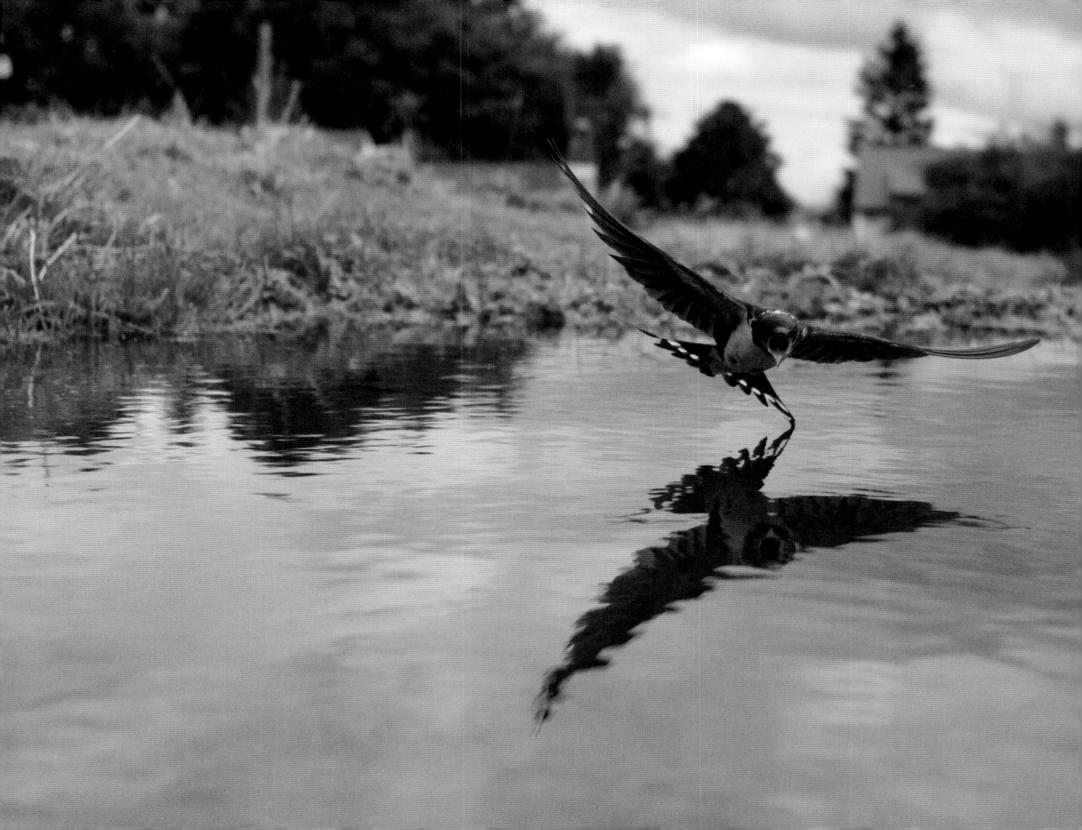

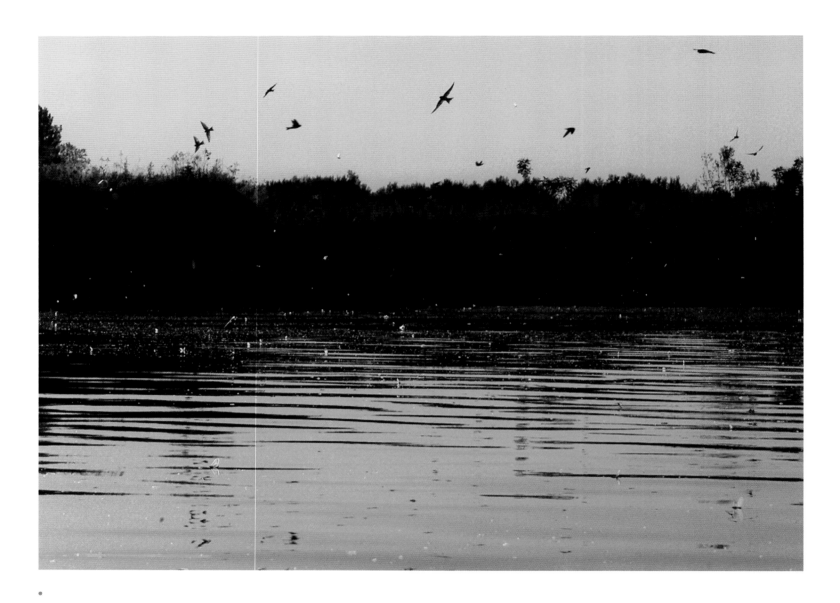

SAND MARTIN, Tisza River, Hungary
Recently arrived from Africa, sand martins feast on the
'Tisza River flowering' – not a blooming of plants, but the
sudden if brief mass emergence of long-tailed mayflies.

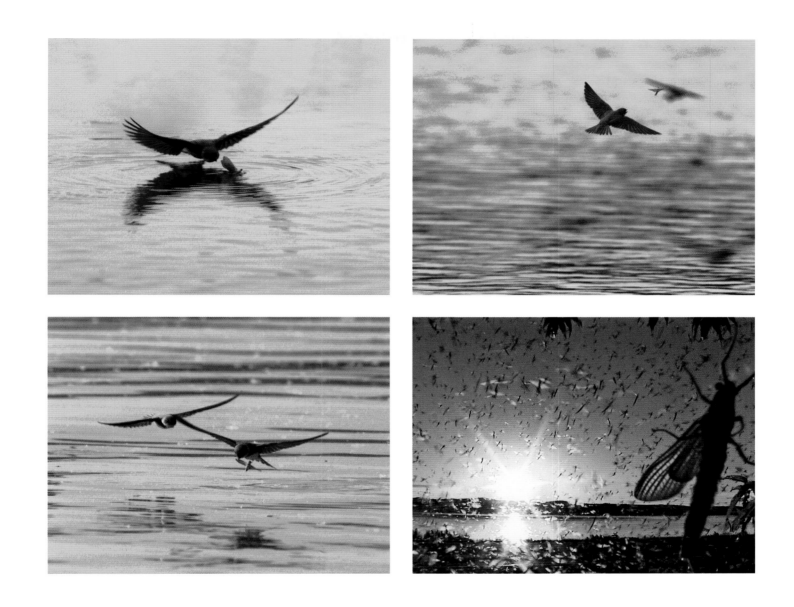

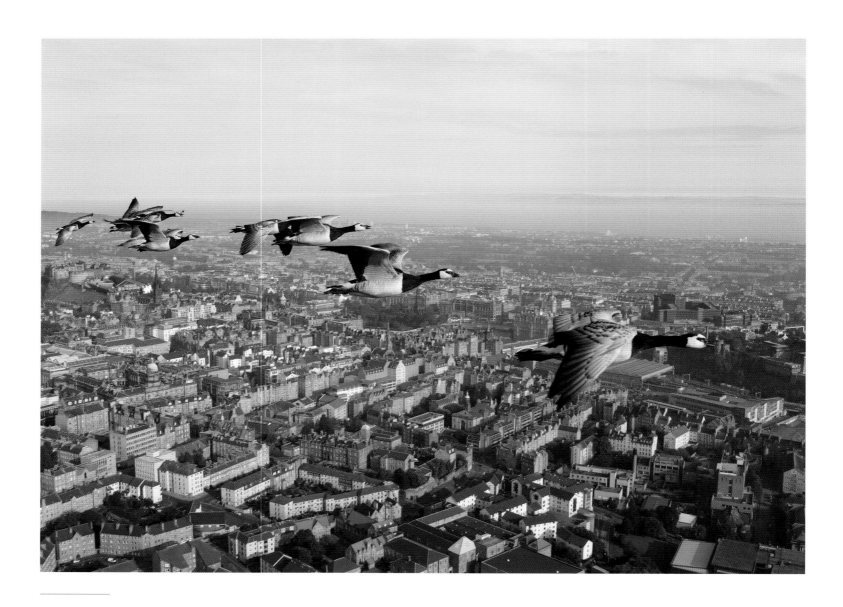

BARNACLE GOOSE, Edinburgh (above) and Stirling Castle (right), Scotland
In late April and early May, the entire 29,000-strong Solway Firth winter
population crosses Scotland on its way to Svalbard where it nests during
the short Arctic summer.

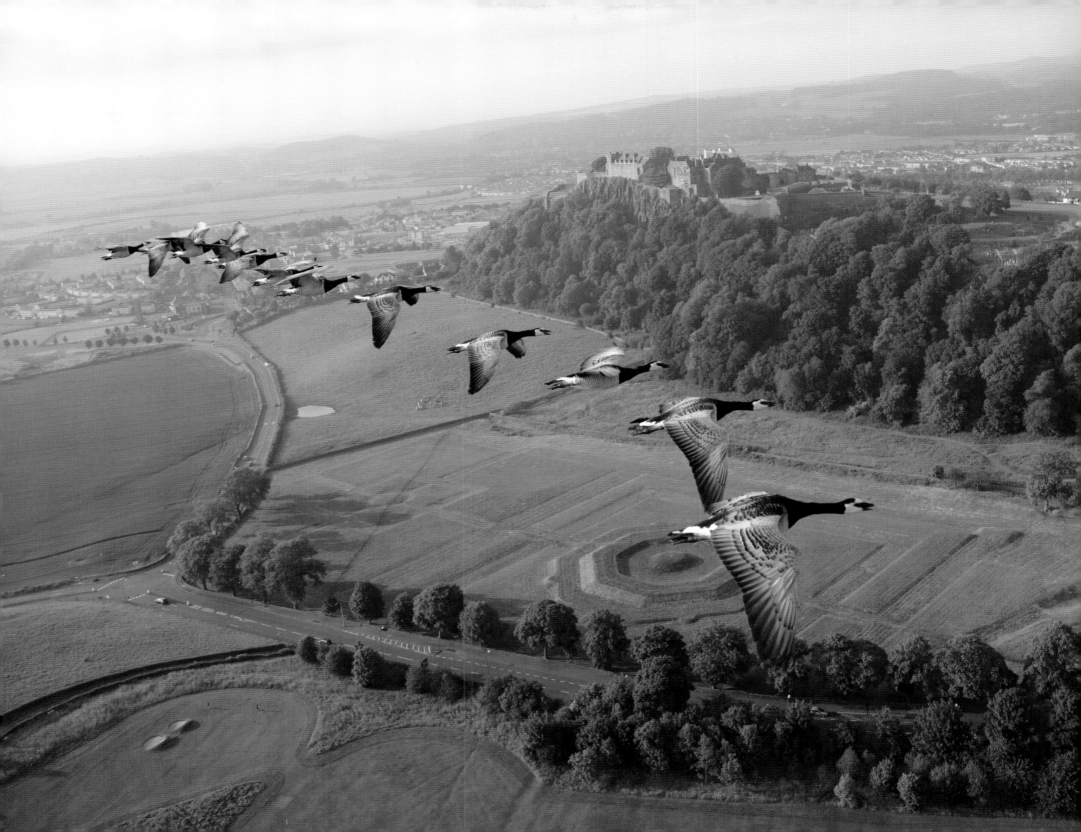

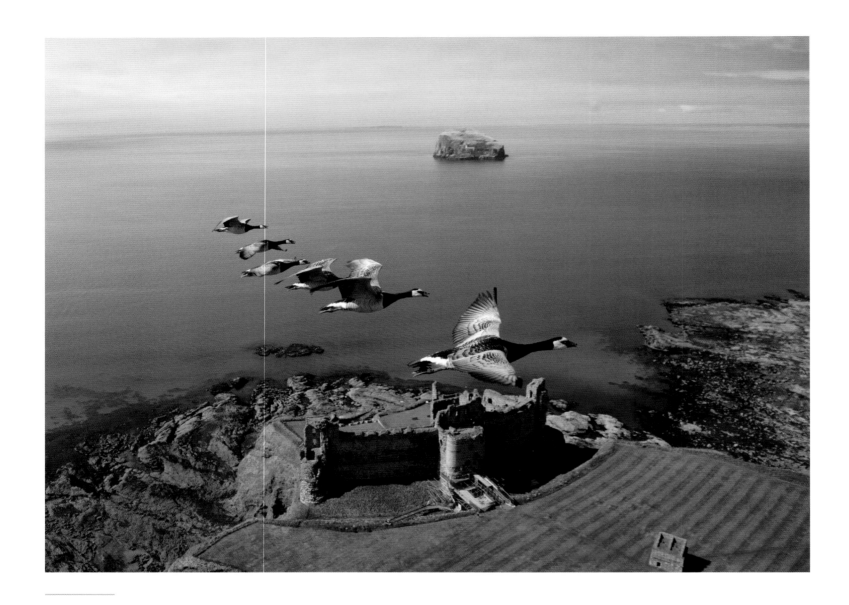

BARNACLE GOOSE, Bass Rock and Tantallon Castle, Scotland
Fresh spring grass provides the fuel for the population's journey,
with females tending to carry more fat reserves than males because
they will start egg laying as soon as they reach Svalbard.

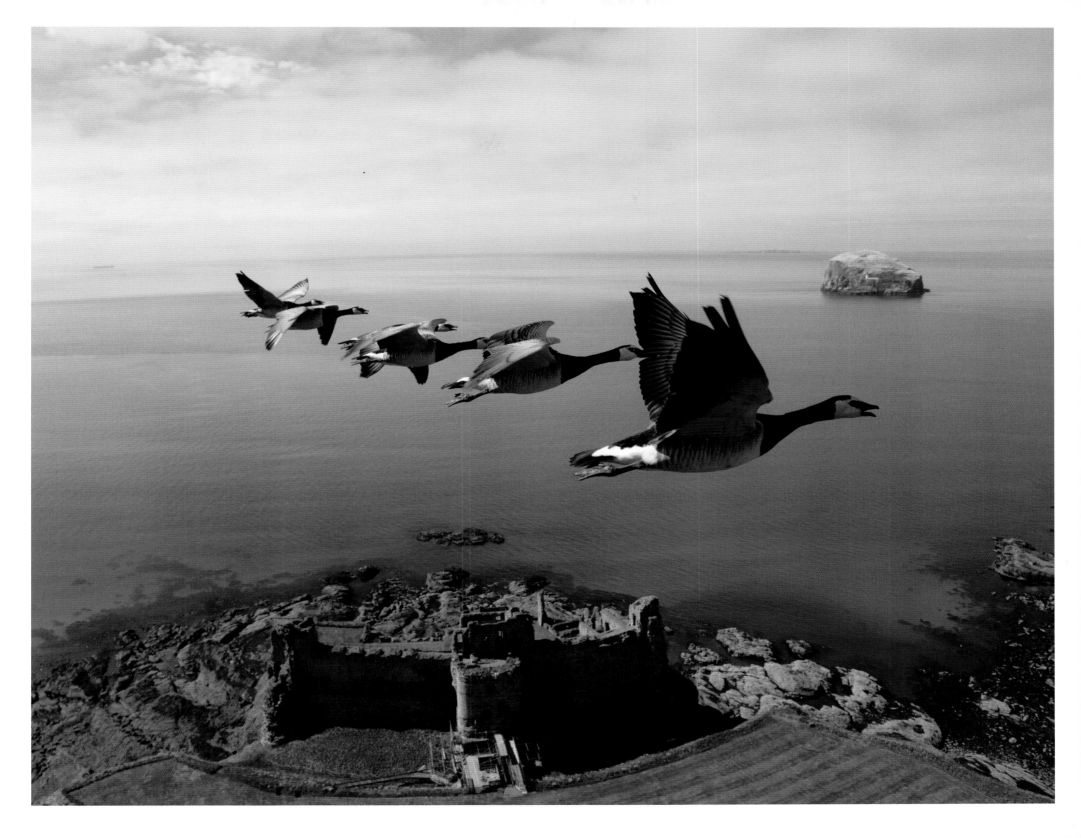

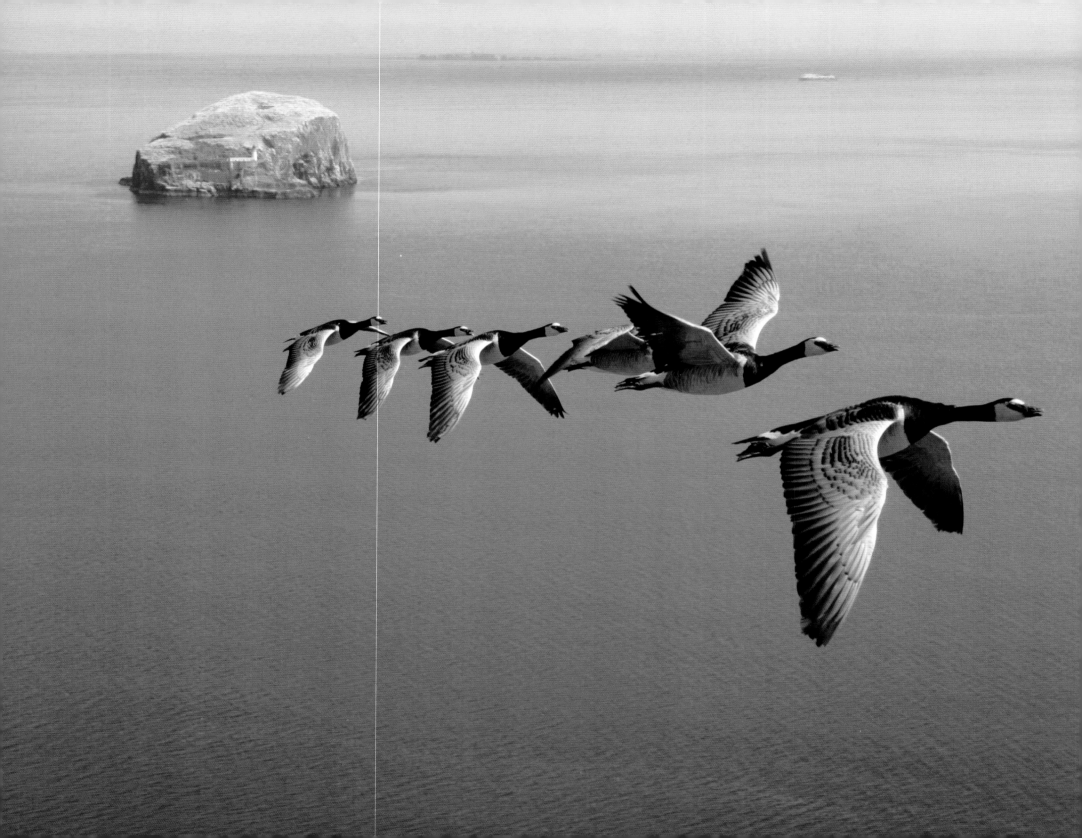

BARNACLE GOOSE, Bass Rock, Scotland
High above Scotland's rocky east coast, the birds fly over Bass Rock, breeding site for the largest single island gannet colony in the world.

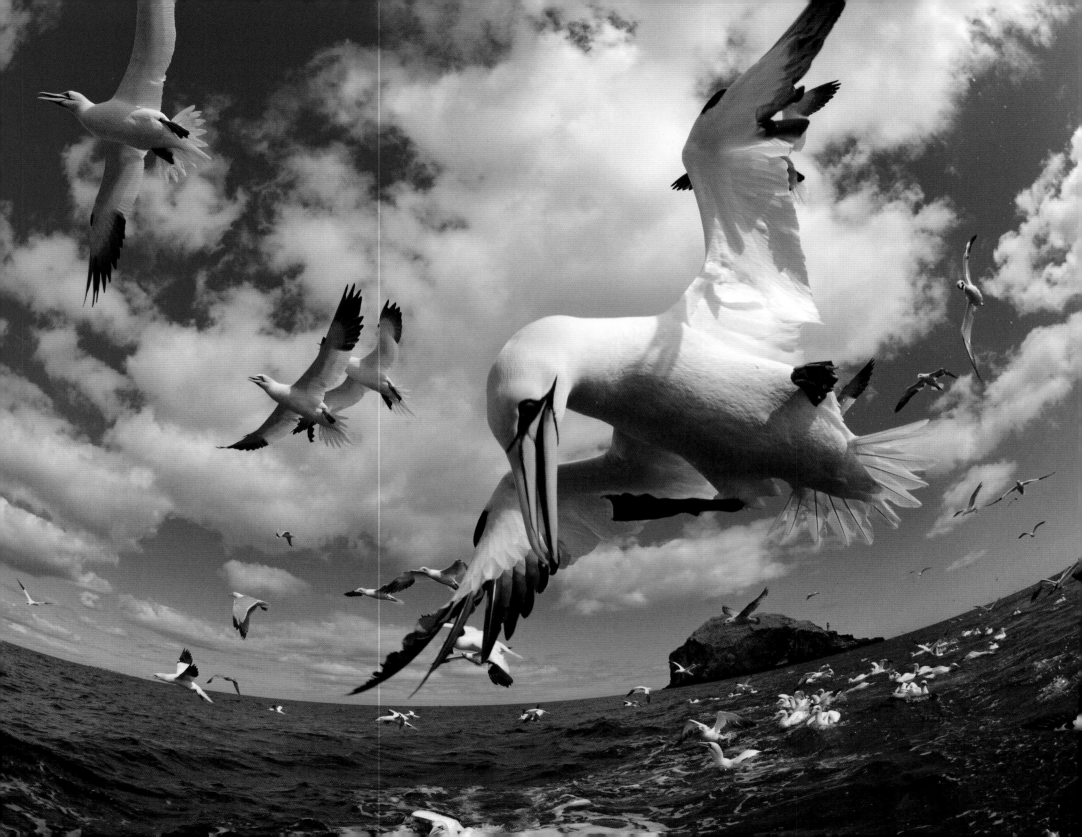

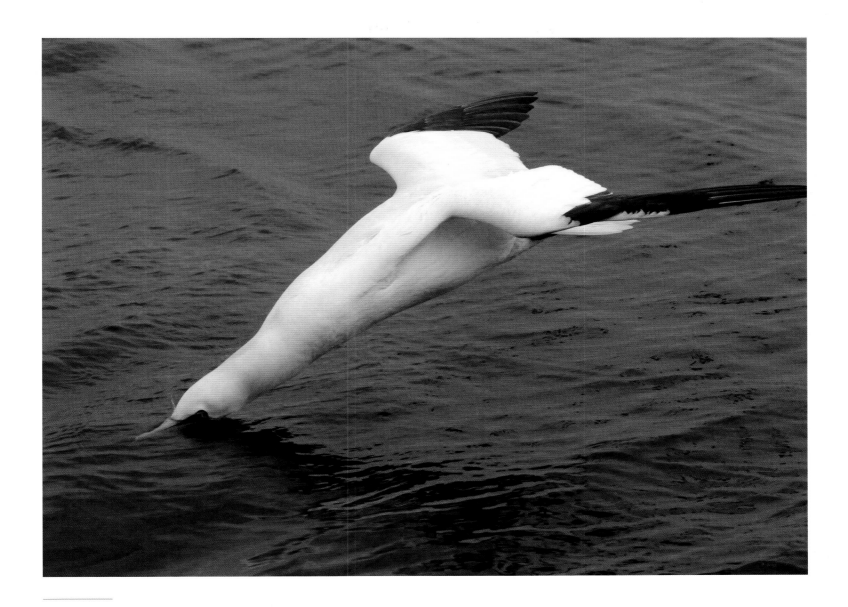

NORTHERN GANNET, Bass Rock, Scotland
The gannets return from the open sea in January to nest on
the rock and feed by plunge diving on fish shoals. In October,
young birds may fly as far away as West Africa for the winter.

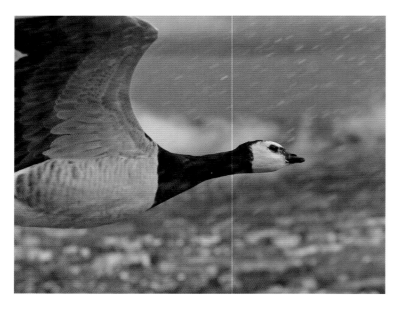

BARNACLE GOOSE, Loch Ness, Scotland
Bad weather can delay the spring departure, as the birds head further north towards the Scandinavian coast. Especially fit birds may fly non-stop for 24 hours over the North Sea.

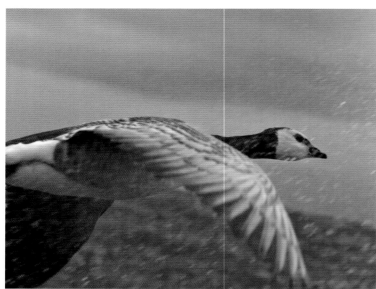

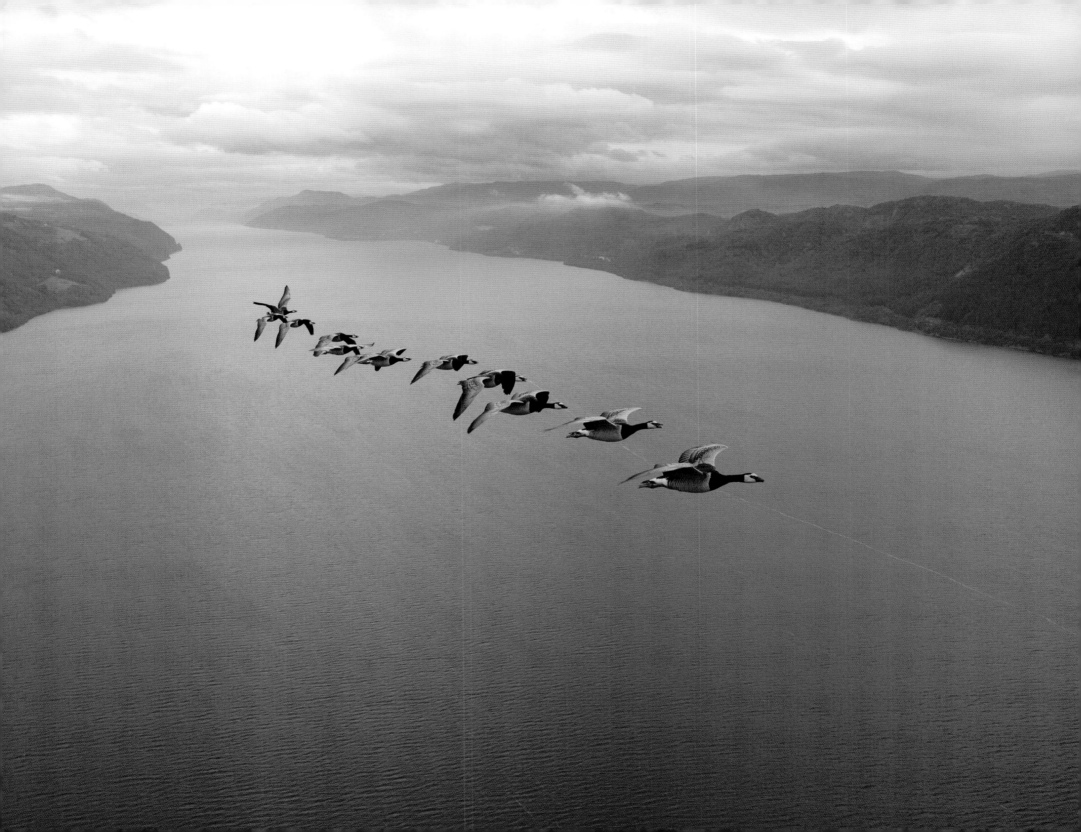

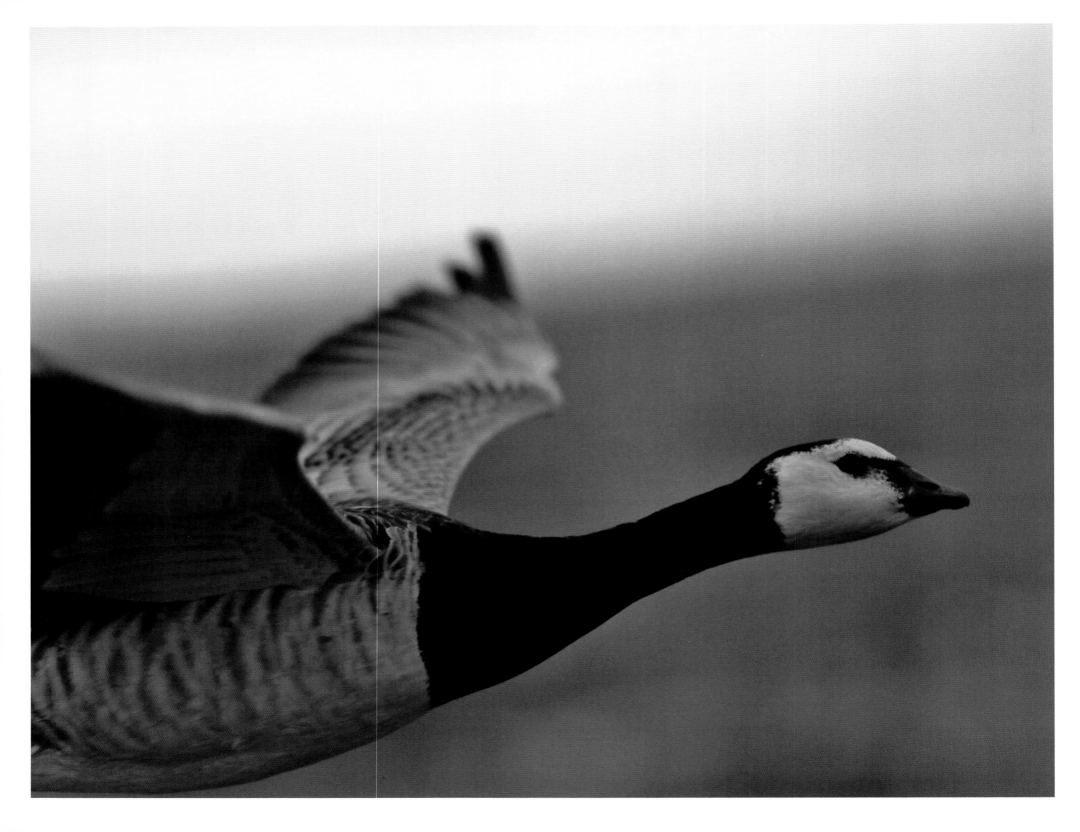

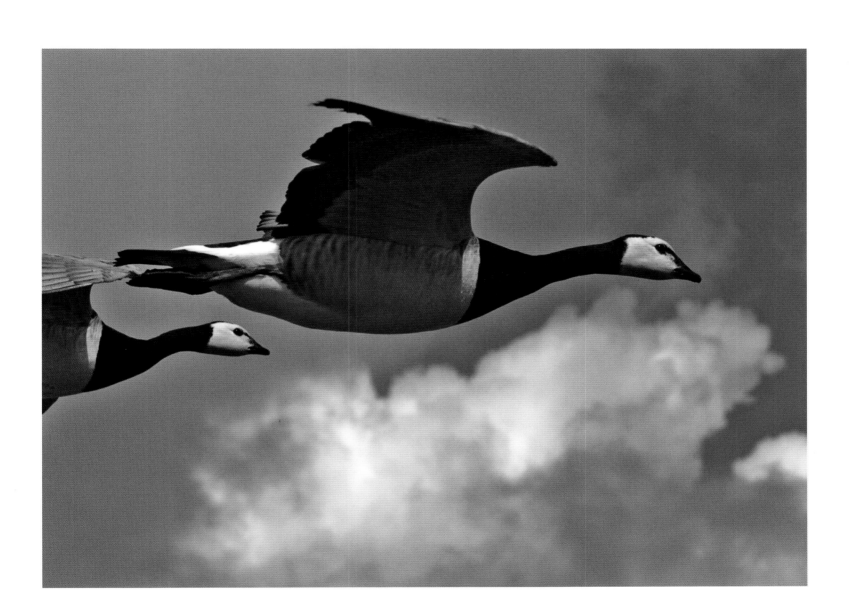

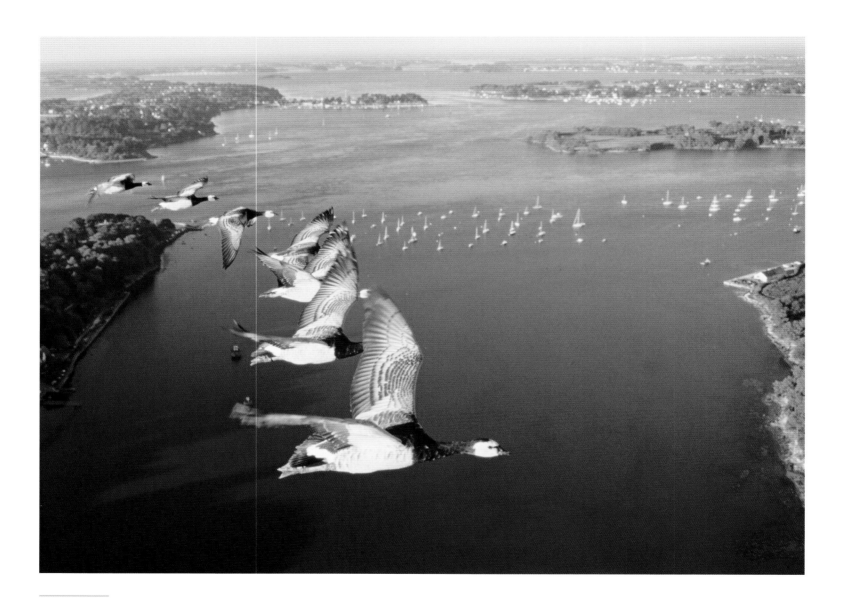

BARNACLE GOOSE, southern coast, Sweden
The geese fly over the coast of Sweden on their journey
north, continuing onwards to the snowy climes of their
final destination – nesting sites in Svalbard, Norway.

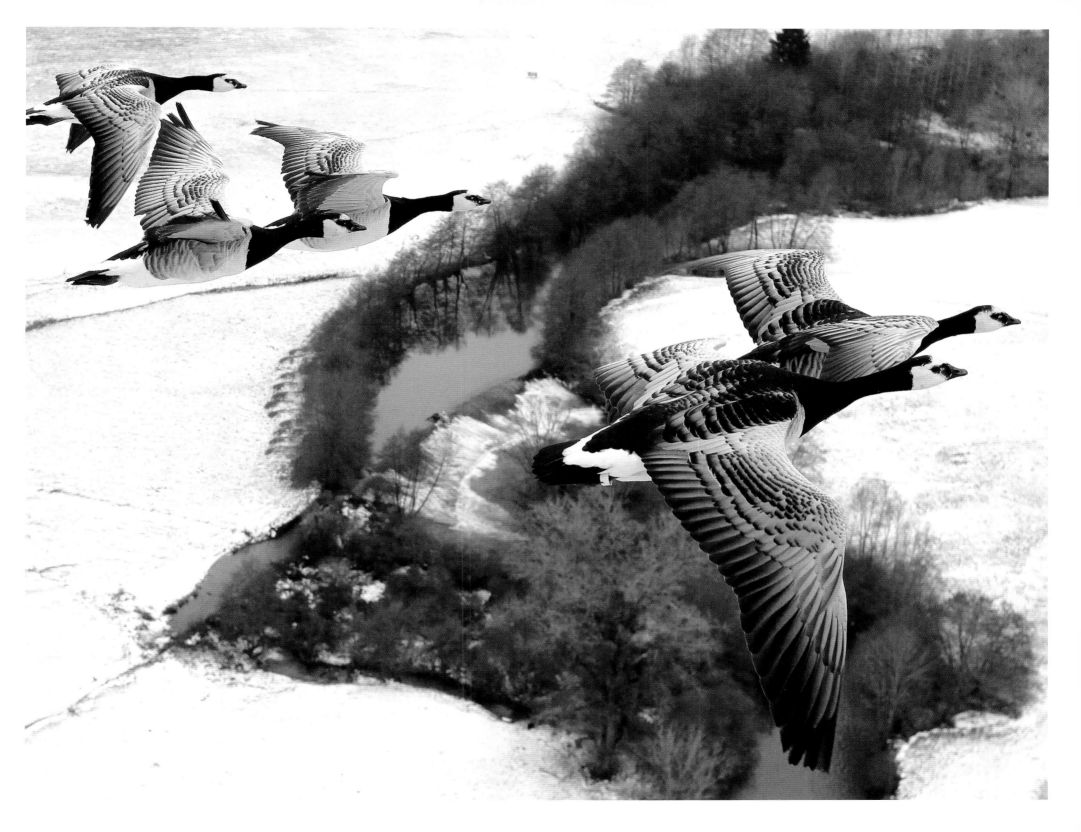

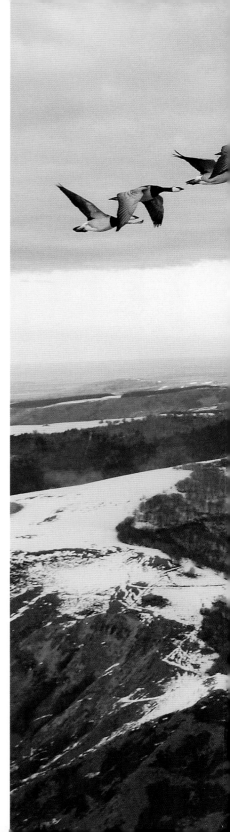

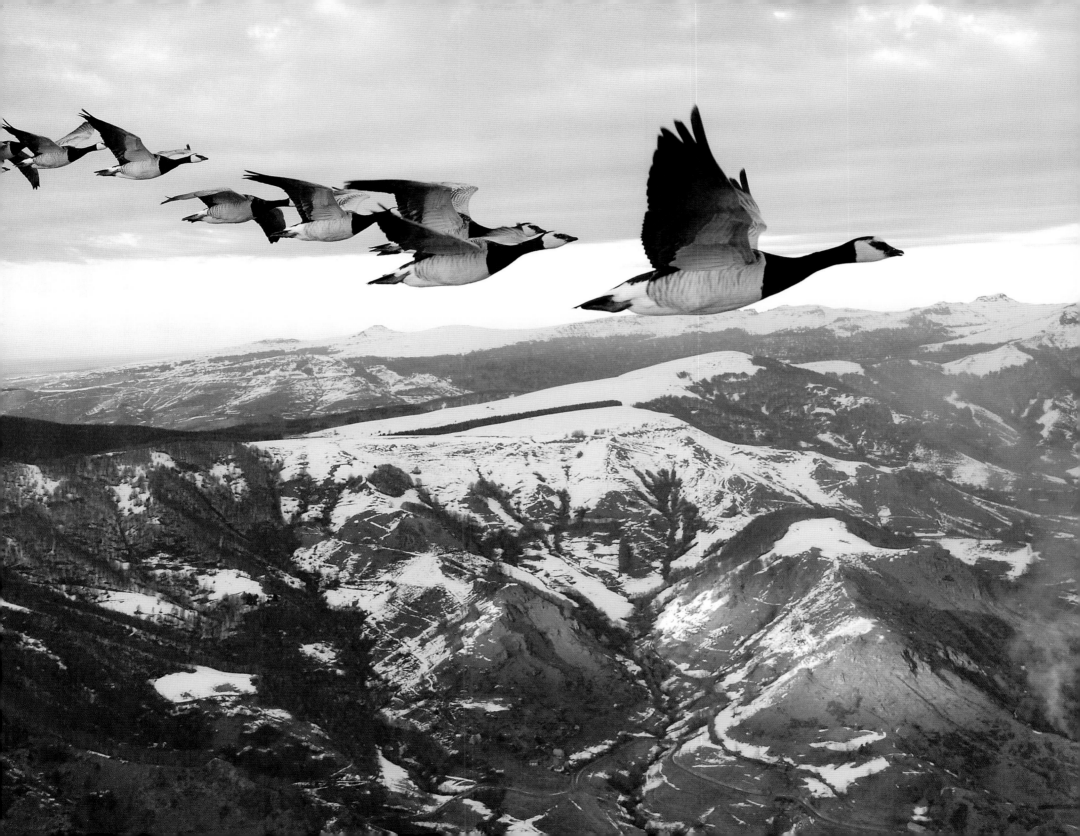

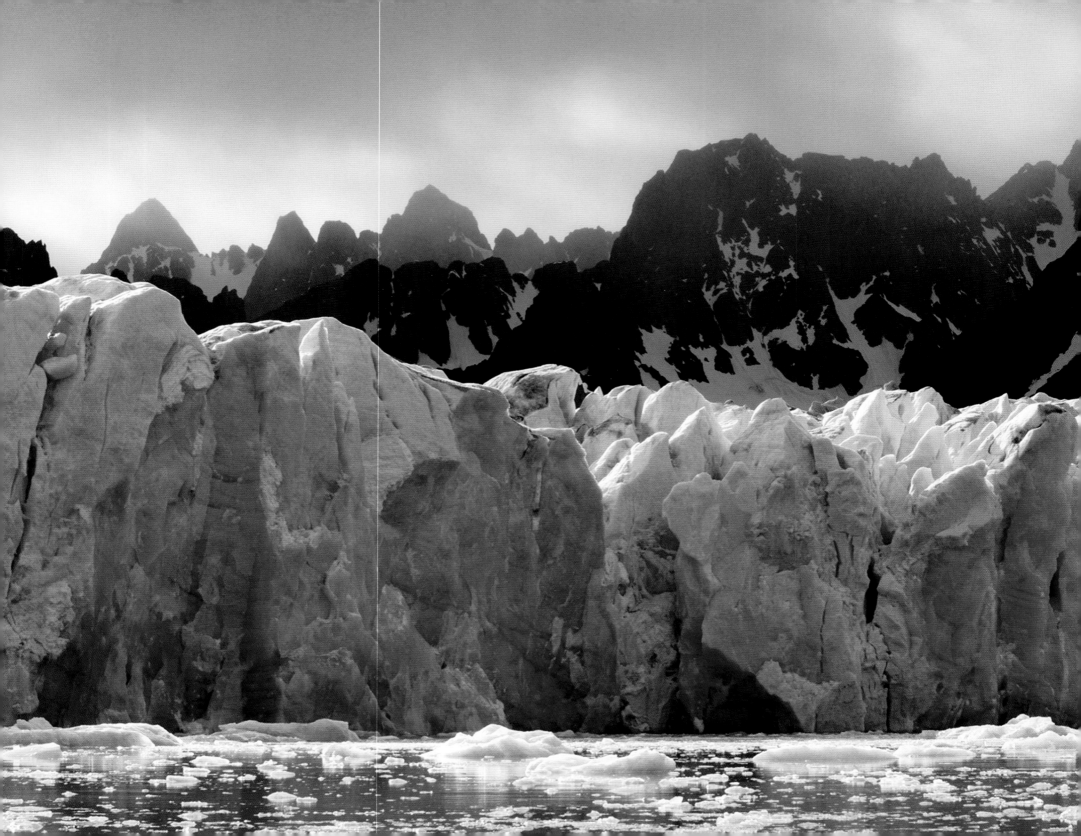

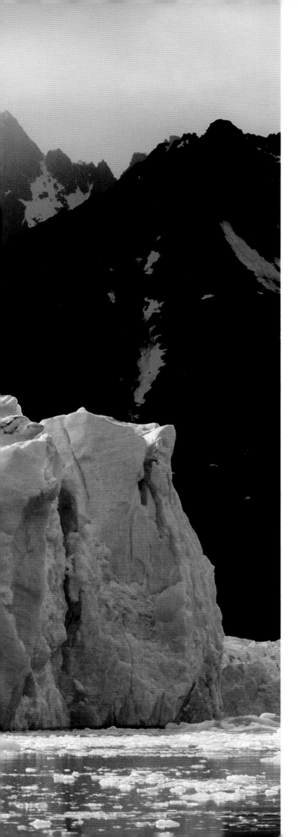

GLACIER MOUTH, Svalbard, Norway
Svalbard is an unforgiving place and may seem a strange choice of breeding ground for the geese, yet in a good year up to 25 per cent of the Solway Firth population of barnacle geese comprises young birds reared here.

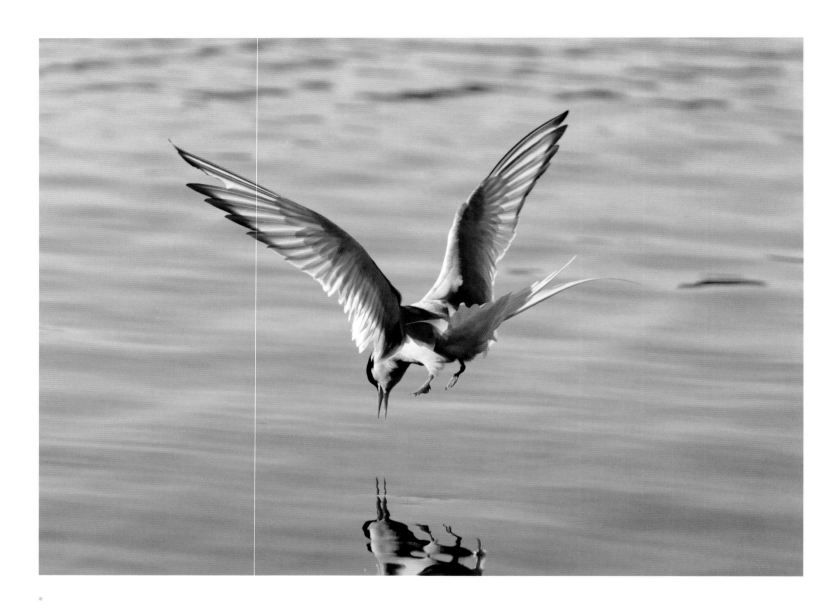

ARCTIC TERN, Svalbard, Norway
Barnacle geese share their island breeding sites with
Arctic terns. These birds have flown in from the Antarctic,
an entire world away.

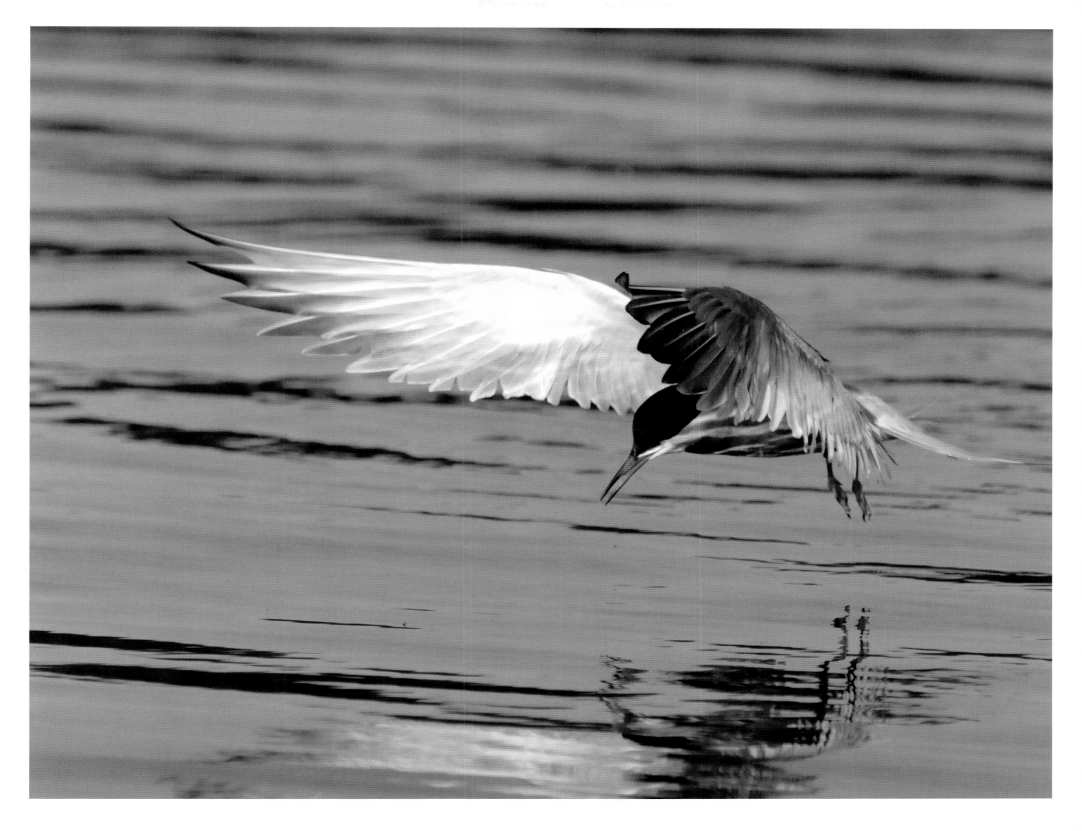

AFRICA

Think of Africa and an image that might come to mind is that of swathes of flamingos standing stock still in soda lakes, but in making *Earthflight*, we discovered that there's more to the migratory behaviour of these birds than meets the eye.

Despite their image as static, wading birds that do little but mill around the lakes of Africa in huge numbers, flamingos, it turns out, are great travellers. DNA analysis has revealed that the birds we filmed breeding at Kamfers Dam in South Africa – one of only six flamingo breeding centres on the entire continent – are some of the very same birds that visit the Makgadikgadi Pan in the dry heart of the Kalahari Desert of Botswana; and, they don't stop there. A few intrepid individuals fly onwards to Kenya, 3,000 km (1,800 miles) away and, wherever they go, they attract unwelcome attention.

At Lake Nakuru, in Kenya, we saw spotted hyenas brave the caustic waters to grab them; on Lake Bogoria olive baboons would charge into the lake to find the weaker birds, making flying leaps to pluck them from the air; and on all the lakes African fish eagles were on the hunt – circling the flock to pick a victim before striking with ruthless efficiency. The flamingos' problems didn't end there either, with opportunist marabou storks and steppe eagles keeping a close eye on the fish eagle hunts. Just as fish eagles study the flamingos, the storks and steppe eagles watch the hunt intently, waiting to steal their catch. The sort of canny behaviour displayed by these birds was something that we came across more than once, and would influence greatly the way in which we filmed *Earthflight*.

Not far from Cape Town, kelp gulls fly out to the channel between Dyer Island and Geyser Rock on a mission for food. Geyser Rock is filled beyond capacity by a rookery of 50,000 Cape fur seals, and when the pups make their first forays into the sea, they swim straight into danger, for waiting in the channel are the world's largest predatory fish – great white sharks.

The gulls appear to ignore most of the seals, focusing on a single novice swimmer. What they observe is unclear, but scientists have a hunch. Adult seals tend to set a zigzag course away from the islands in order to avoid the sharks, whereas young seals swim in a predictable straight line. Whatever the cue, the gulls are always right, and a shark races up from the depths and slams into its victim, sometimes leaving the water in spectacular fashion. The gulls pick up any leftovers, and then look for the next hit.

Perhaps the most spectacular example of this behaviour that we filmed occurs off the east coast of South Africa, where snow-white Cape gannets nest on Bird Island in Algoa Bay. During the September breeding season, adult birds find the South African sardines needed to feed their growing chicks right on the doorstep and in relatively shallow water where they're easy to spot. However, by the time the young gannets have fledged, the sardines move offshore and southwards to the Agulhas Bank to spawn. Here, in deeper water they are less easy to see from the air, but the birds have a Plan B: they watch dolphins.

Equipped with a very sophisticated echo-location system, the dolphins find the vast shoals and herd them into tight bait balls. The gannets rain down on the fish in spectacular plunge dives, while dolphins and sharks attack from below. By May, the entire procession of prey and predators moves gradually northwards, easing itself up a narrow corridor of cold water along Africa's southeast coast and huge shoals of sardines, sometimes seven kilometres (over four miles) long, begin to form – the so-called 'sardine run'. The dolphins and whales are close behind, followed by the gannets.

The interaction of birds with the wildlife around them isn't restricted to sea birds. Inland, we followed vultures as they soared high above the African plains, searching for pickings from kills made by other animals.

The remarkable thing about feeding events like these is that they are the direct result of different species carefully watching each other's behaviour. It's a cunning shortcut to obtain a meal, and many different species of birds use it. We learned to use it too. By watching the birds, the film crew was led directly into the thick of the action.

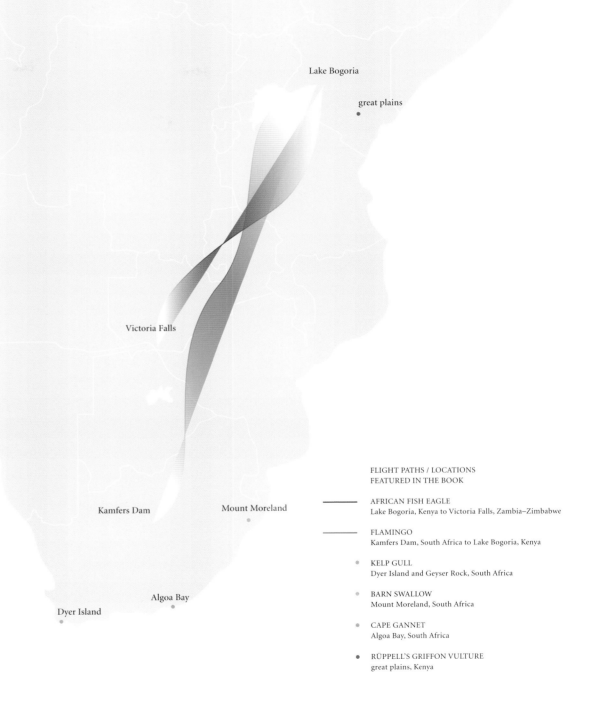

Lake Bogoria

great plains

Victoria Falls

Kamfers Dam

Mount Moreland

Dyer Island

Algoa Bay

FLIGHT PATHS / LOCATIONS
FEATURED IN THE BOOK

——— AFRICAN FISH EAGLE
Lake Bogoria, Kenya to Victoria Falls, Zambia–Zimbabwe

——— FLAMINGO
Kamfers Dam, South Africa to Lake Bogoria, Kenya

•   KELP GULL
Dyer Island and Geyser Rock, South Africa

•   BARN SWALLOW
Mount Moreland, South Africa

•   CAPE GANNET
Algoa Bay, South Africa

•   RÜPPELL'S GRIFFON VULTURE
great plains, Kenya

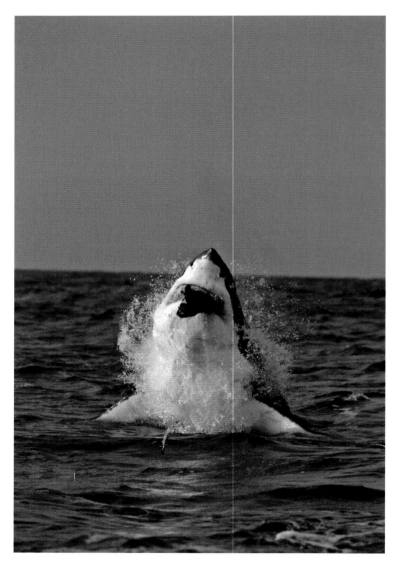

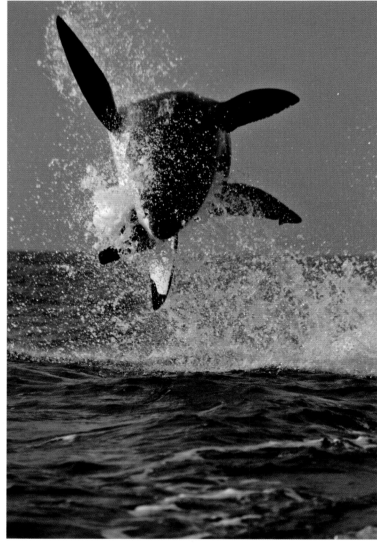

KELP GULL, Dyer Island and Geyser Rock, South Africa
Gulls seem to know where and when a great white shark
will slam spectacularly into a young fur seal, and are ready
and waiting to feast on the leftover scraps.

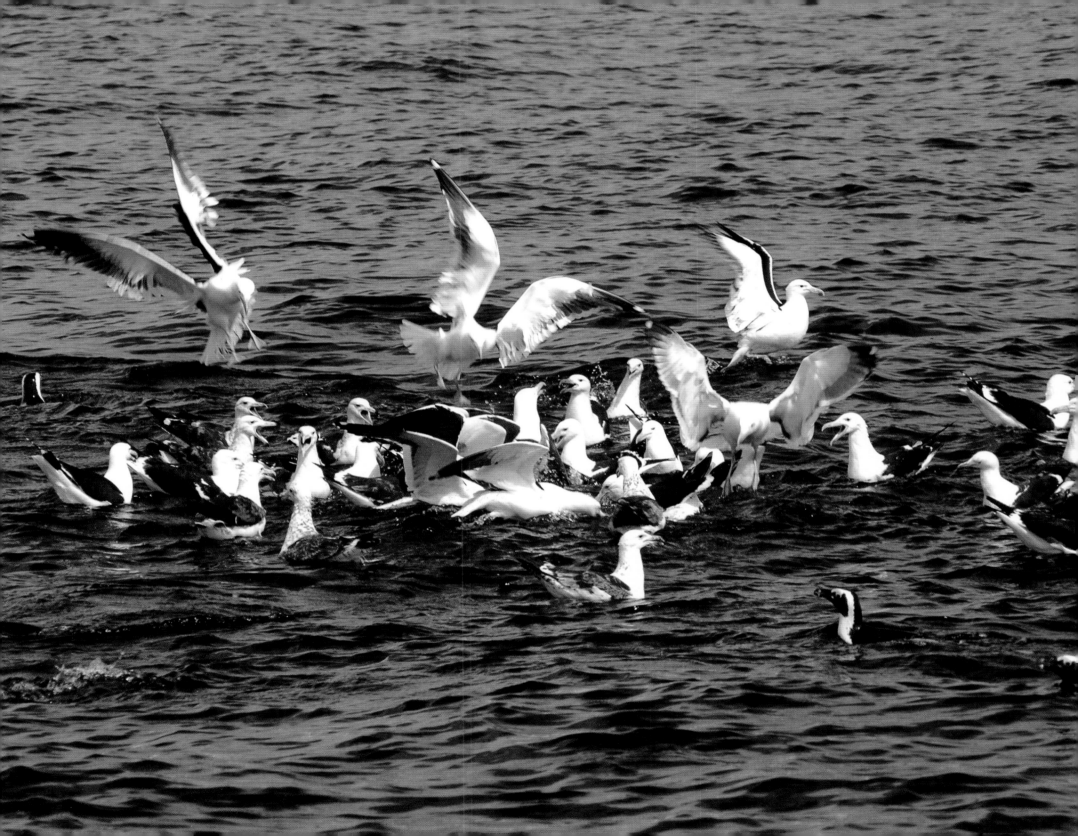

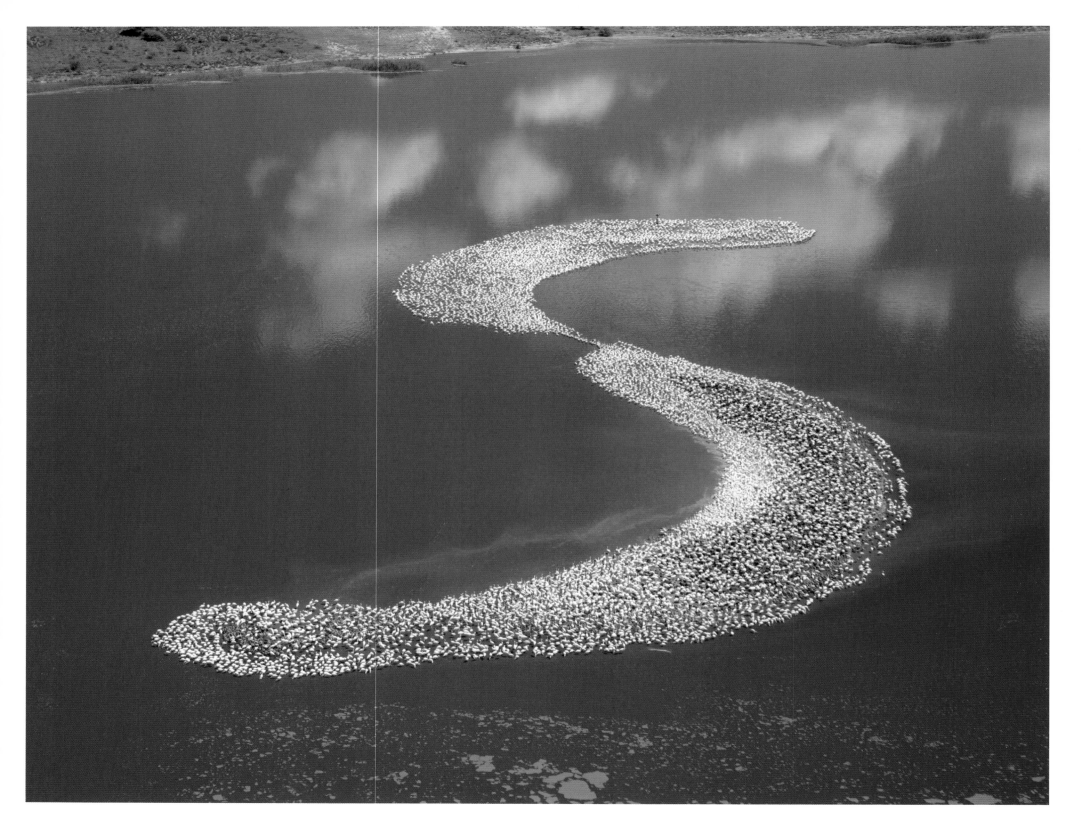

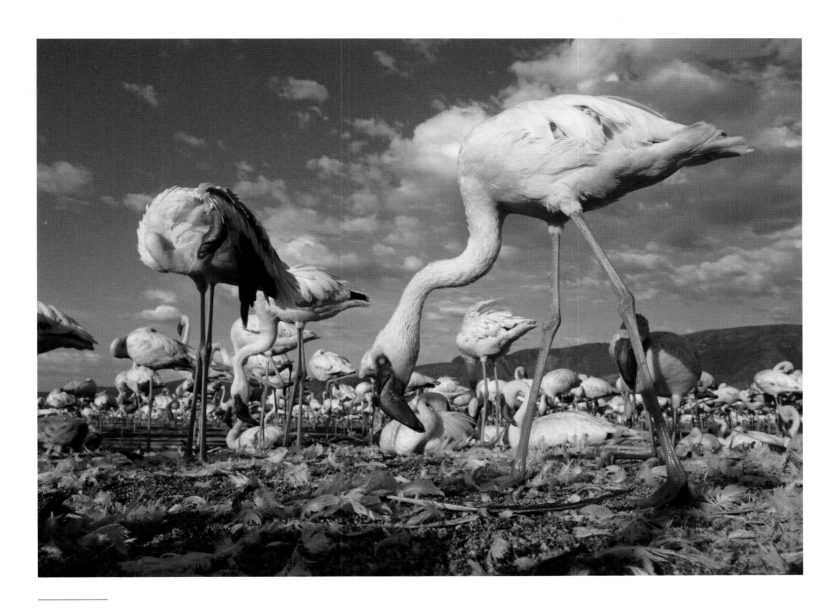

LESSER FLAMINGO, Kamfers Dam, South Africa
The flamingos nest on an artificial S-shaped island built in
2006 by a local mining company. During the first year, 10,000
birds arrived seemingly from nowhere, and 20,000 the year
after; currently, up to 50,000 birds breed here.

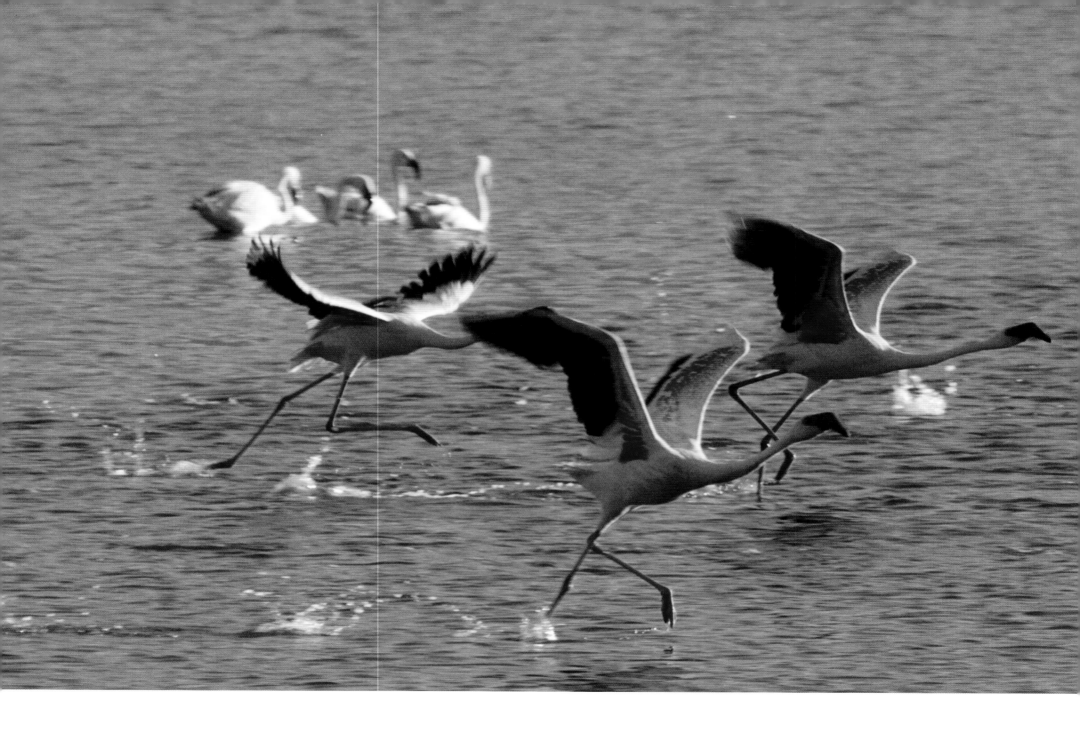

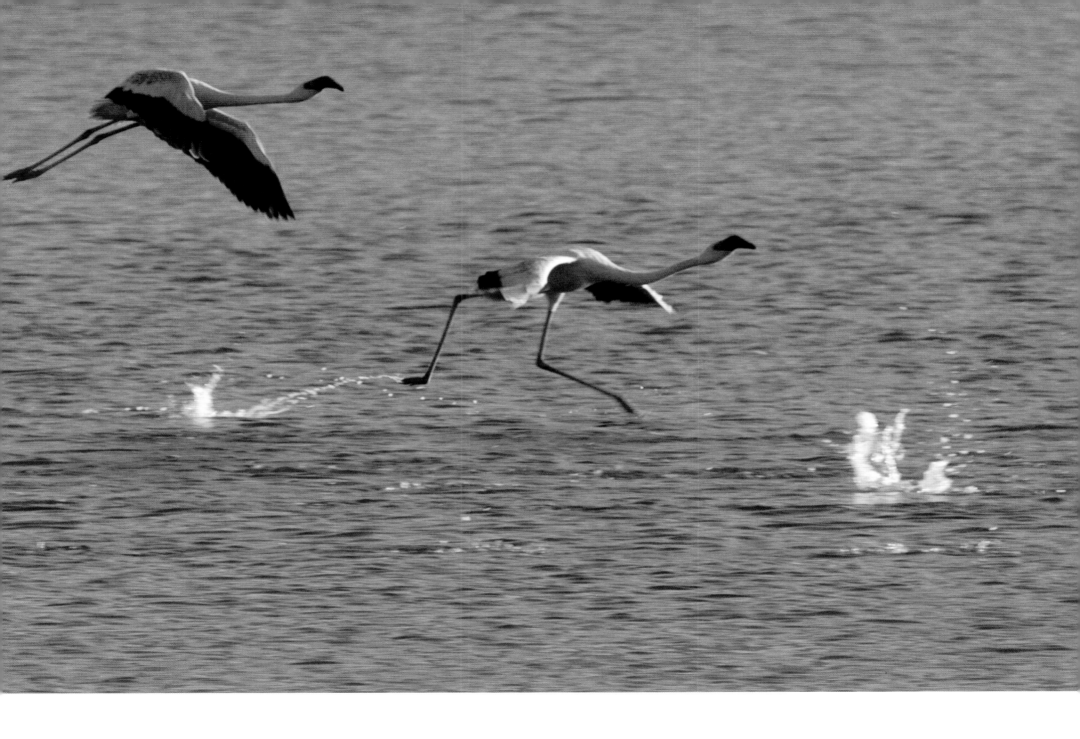

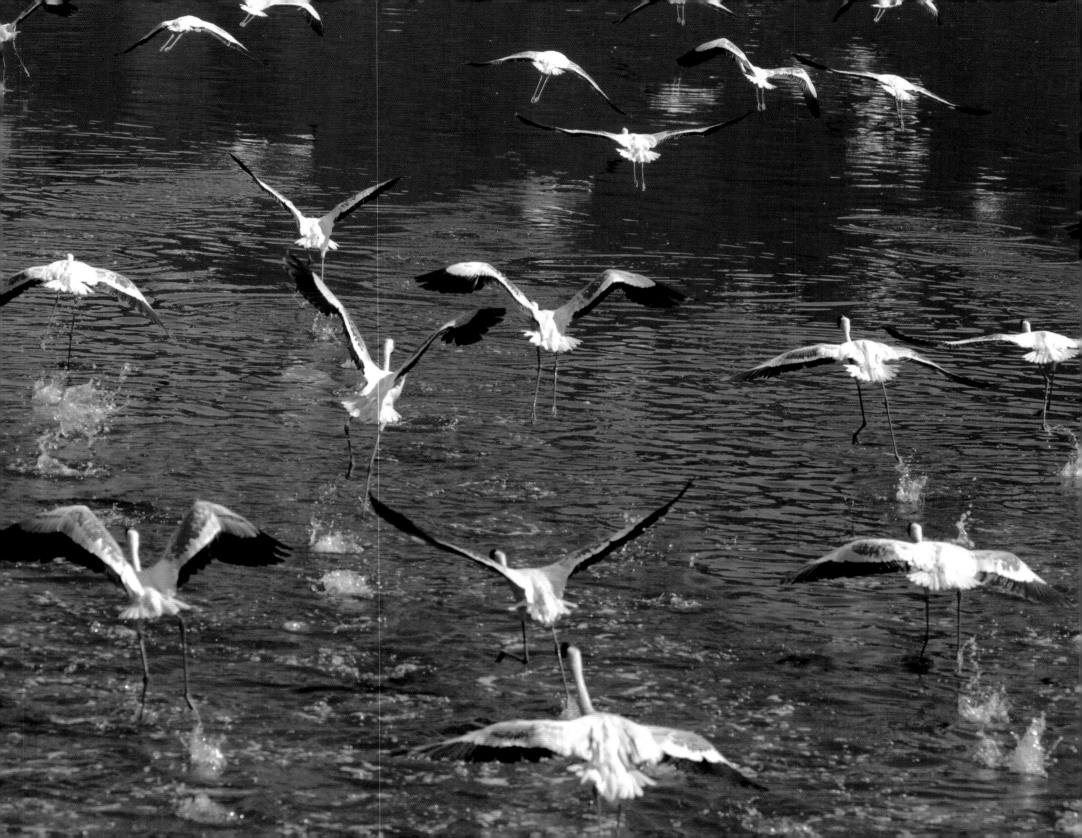

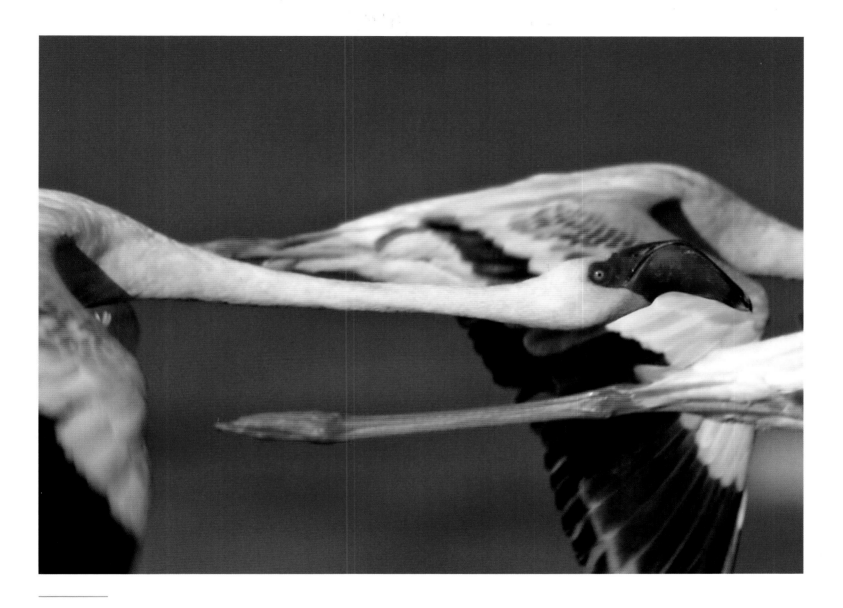

LESSER FLAMINGO, Kamfers Dam, South Africa
The flamingos leave the dam and fly off to nearby lakes,
though some will continue as far as Lake Bogoria in Kenya.

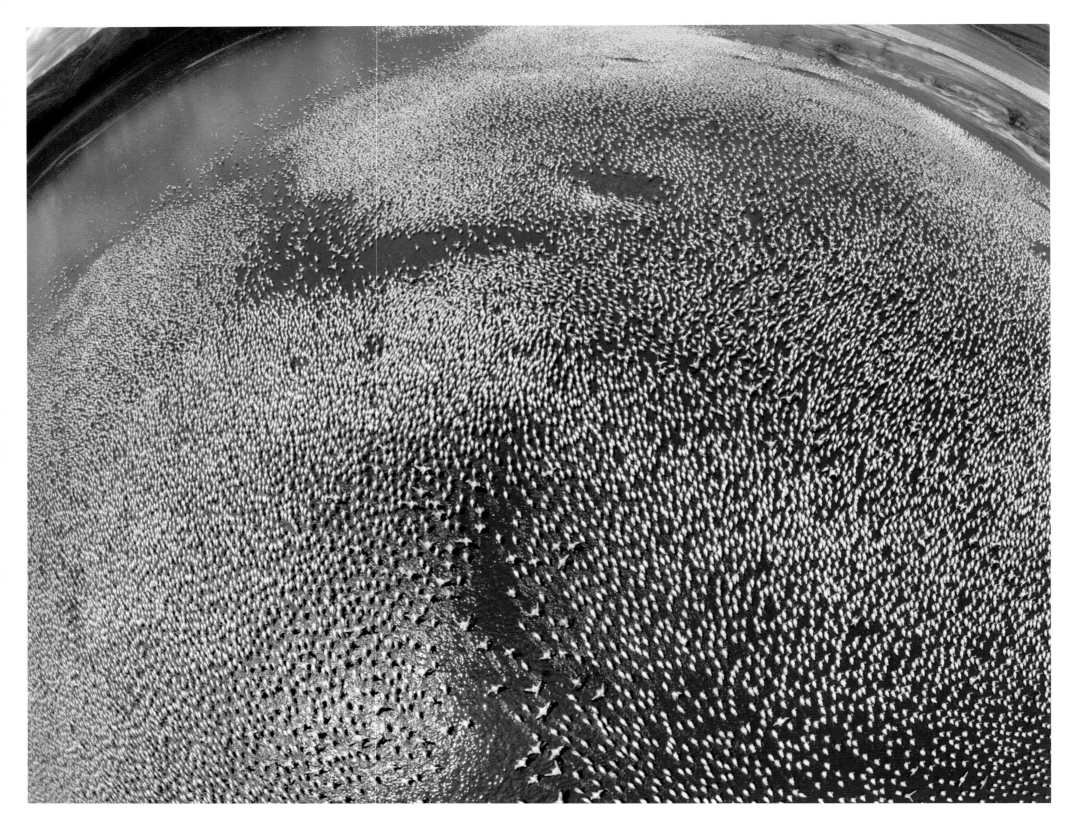

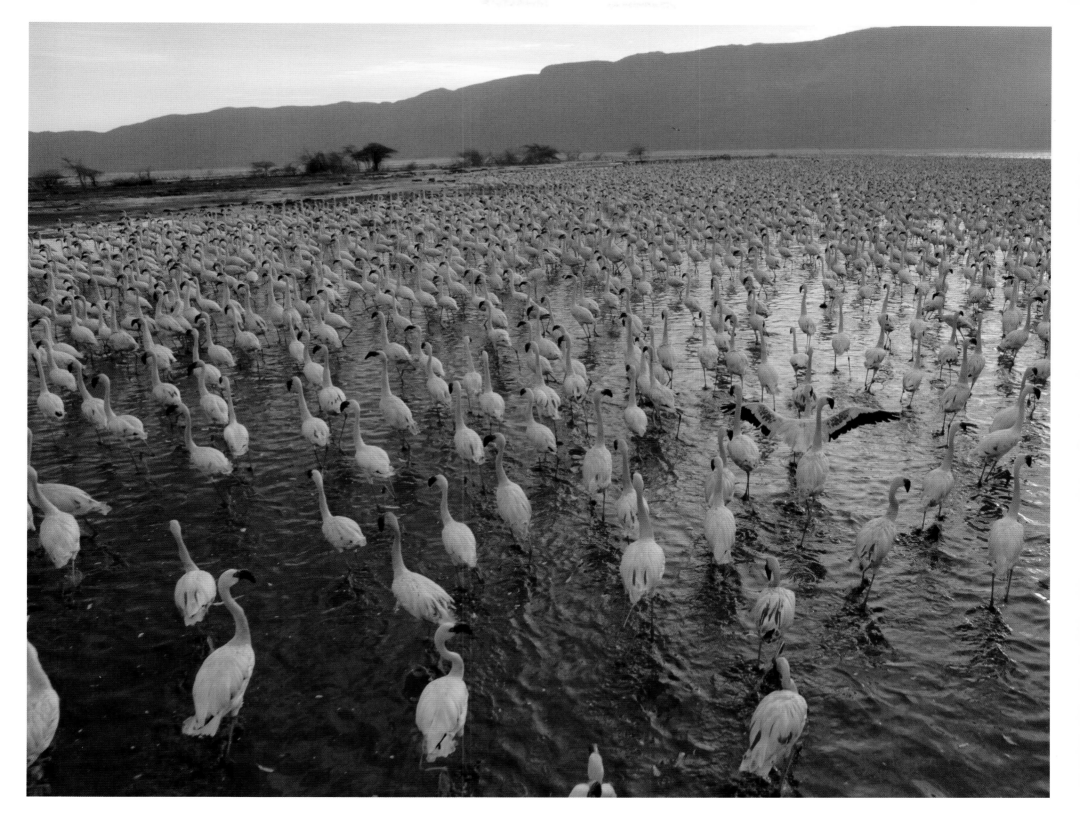

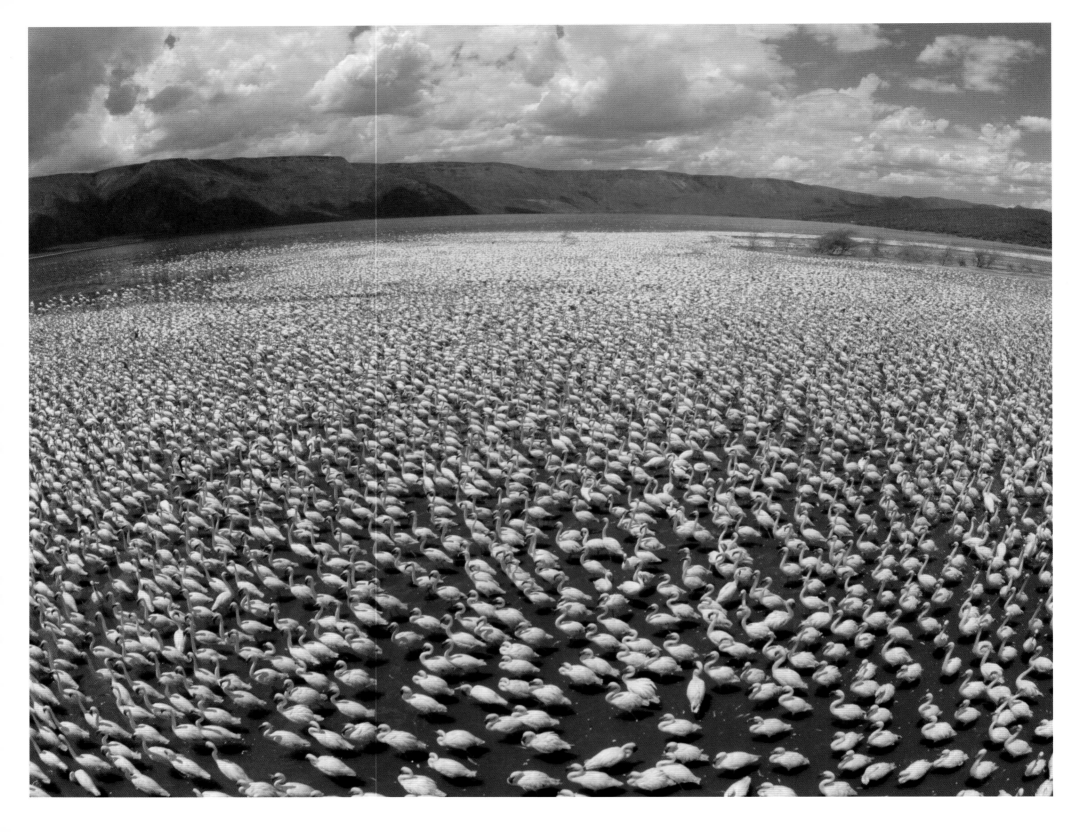

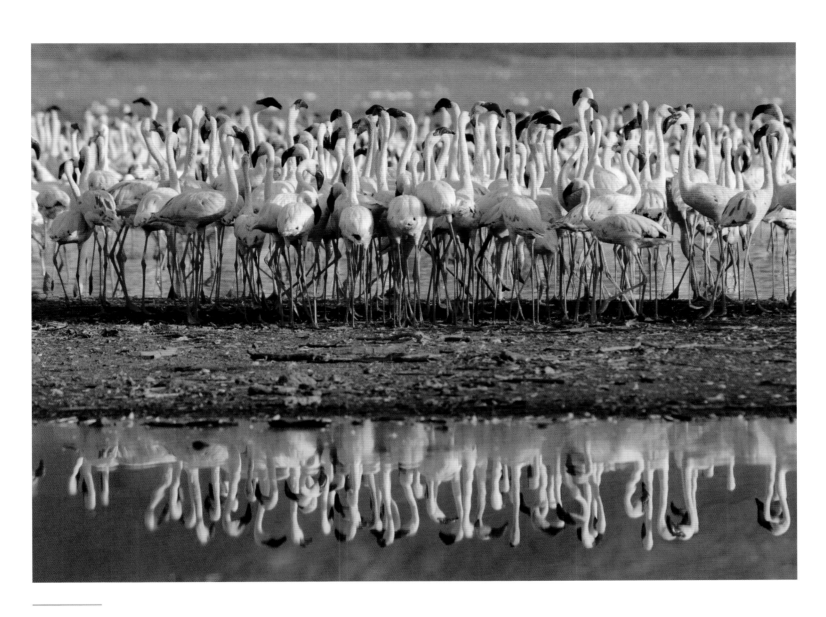

LESSER AND GREATER FLAMINGOS, Lake Bogoria, Kenya
Arriving at Lake Bogoria to feed are more than a million
migratory lesser flamingos. They feed on spirulina,
a blue-green algae that thrives here.

LESSER AND GREATER FLAMINGOS, Lake Bogoria, Kenya
While searching for the best places to feed, most flamingos will only travel as far as the next lake, but we discovered that some of these birds had travelled thousands of miles.

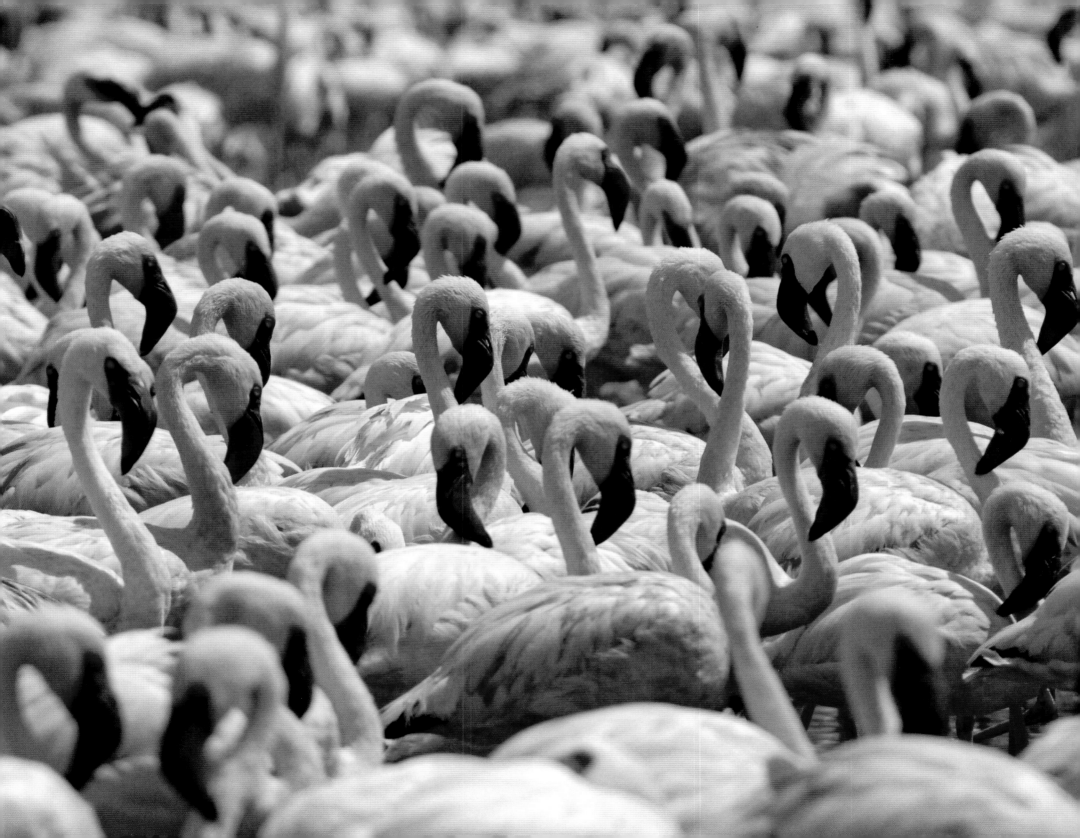

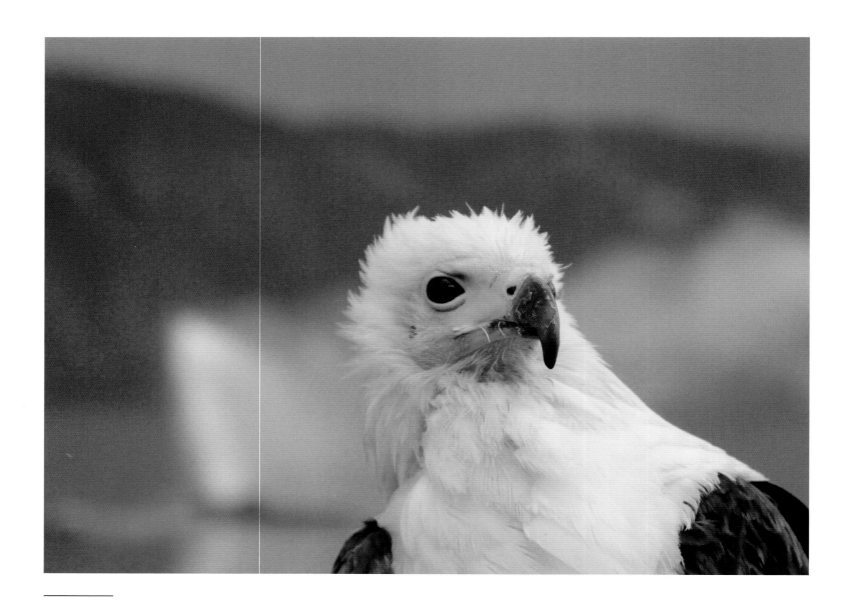

AFRICAN FISH EAGLE, Lake Bogoria, Kenya
The fish eagle, related to North America's bald eagle,
is found throughout sub-Saharan Africa, but always
close to lakes, rivers and swamps.

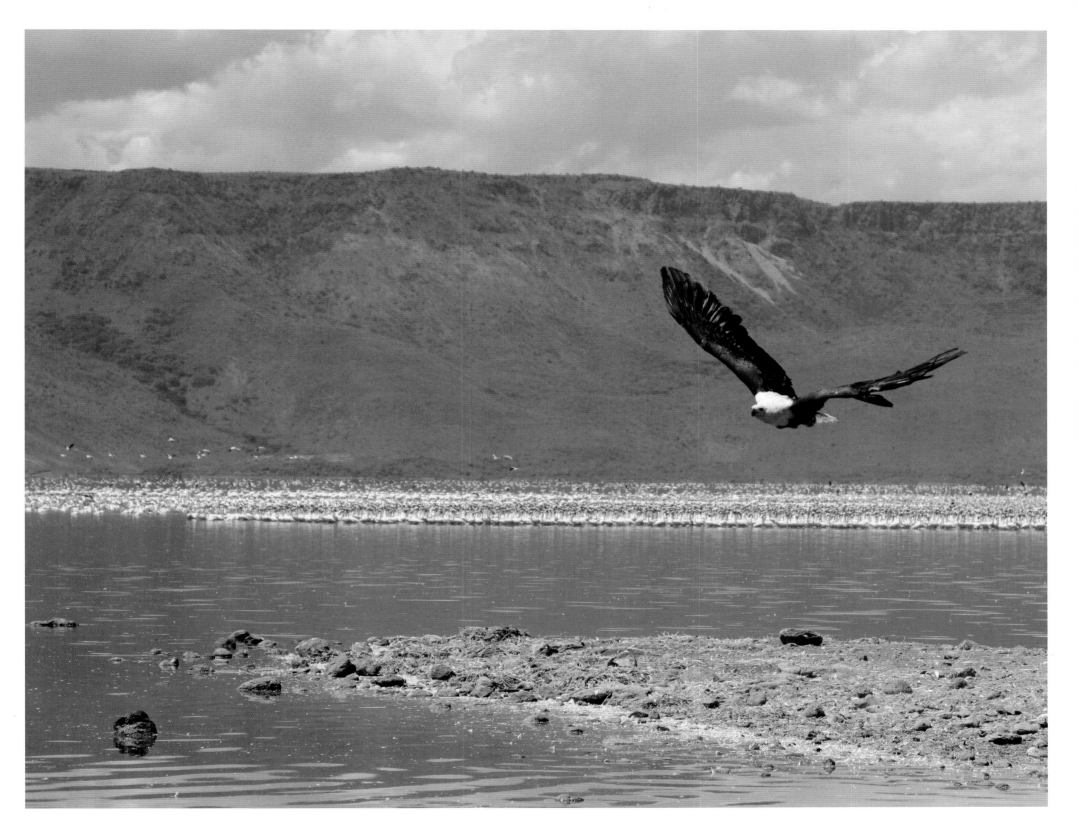

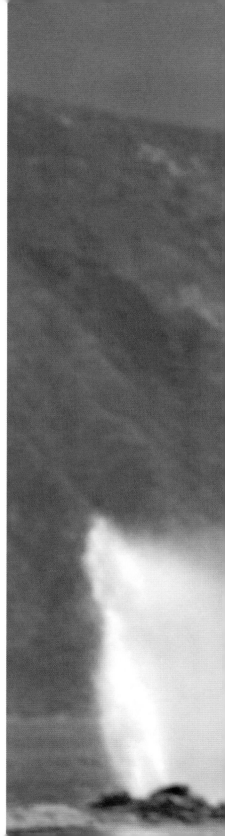

AFRICAN FISH EAGLE, Lake Bogoria, Kenya
These large eagles are opportunists. Although mainly
fish-eaters, they will hunt waterbirds, including young
or ailing flamingos.

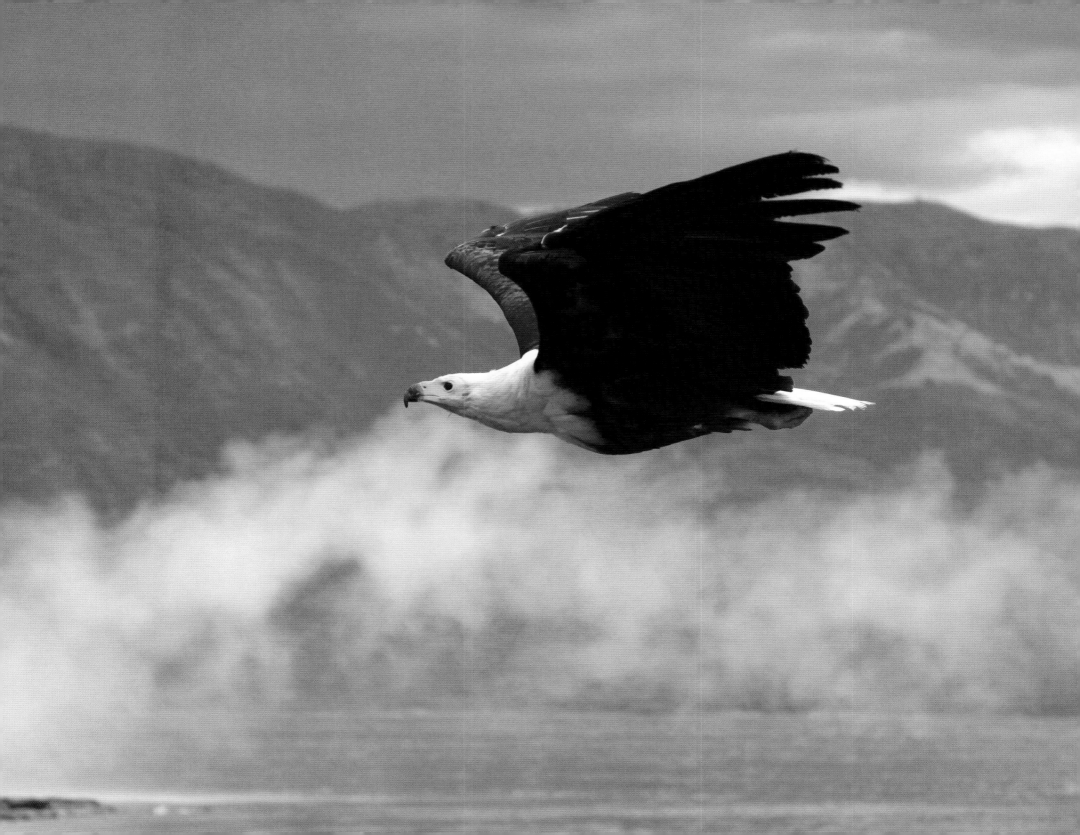

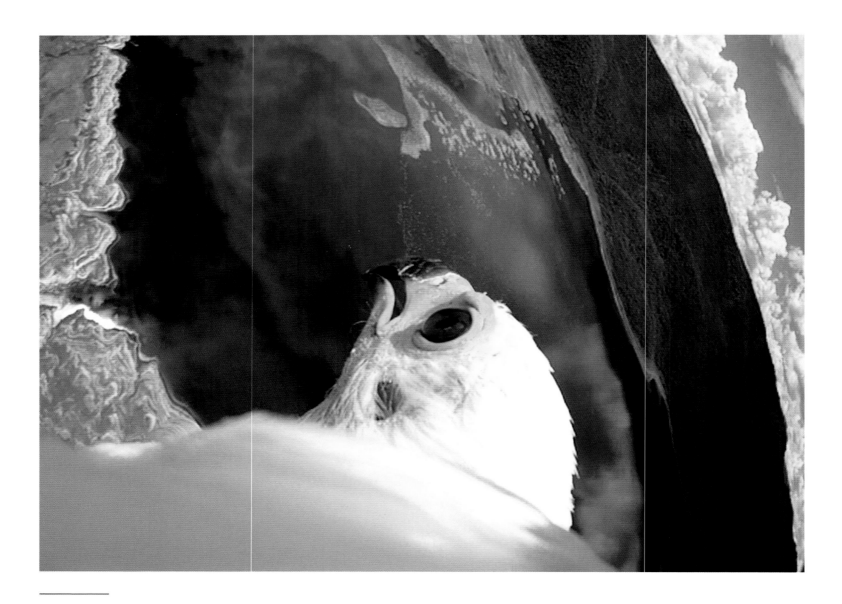

AFRICAN FISH EAGLE, Lake Bogoria, Kenya
From the eagle's point of view, the flamingos appear as a great
pink stain along the shallow shoreline, but with its acute vision the
predator is adept at picking out a vulnerable target from the crowd.

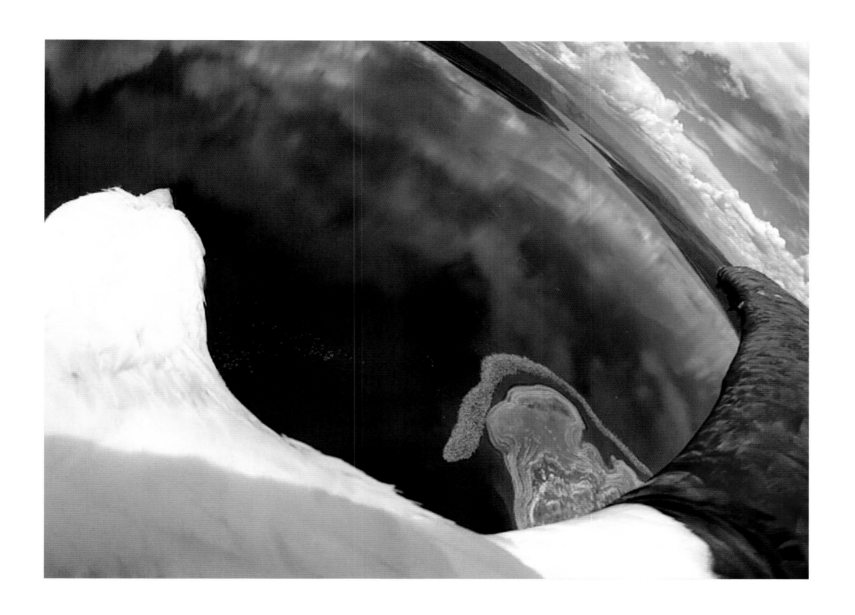

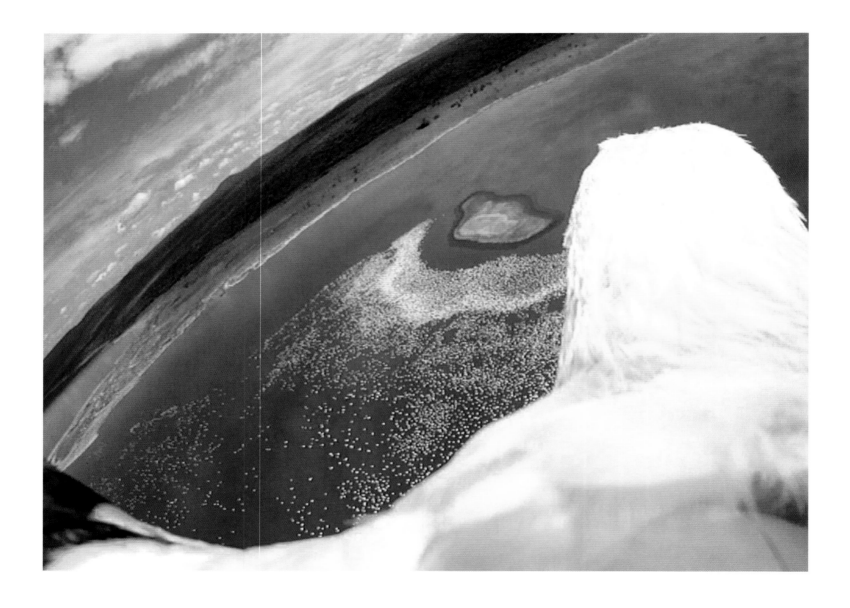

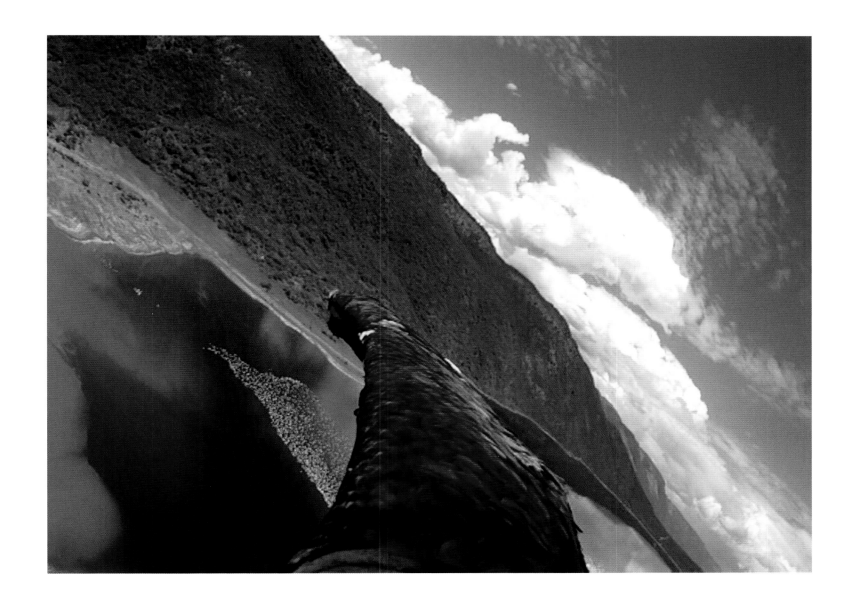

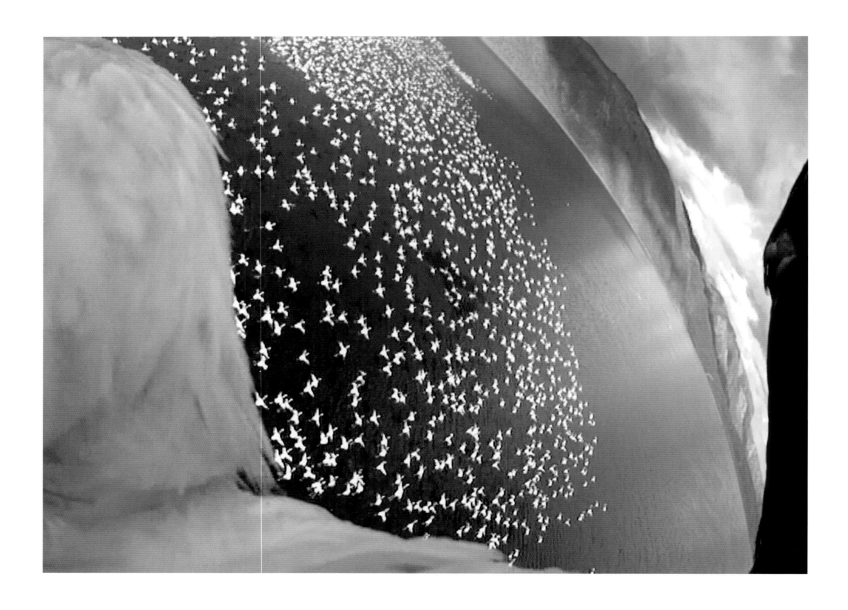

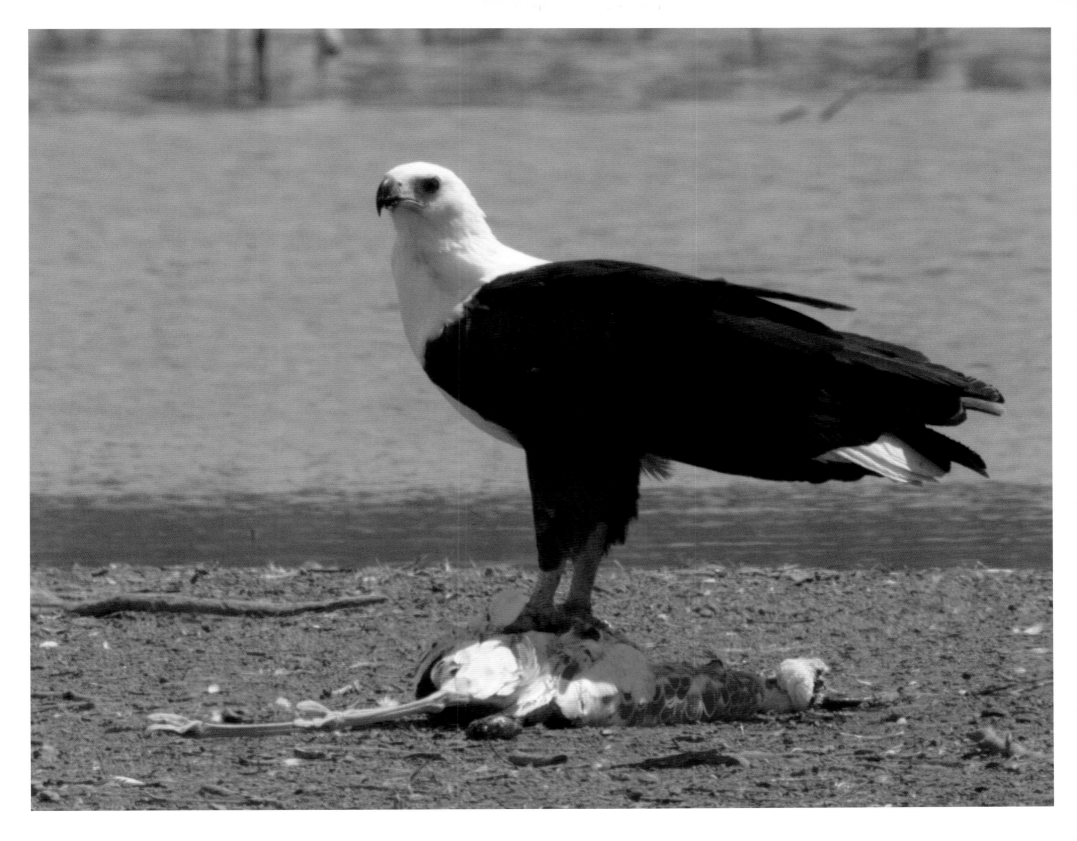

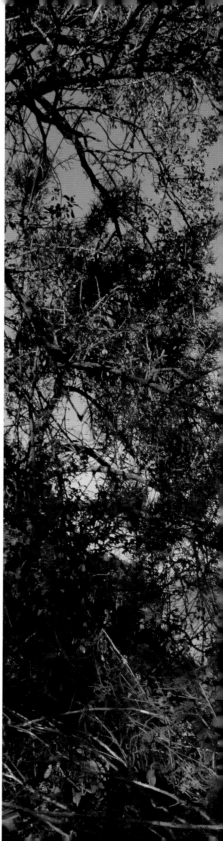

AFRICAN FISH EAGLE, Victoria Falls, Zambia–Zimbabwe
Some fish eagles migrate seasonally to avoid areas affected by
particularly heavy rain, while those in drier areas stay put all
year round. The Victoria Falls offers especially rich pickings.

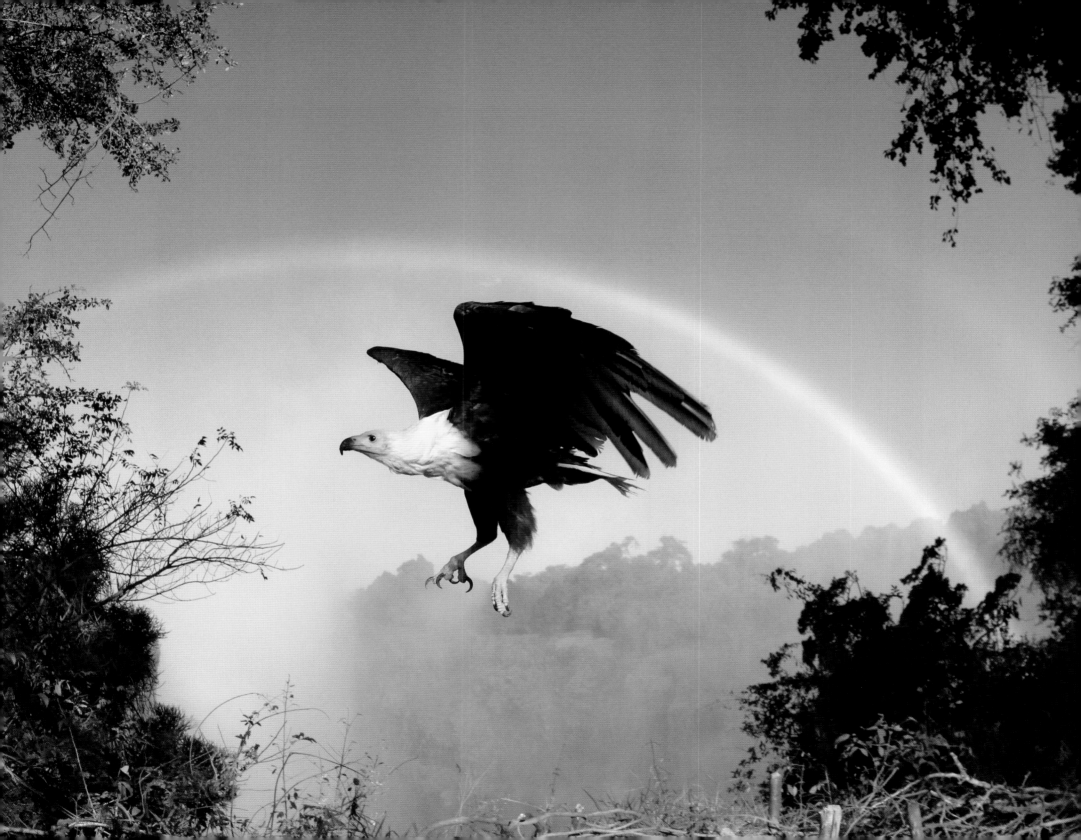

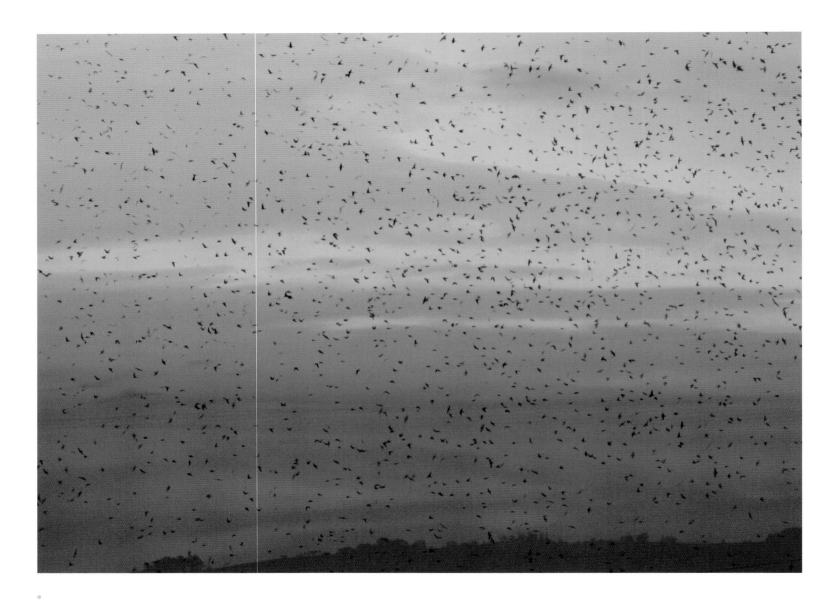

BARN SWALLOW, Mount Moreland, South Africa
From October, the Lake Victoria wetland is host
to three million swallows en route from Europe back
to South Africa.

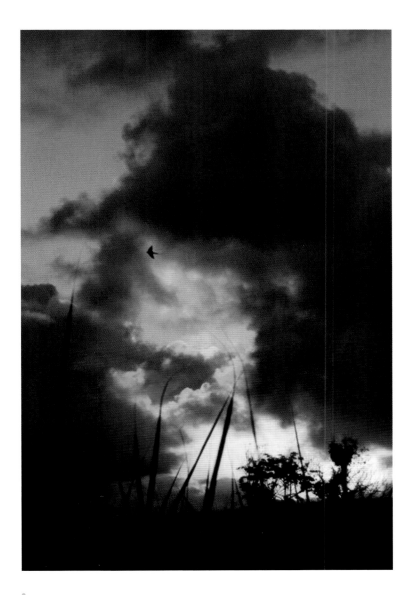
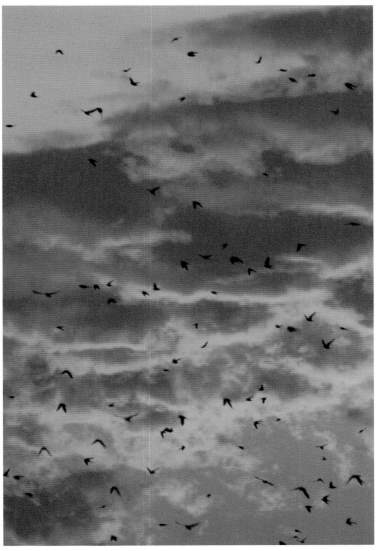

BARN SWALLOW, Mount Moreland, South Africa
In April they leave Africa for their long migration to Europe,
with some birds flying over 10,000 km (6,200 miles) to Nilsia
in Finland.

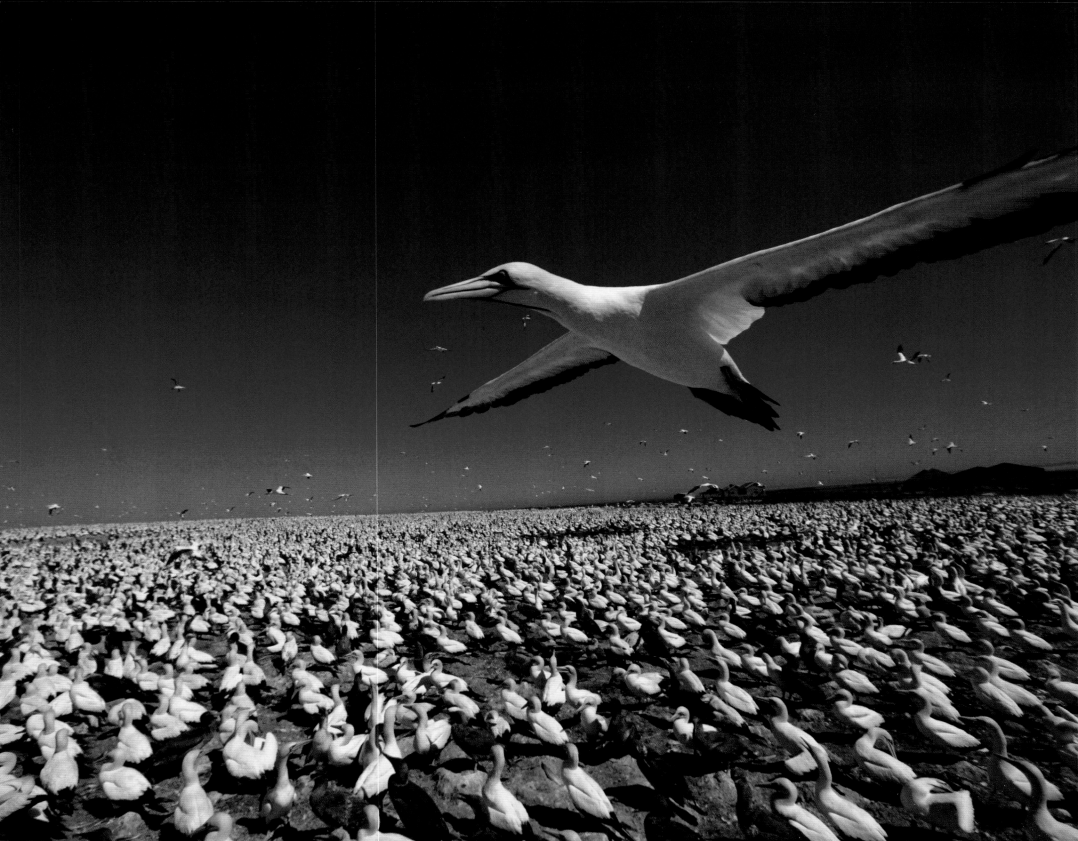

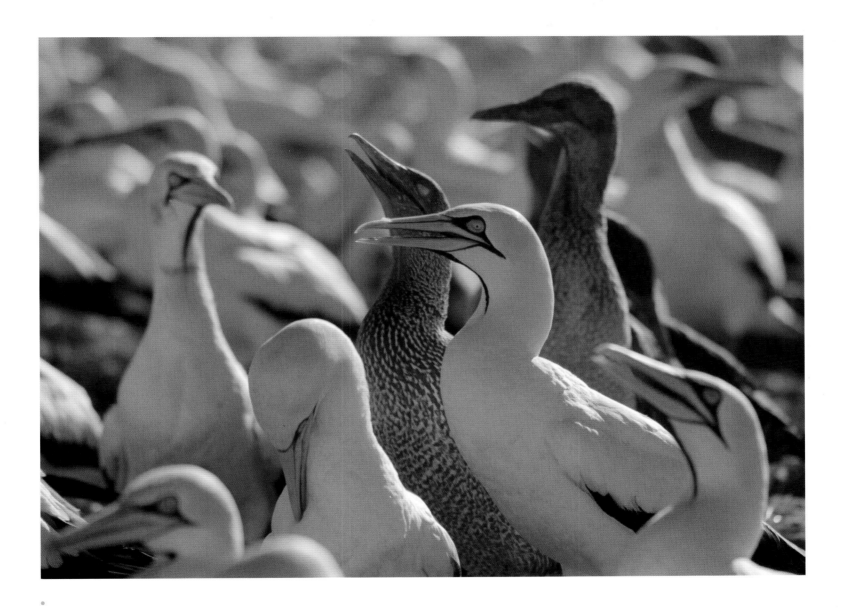

CAPE GANNET, Algoa Bay, South Africa
With upwards of 65,000 breeding pairs packed into
2.4 hectares, the aptly named Bird Island of Algoa Bay
hosts the largest gannet colony in the world.

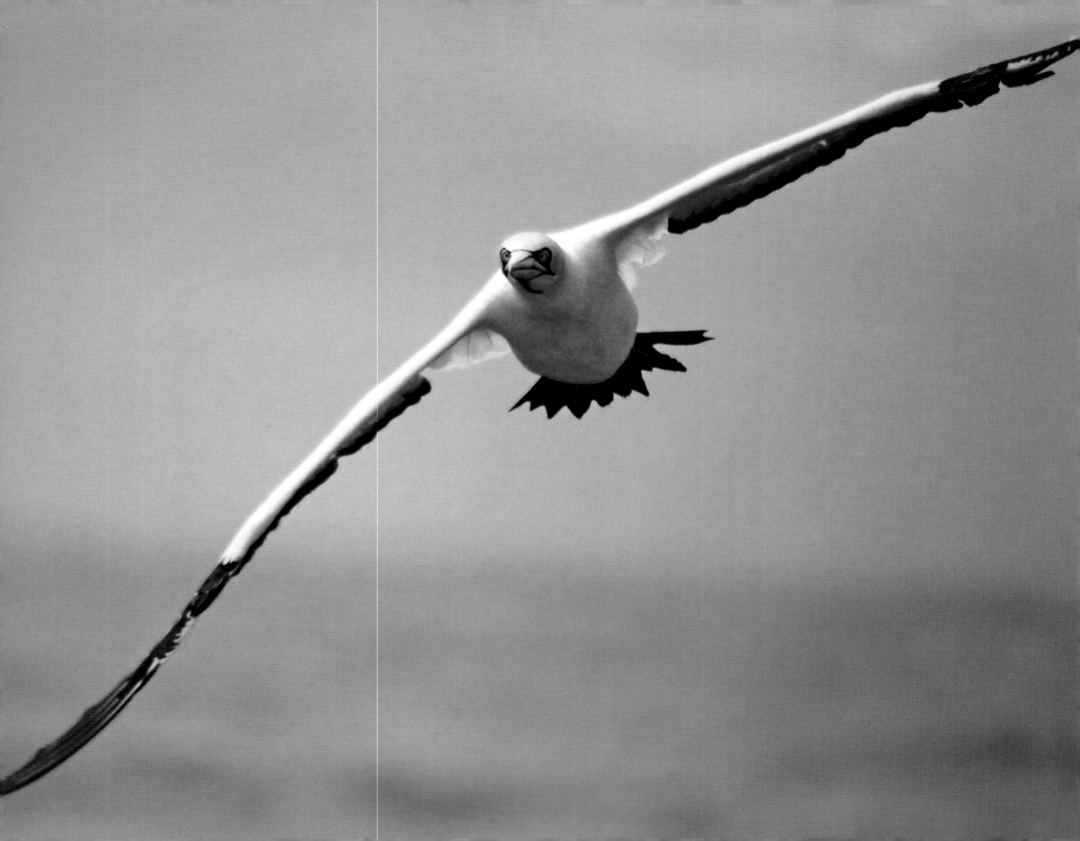

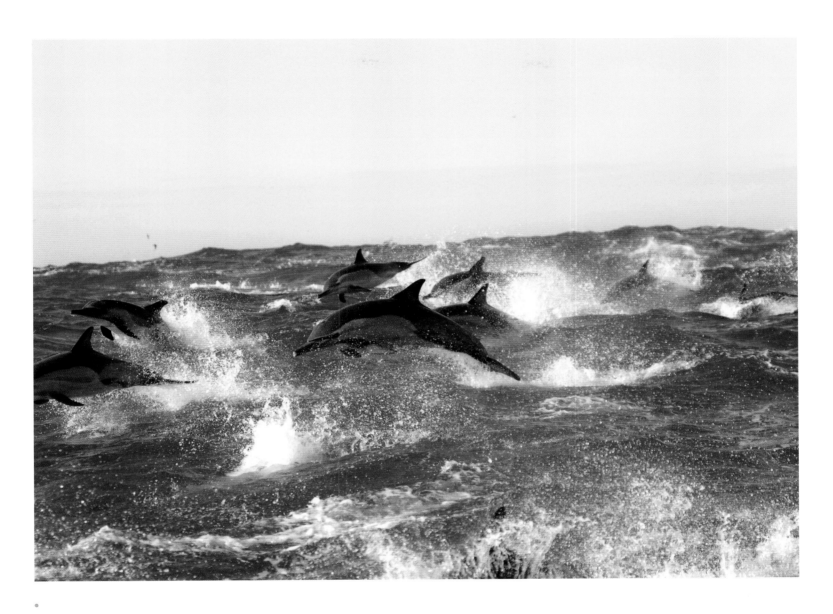

CAPE GANNET, off South African coast
The gannets follow the 'sardine run', watching the dolphins and
Bryde's whales that lead them to the monstrous shoals of fish.
The birds plunge-dive, hitting the water at up to 120 kph (75 mph).

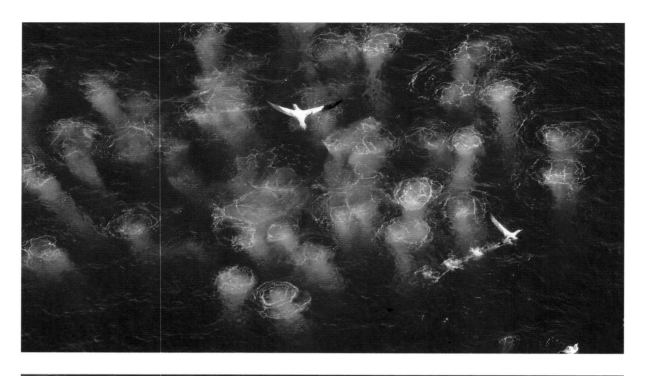

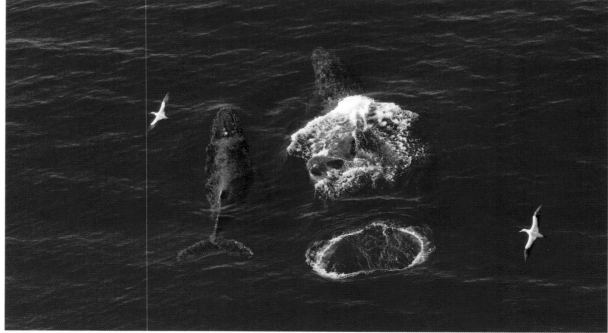

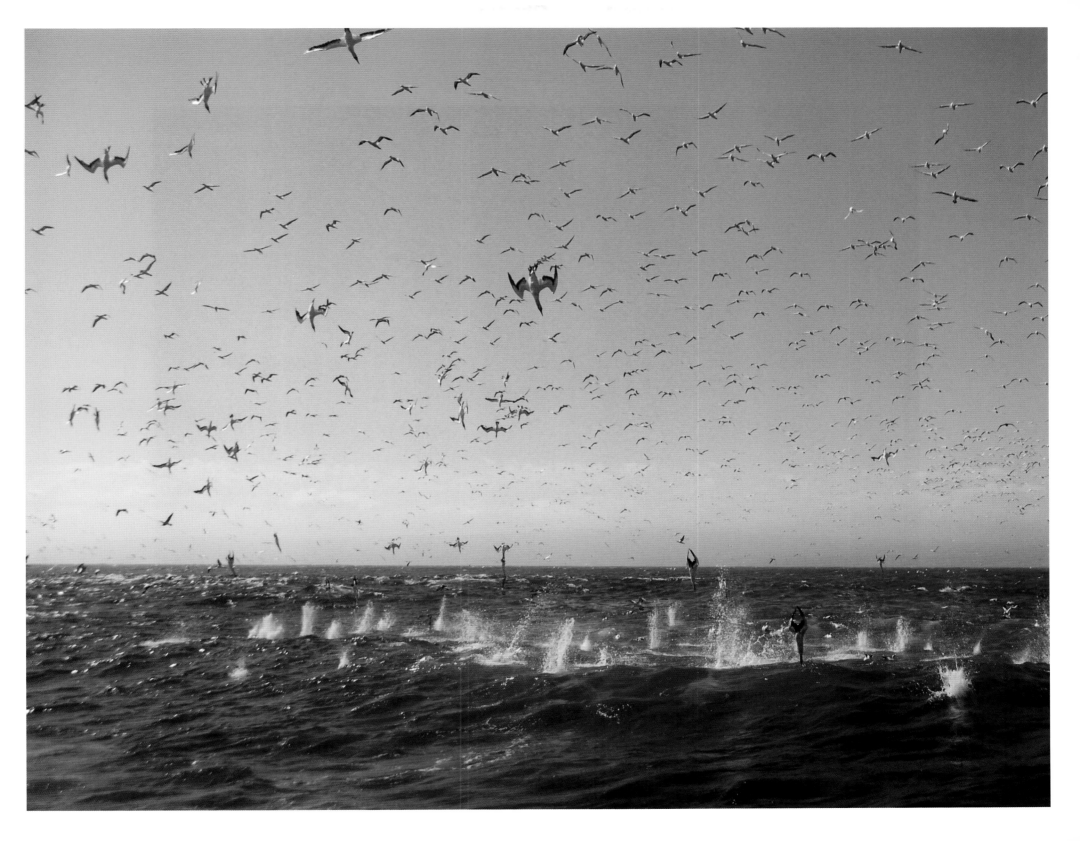

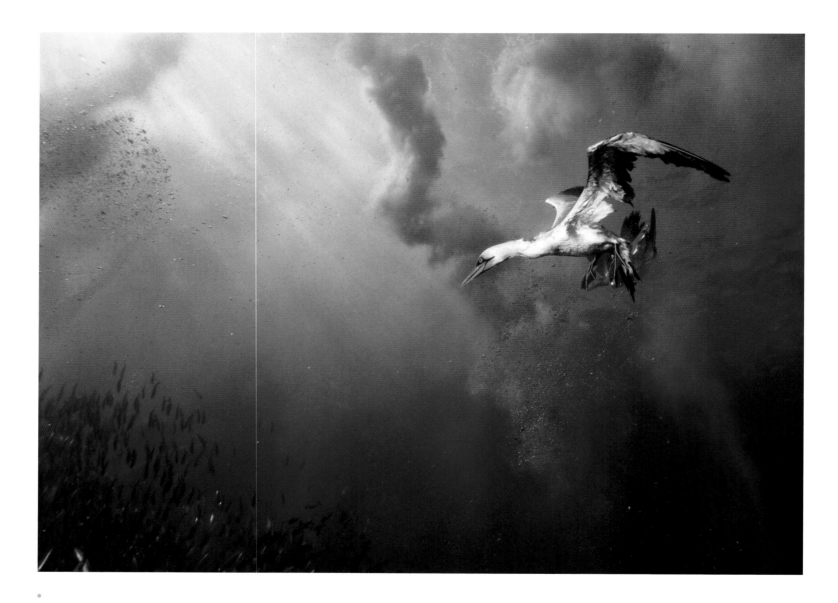

CAPE GANNET, off South African coast
Below the surface, the gannets catch anchovies and sardines
– not on their high-speed entry, but on their way back to
the surface.

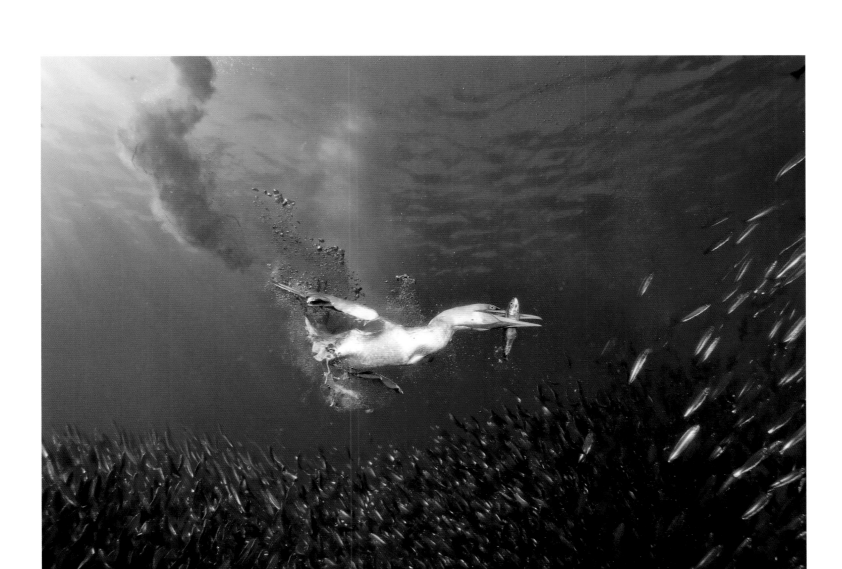

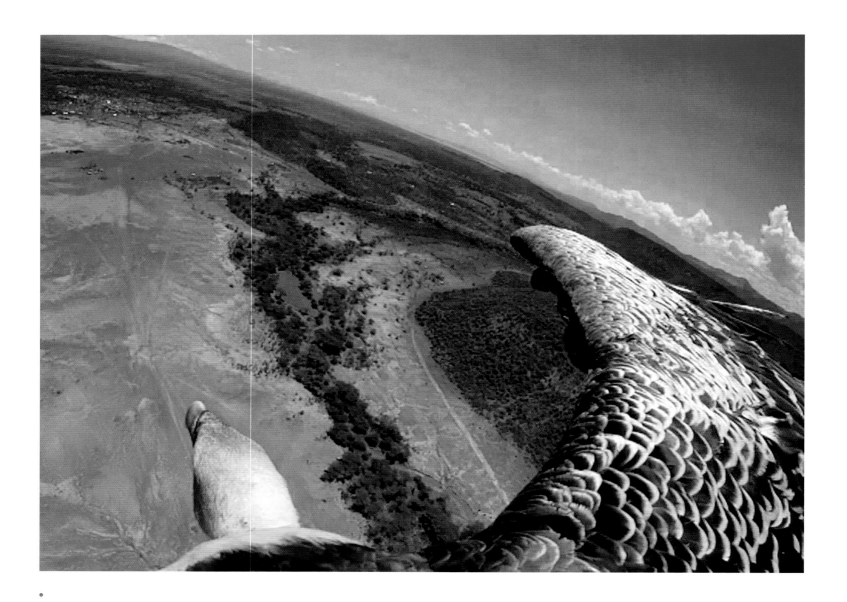

RÜPPELL'S GRIFFON VULTURE, great plains, Kenya
With eyes that are said to see a carcass from over six kilometres
(nearly four miles) away, the vulture is quick to spot a lion kill
or the commotion of a crocodile attack in the rivers below.

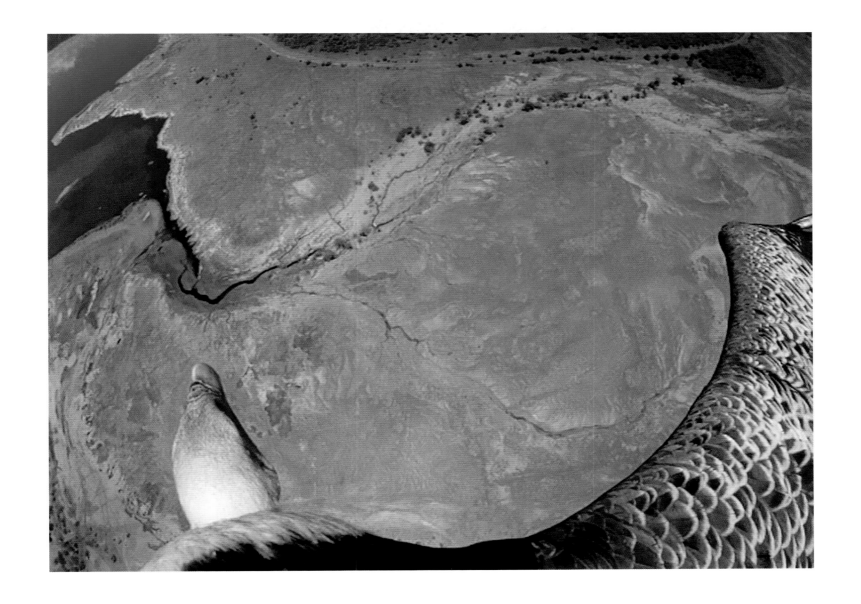

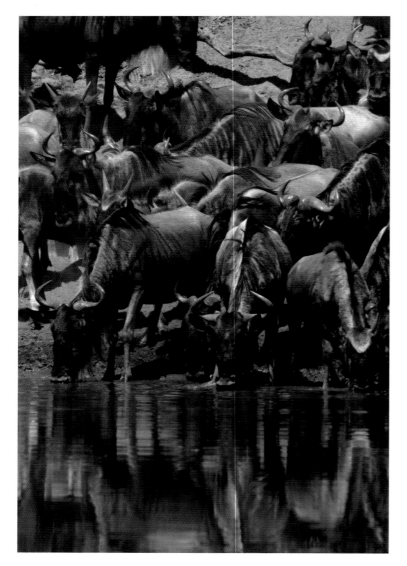
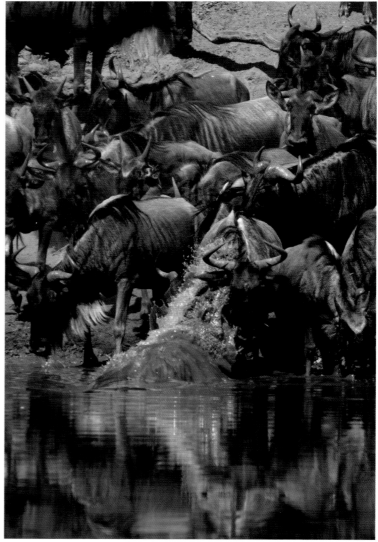

NILE CROCODILES AND WILDEBEEST, Grumeti River, Tanzania
Crocodiles are an everyday hazard for the vast herds of wildebeest on
their annual migration around the Serengeti, and where there are feeding
crocodiles there are certain to be leftovers for vultures.

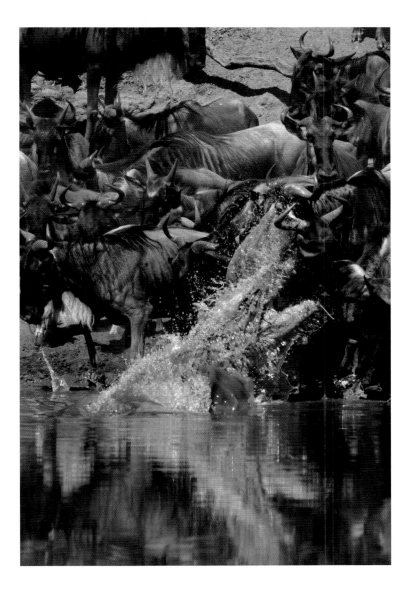
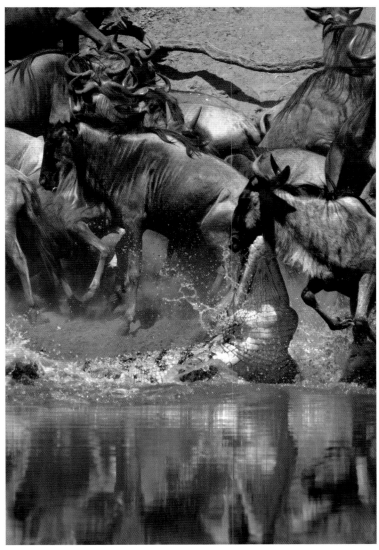

NORTH AMERICA

The great, iconic North American landscape provides the backdrop to a breathtakingly intricate network of criss-crossing migrations, as species after species of bird time their great journeys to coincide with some of nature's key events.

Birds work to punishing schedules. Each spring, more than five million snow geese set out from overwintering grounds along the Gulf of Mexico on a 5,000 km (3,000 mile) journey across the North American countryside and cityscapes to the Arctic, where they nest and bring up their young. They stream northwards in flocks many thousand strong, following traditional flyways across the continent. The geese stop off to refuel at key sites, such as the Platte River area on the Central Flyway, but such is their urgency to breed, the frontrunners literally follow the melting snows. One group heads up the East Coast Flyway, stopping to feed around Delaware Bay, and when they leave, others arrive to take their place.

For birds on migration, timing is critical. Without sustenance, it would be impossible for many species to complete the gruelling journeys required of them. The source of this sustenance is often tied inextricably to the life cycle of another species, and so birds must travel in a carefully managed window of time in order to make the most of the food available. California's brown pelicans, for example, head for the Gulf of California. The bordering lands may be dry and rugged, but the sea is teeming with life. The nutrient-rich waters provide food for all manner of creatures, from seabirds to humpback whales, and the pelicans have discovered another of nature's unusual events.

At a certain time on high spring tides, small fish called grunion are swept up the beach by the waves to deposit their eggs along the tideline. All the brown pelicans should need to do is scoop them up, but their bills are the wrong shape. If they tried for the beached fish, they would simply get a mouthful of sand. Instead, they turn their backs on the stranded fish and try to catch those arriving or leaving in the surf – no mean feat in itself, for their bag-like pouch is awkward in the turbulent water. Arriving at the right place and at just the right time to partake in this breeding frenzy is crucial to the pelicans' survival, and is just one example that we filmed of birds working within a complicated timeframe of natural events.

Near the USA's southern border with Mexico, red-tailed hawks are among the mass exodus of raptors from South to North America each spring. Some head for Bracken Cave near San Antonio, Texas, and they've not come for the fishing, but for meat – bat meat.

The bats in question are free-tailed bats, and an estimated 20 million of them roost in the caves in summer – the biggest congregation in the world. Each evening they stream out of the cave entrance to catch insects in the surrounding countryside, and the hawks stand around as inconspicuously as they can waiting for them to emerge. The first sign is a couple of scout

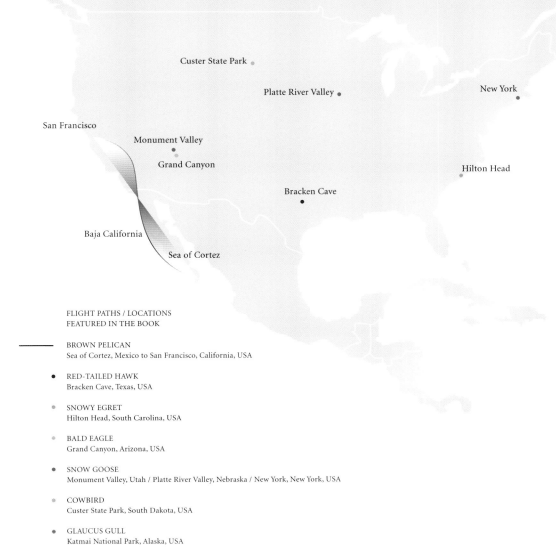

bats that fly out and around the immediate vicinity, checking where the predators might be. They return to the cave and the exodus begins.

The bats emerge in pulses, filling the air and blotting out the setting sun. The hawks tear into the swarm, but there are so many bats most avoid being caught in the confusion. And, if a storm is brewing, with thunder and lightning on the distant horizon, the bats emerge all at once in a bat 'explosion'. It is a rare event, and the hawks barely have time to react. The bats, though, are on the wing and racing off to their hunting grounds before either the storm or the predators can catch them.

In the creeks of the Carolinas, egrets have latched onto an easier fast-food outlet: they watch dolphins. The egrets line up at key spots on the muddy banks about an hour either side of low tide, and regular as clockwork, pods of bottlenose dolphins appear. The dolphins herd entire shoals of fish up onto the mud – a behaviour known as 'strand feeding' – and the birds steal as many fish as they can before they slither back into the river.

Finally, we watched in the parks of Alaska as bald eagles and glaucus gulls join wild bears on the salmon run, picking off the fish as they leap upstream on their own exhausting journey. Time and again, we came across key events such as this, locked into an intricate timetable of migration, feeding and breeding.

Katmai National Park

Custer State Park

Platte River Valley

New York

San Francisco

Monument Valley

Grand Canyon

Hilton Head

Bracken Cave

Baja California

Sea of Cortez

FLIGHT PATHS / LOCATIONS
FEATURED IN THE BOOK

BROWN PELICAN
Sea of Cortez, Mexico to San Francisco, California, USA

RED-TAILED HAWK
Bracken Cave, Texas, USA

SNOWY EGRET
Hilton Head, South Carolina, USA

BALD EAGLE
Grand Canyon, Arizona, USA

SNOW GOOSE
Monument Valley, Utah / Platte River Valley, Nebraska / New York, New York, USA

COWBIRD
Custer State Park, South Dakota, USA

GLAUCUS GULL
Katmai National Park, Alaska, USA

BROWN PELICAN, Sea of Cortez, Mexico
Pelicans and humpback whales not only patrol the same
waters, but also share a bag-like lower jaw mechanism
to engulf large volumes of water containing food –
an example of convergent evolution.

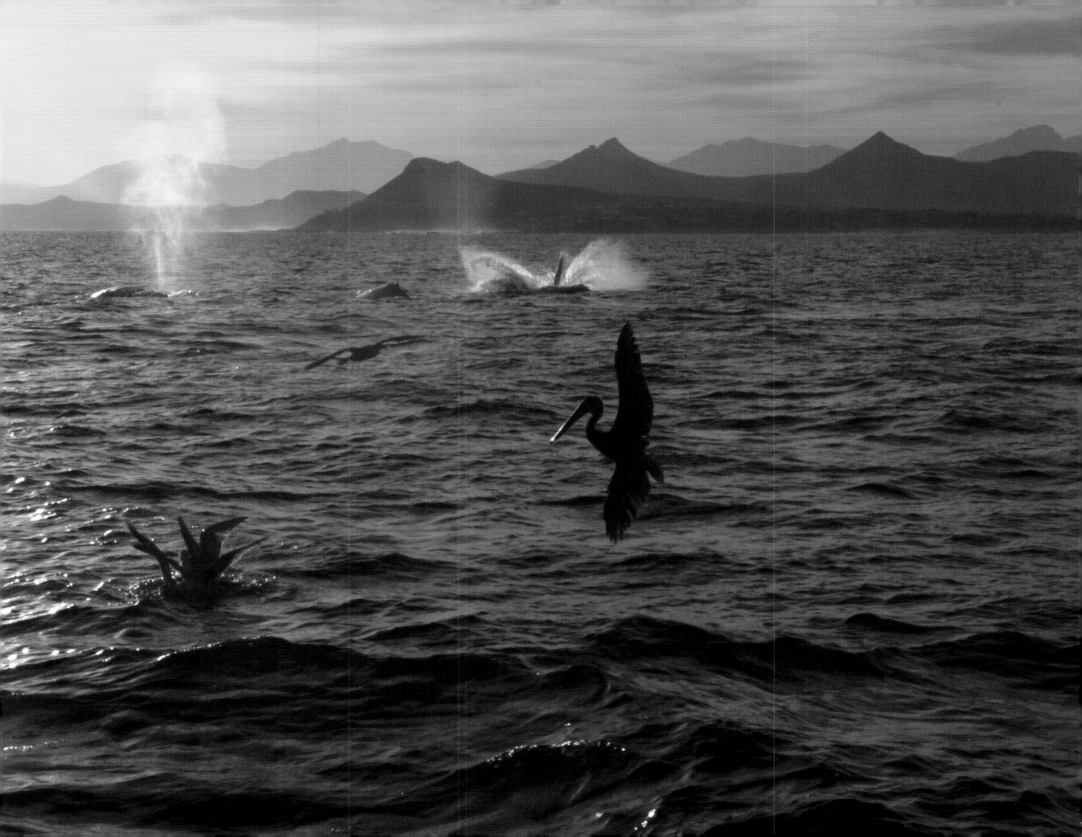

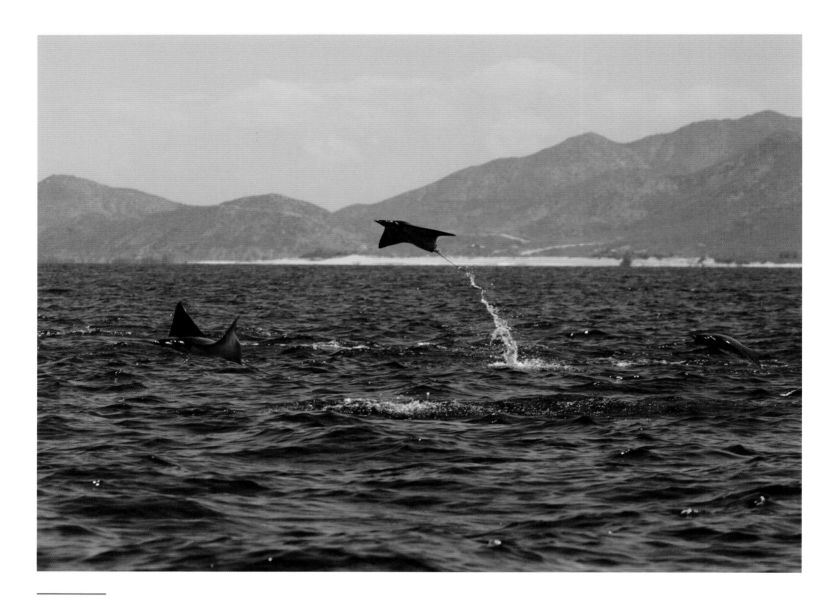

MOBULA RAY, Sea of Cortez, Mexico
These rays leap clear of the water and travel a few metres
in the air, moving their 'wings' (pectoral fins) as if flying.

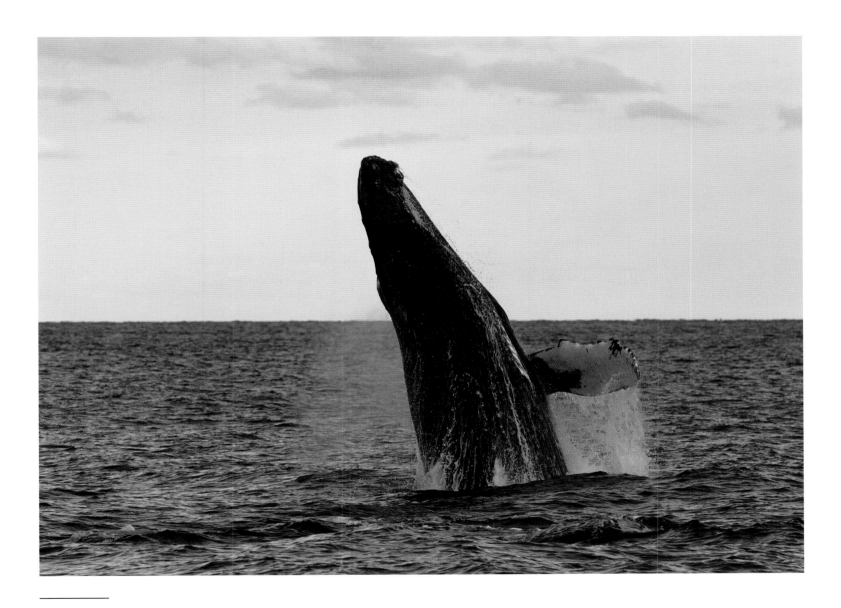

HUMPBACK WHALE, Sea of Cortez, Mexico
Similarly, humpbacks rise out of the water and crash
back down in a behaviour known as breaching.

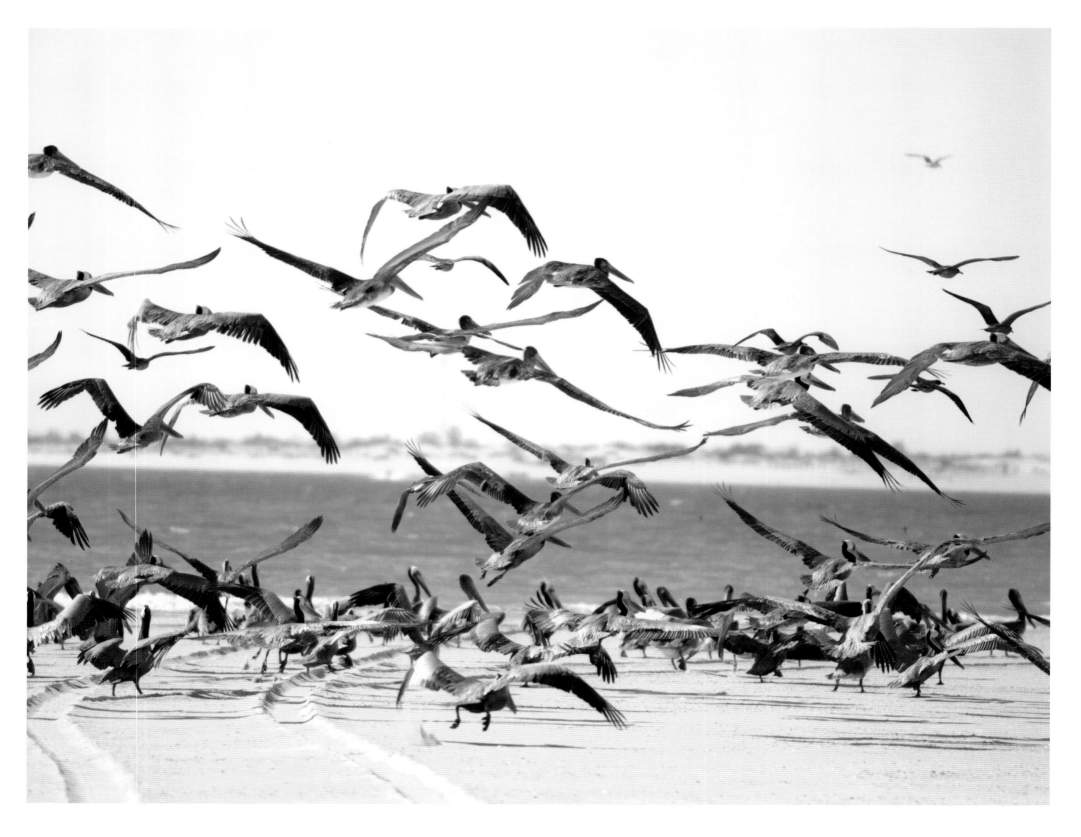

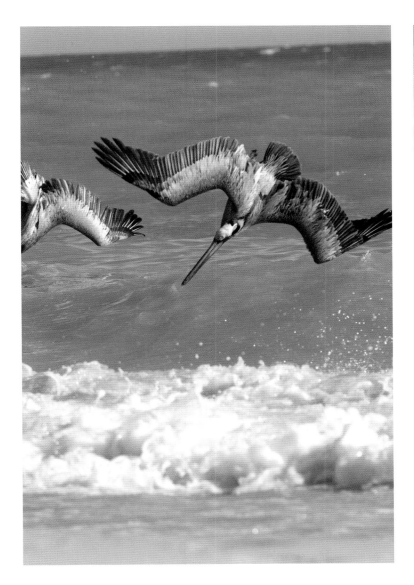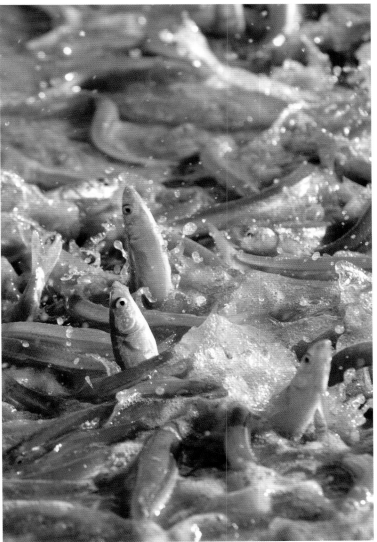

BROWN PELICAN, Sea of Cortez, Mexico
Pelicans feast on small fish known as grunion, and are able to
use their elevated viewpoint to spot where and when the first
batch of prey will emerge.

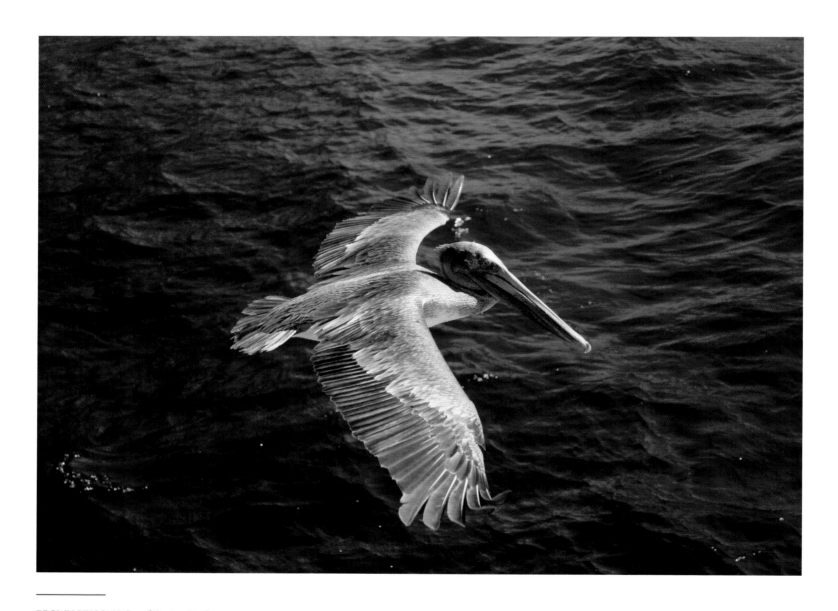

BROWN PELICAN, Sea of Cortez, Mexico
Immediately after breeding in late spring, birds leave the
Sea of Cortez and cross Baja California to the Pacific coast.

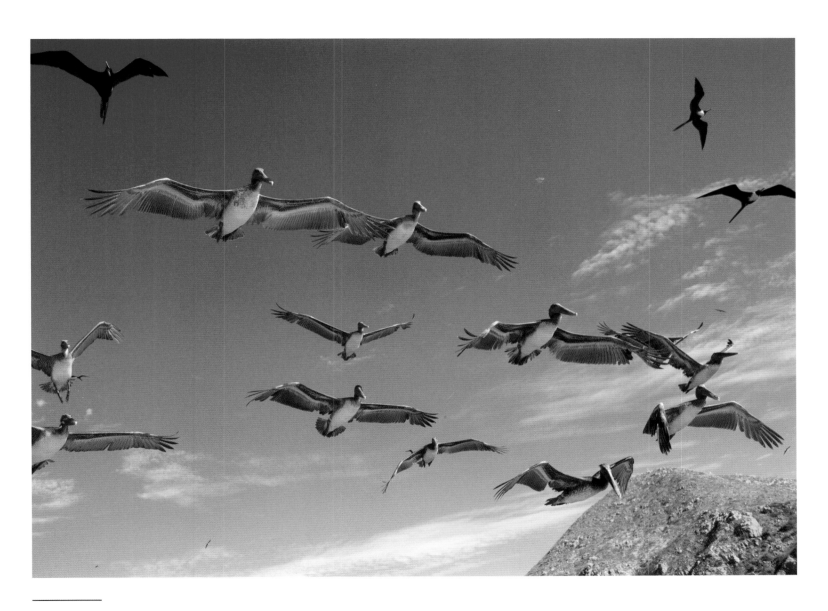

BROWN PELICAN, Baja California, Mexico
One of the main Baja crossing points for pelicans is
Bahía de los Angeles, where the birds use currents of
hot air to soar across the dry and barren land below.

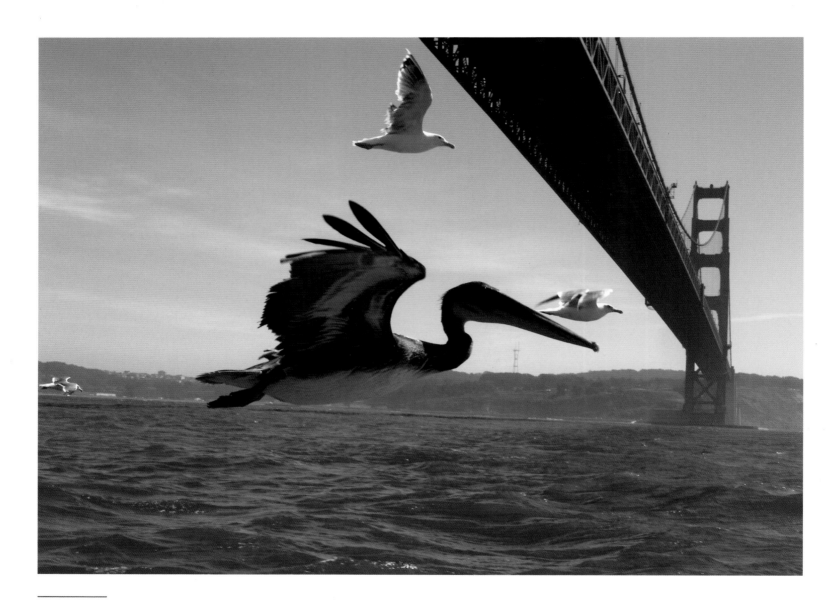

BROWN PELICAN, Golden Gate Bridge, San Francisco, California, USA
Most birds head north, dispersing along the California coast and as far as
Oregon and British Columbia, where they arrive in June just as the baitfish
are schooling.

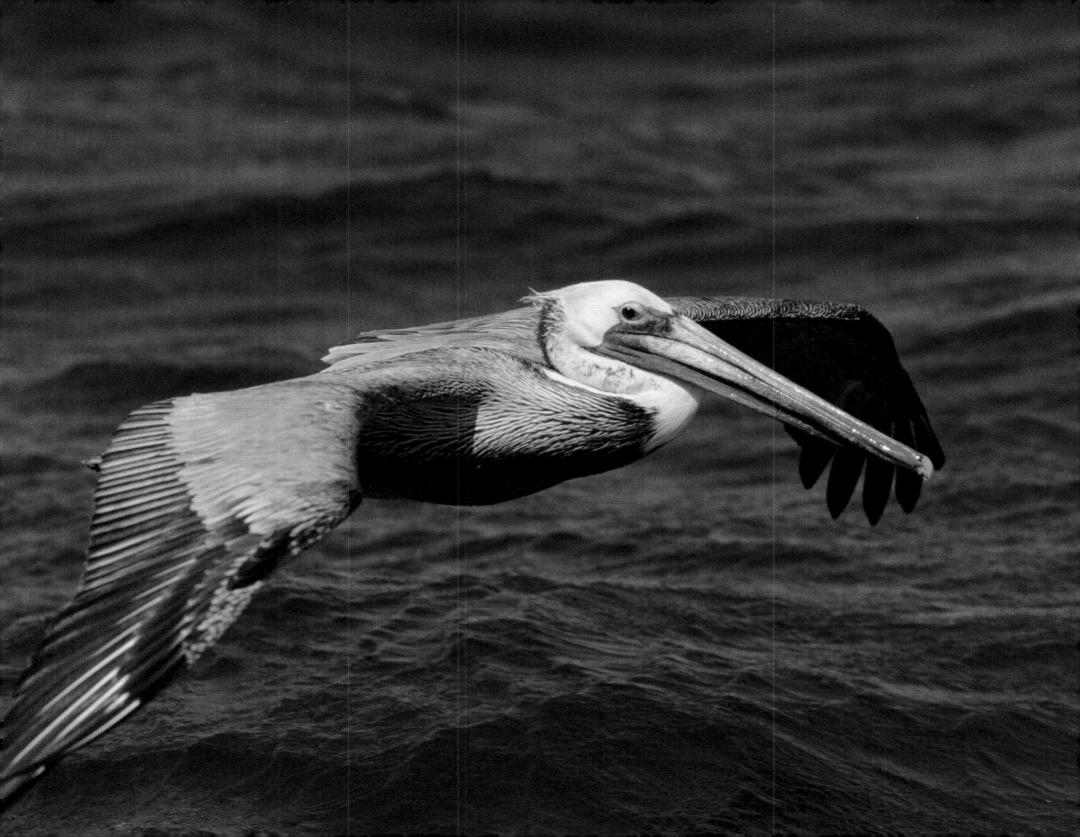

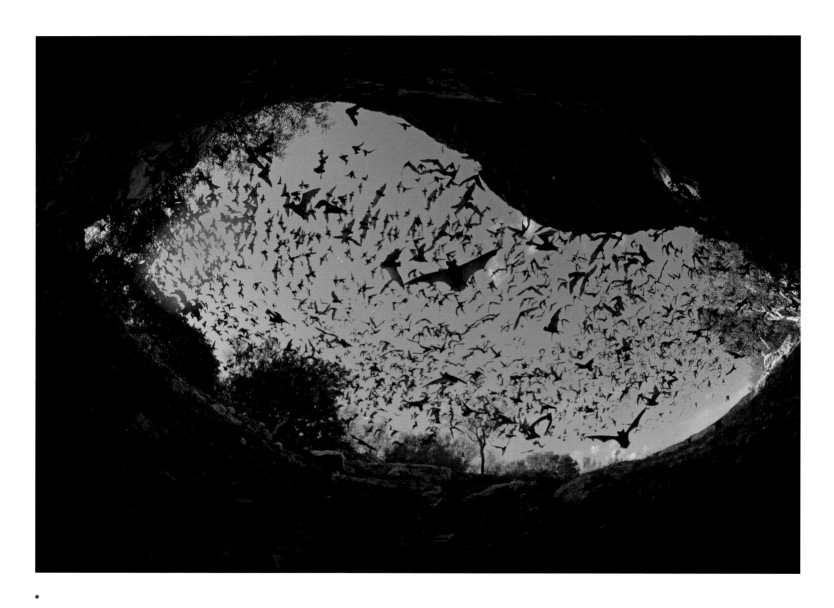

MEXICAN FREE-TAILED BAT, Bracken Cave, Texas, USA
Every evening from March to October, over 20 million bats leave
this cave to hunt in the surrounding countryside, consuming
upwards of 200 tonnes of insects each night.

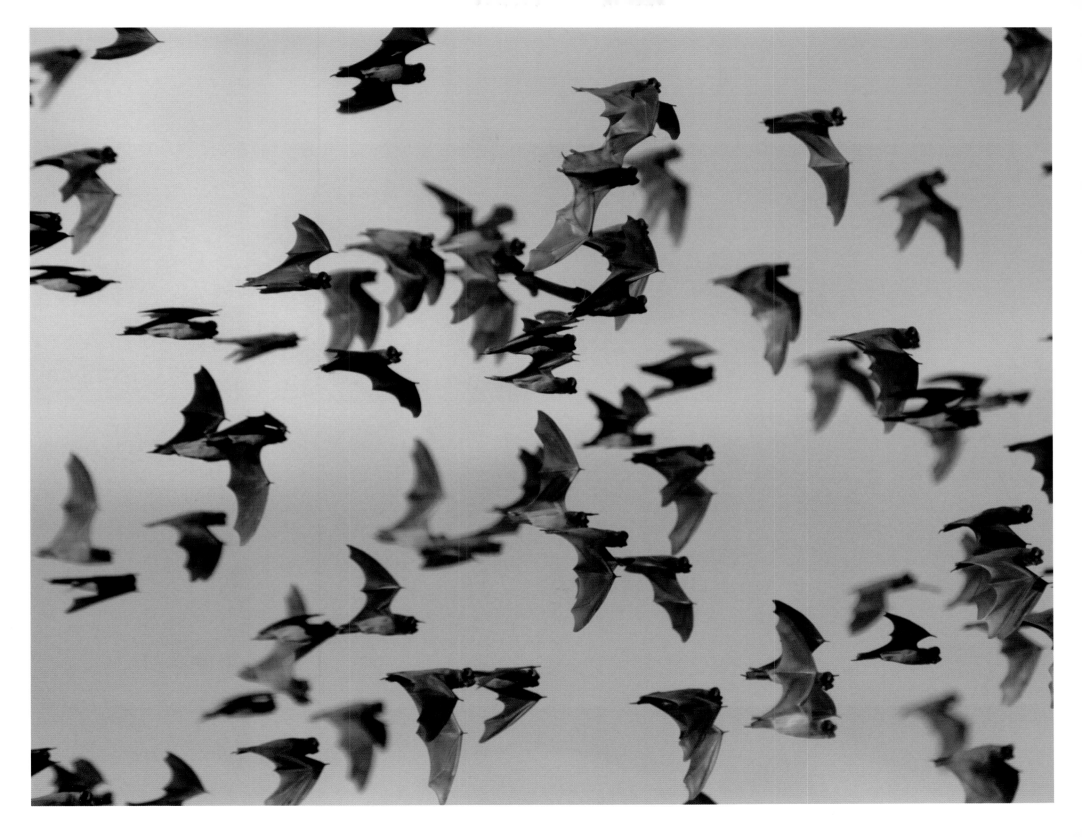

RED-TAILED HAWK, Bracken Cave, Texas, USA
Having flown in from Argentina, red-tailed hawks
stake out the cave entrance to hunt bats as they leave
and return to the cave.

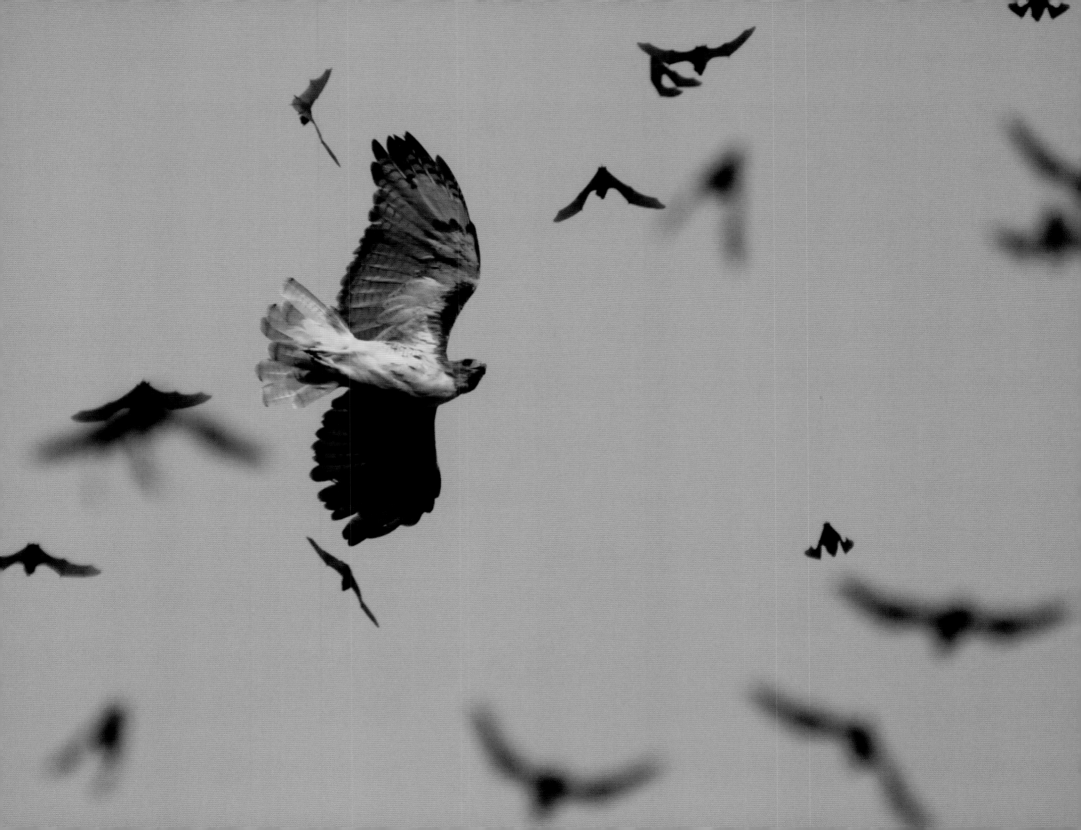

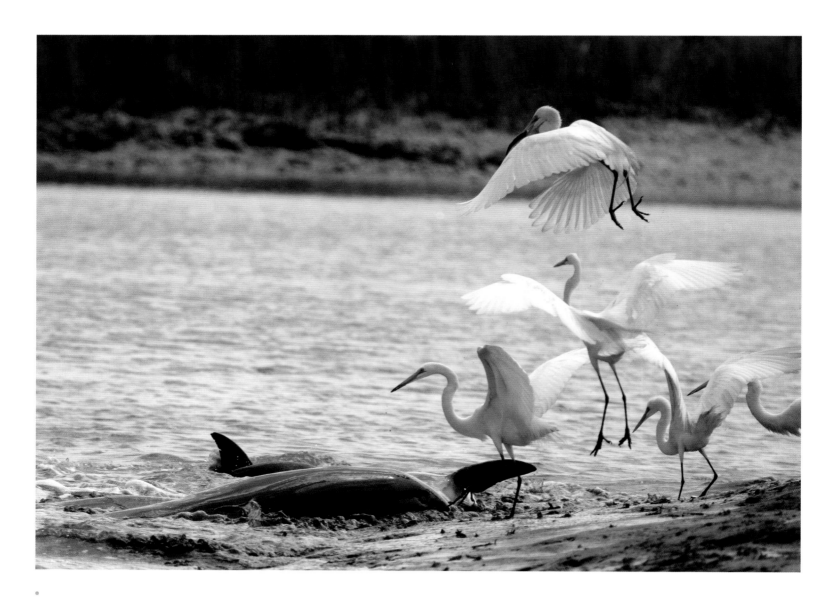

SNOWY EGRET, Hilton Head, South Carolina, USA
Egrets, and the occasional pelican and heron, gather at places in
this estuary where Atlantic bottlenose dolphins drive fish out of
the water and onto mud banks. The birds steal as many as they
can before the fish slither back into the sea.

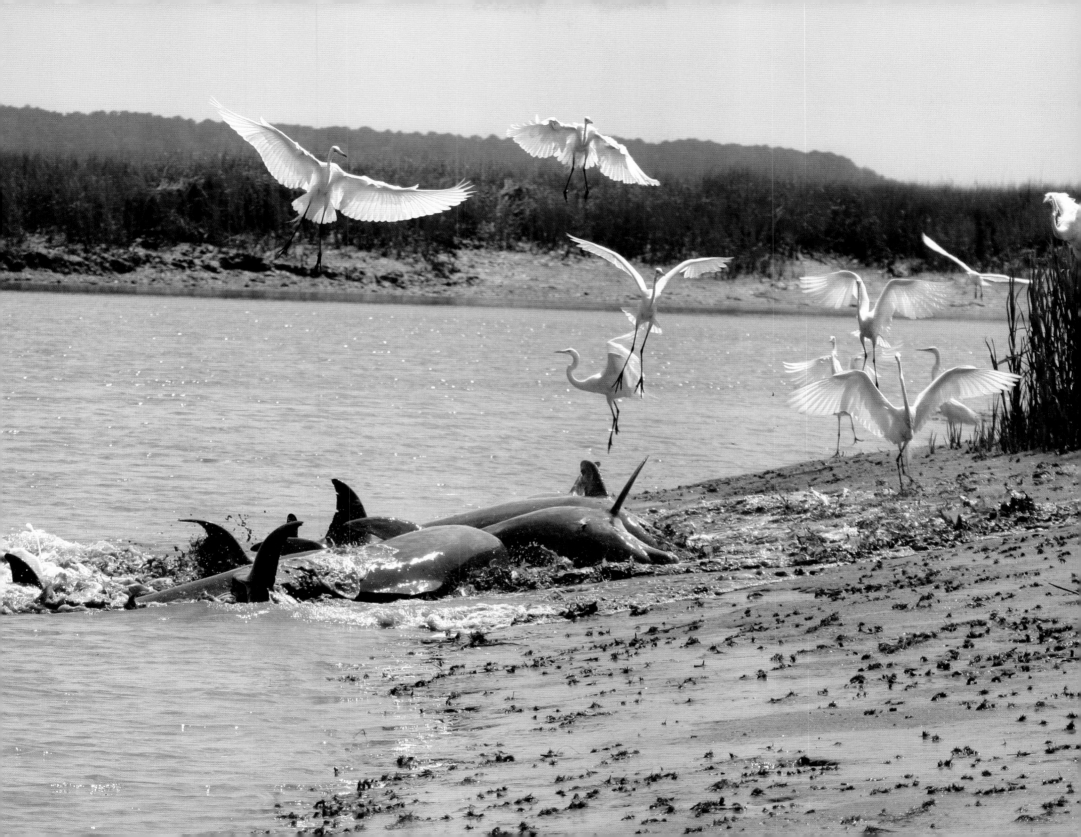

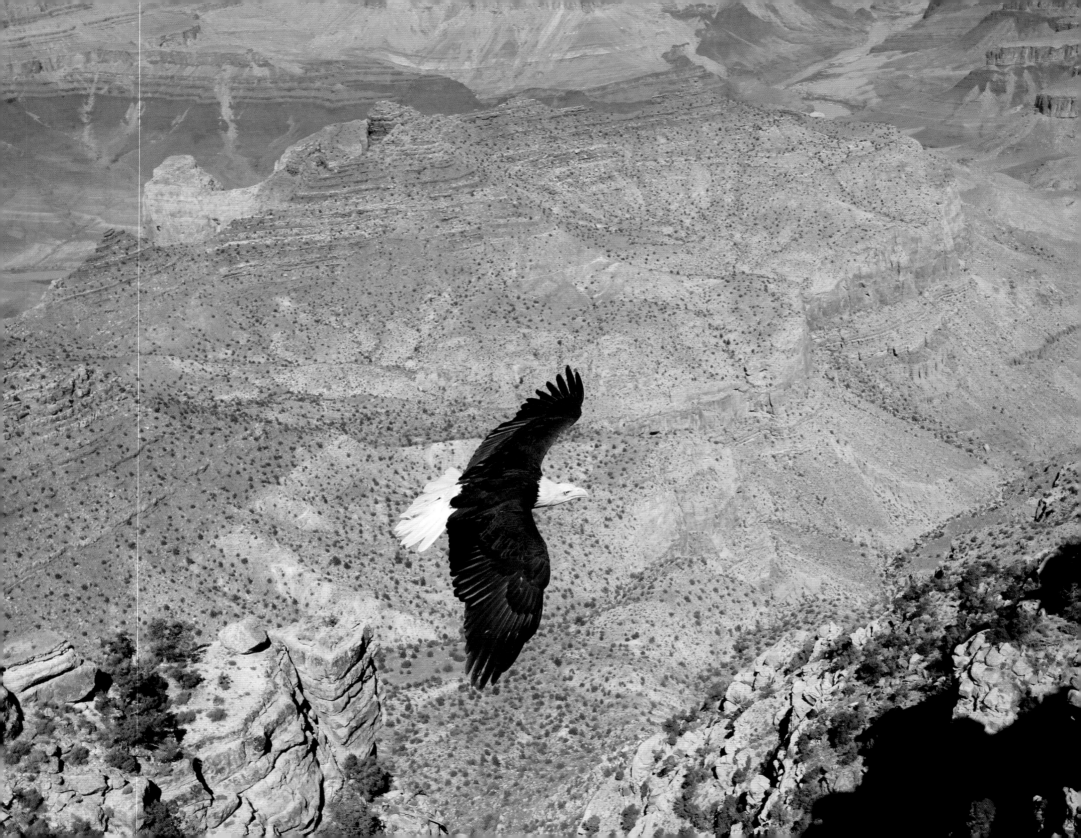

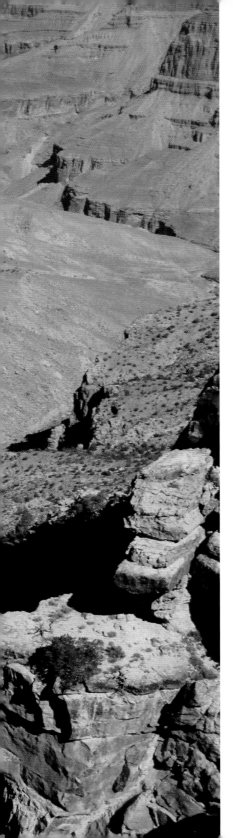

BALD EAGLE, Grand Canyon, Arizona, USA
Since 1985, bald eagles have been spending the winter in the Colorado River corridor, heading to lakes and rivers in the north in spring.

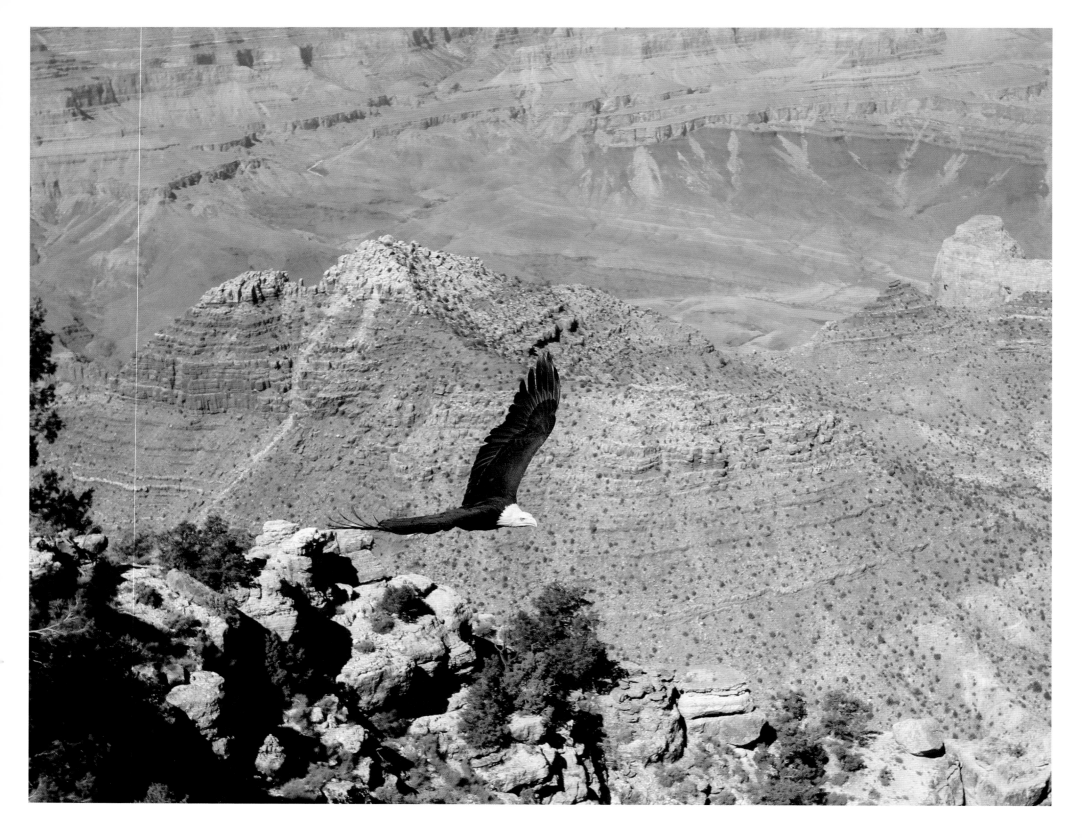

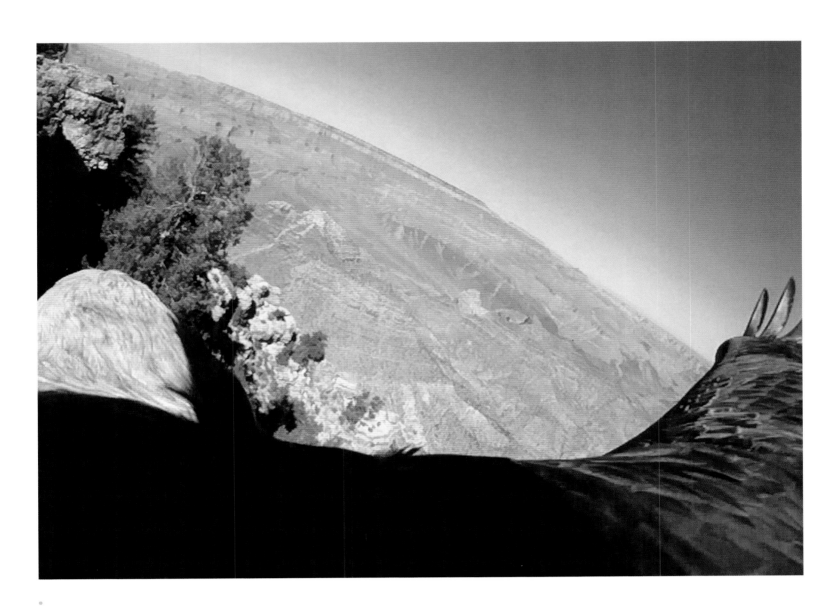

BALD EAGLE, Grand Canyon, Arizona, USA
Eagles on migration speed along at 50 kph (30 mph) and use thermals for a free ride. The birds often travel in loose flocks or 'streams' 30–50 km (18–30 miles) long, with birds up to 1 km (0.6 miles) apart.

SNOW GOOSE, Monument Valley, Utah, USA
Geese on the Pacific Flyway pass through the valley on their annual 8,000 km (5,000 mile) round-trip between wintering sites in California and Mexico, and the Arctic tundra where they breed.

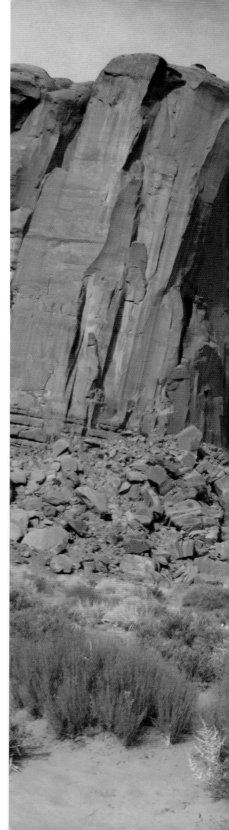

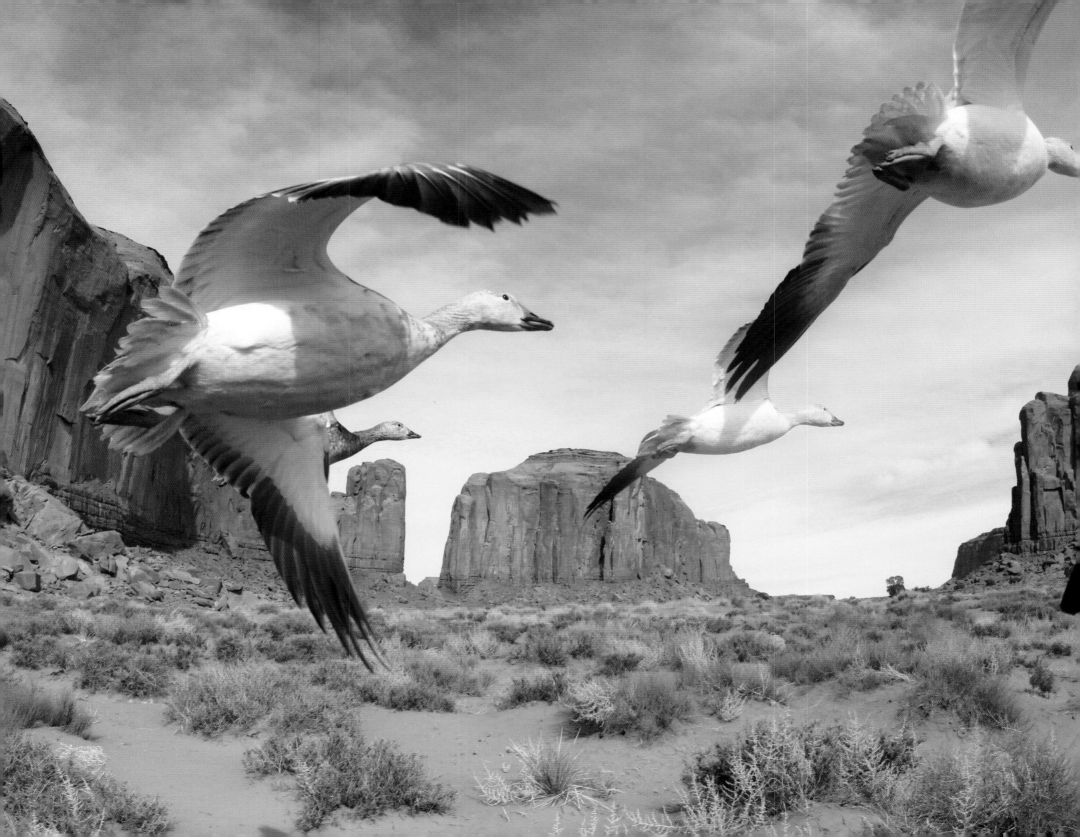

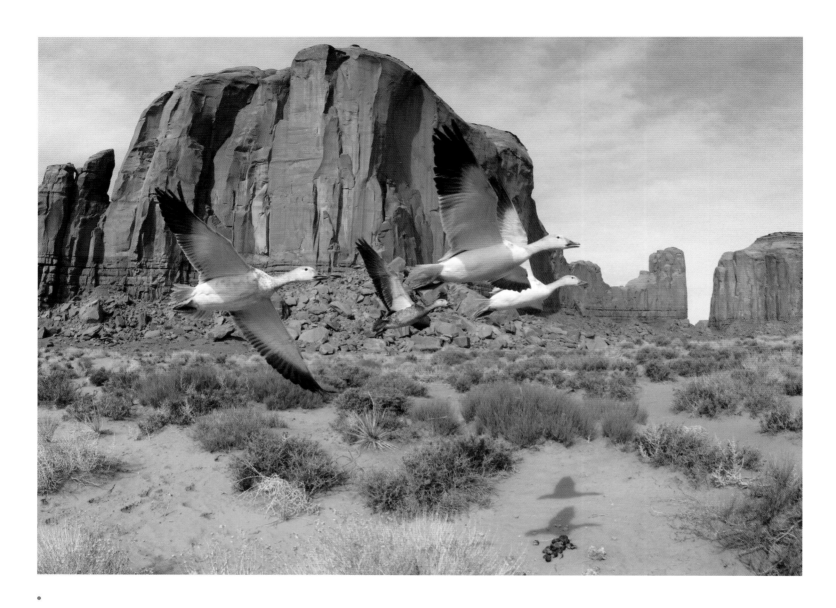

SNOW GOOSE, Monument Valley, Utah, USA
The geese travel high in large flocks and stop frequently to refuel,
so they can spend half of the year on migration.

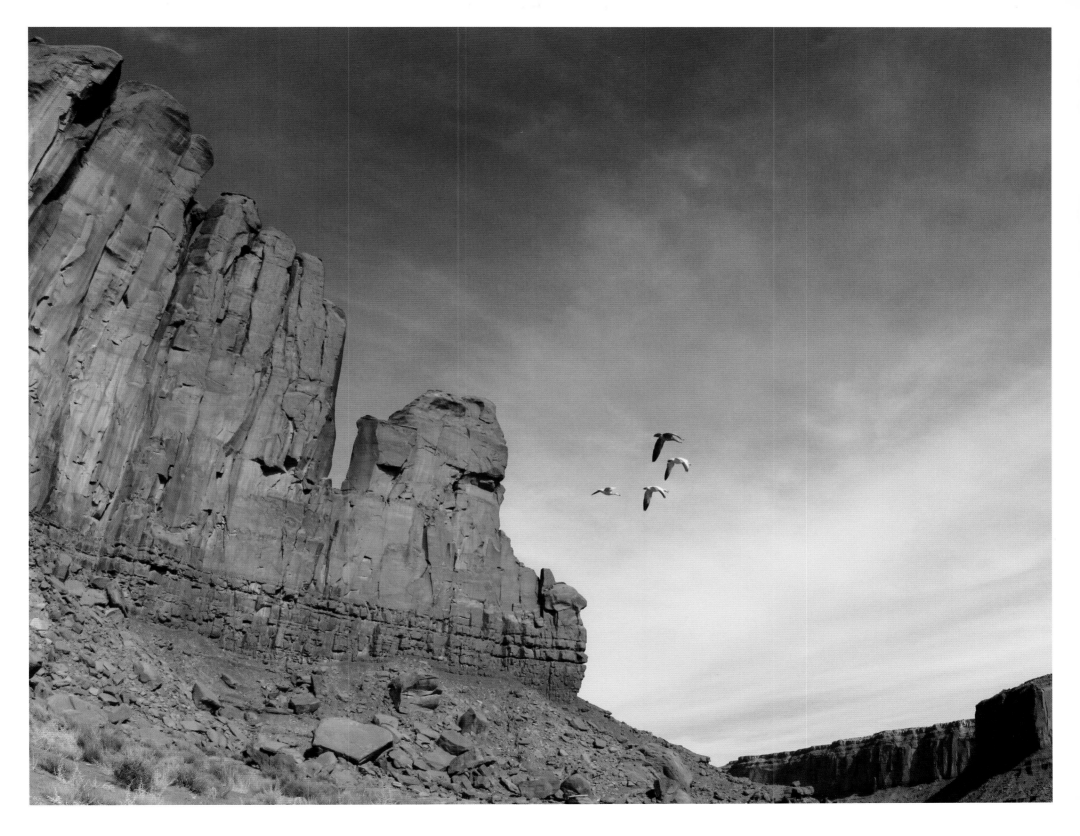

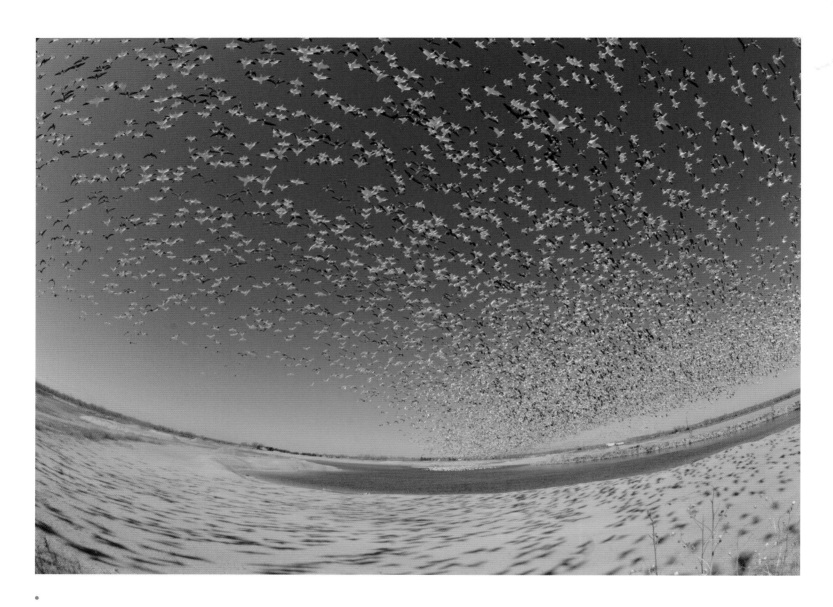

SNOW GOOSE, Platte River Valley, Nebraska, USA
Snow geese stop to refuel in huge numbers at fields and lakes
near the Platte River. There are so many that they exhaust the
area's resources, leaving other species of bird without enough
food to survive their migration.

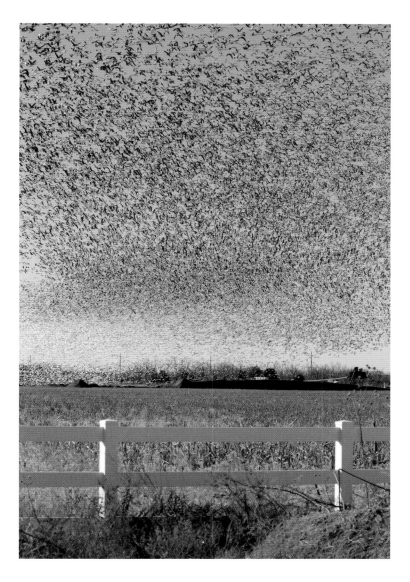
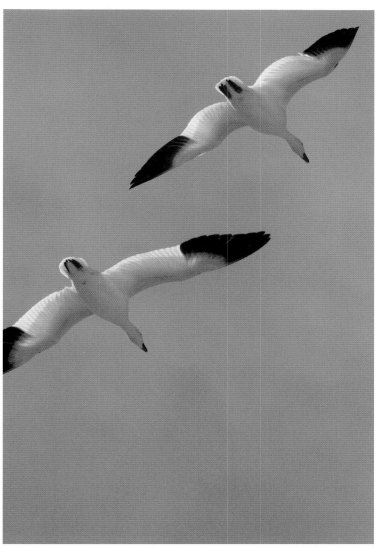

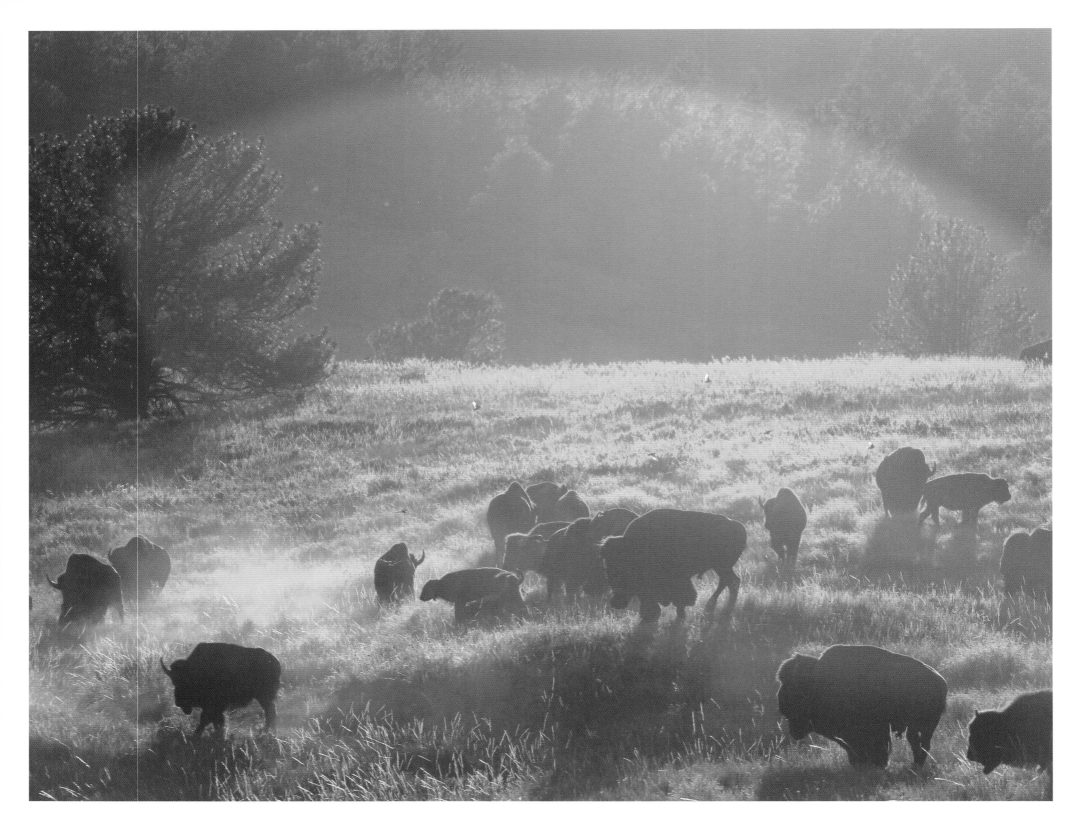

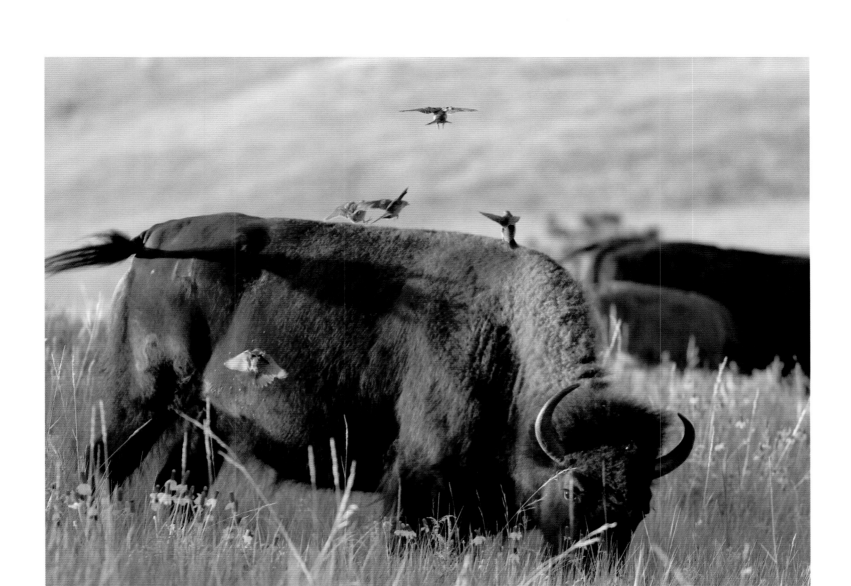

COWBIRD, Custer State Park, South Dakota, USA
Unaware of the snow geese passing high overhead,
cowbirds survive by feasting on the parasites that
live on the North American bison.

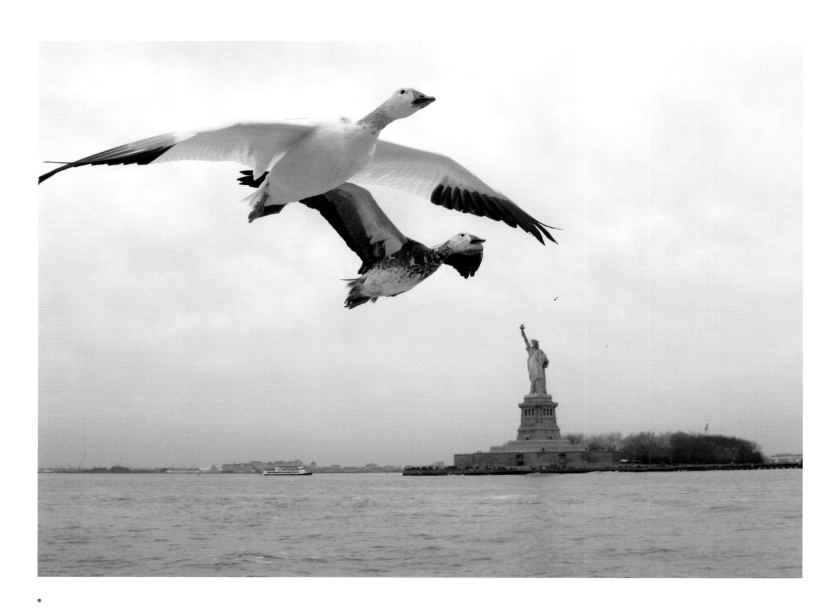

SNOW GOOSE, New York, New York, USA
In spring, over 1.4 million geese leave their wintering sites
in New Jersey, Delaware and Maryland, and travel northwards
via New York to islands in the Canadian Arctic.

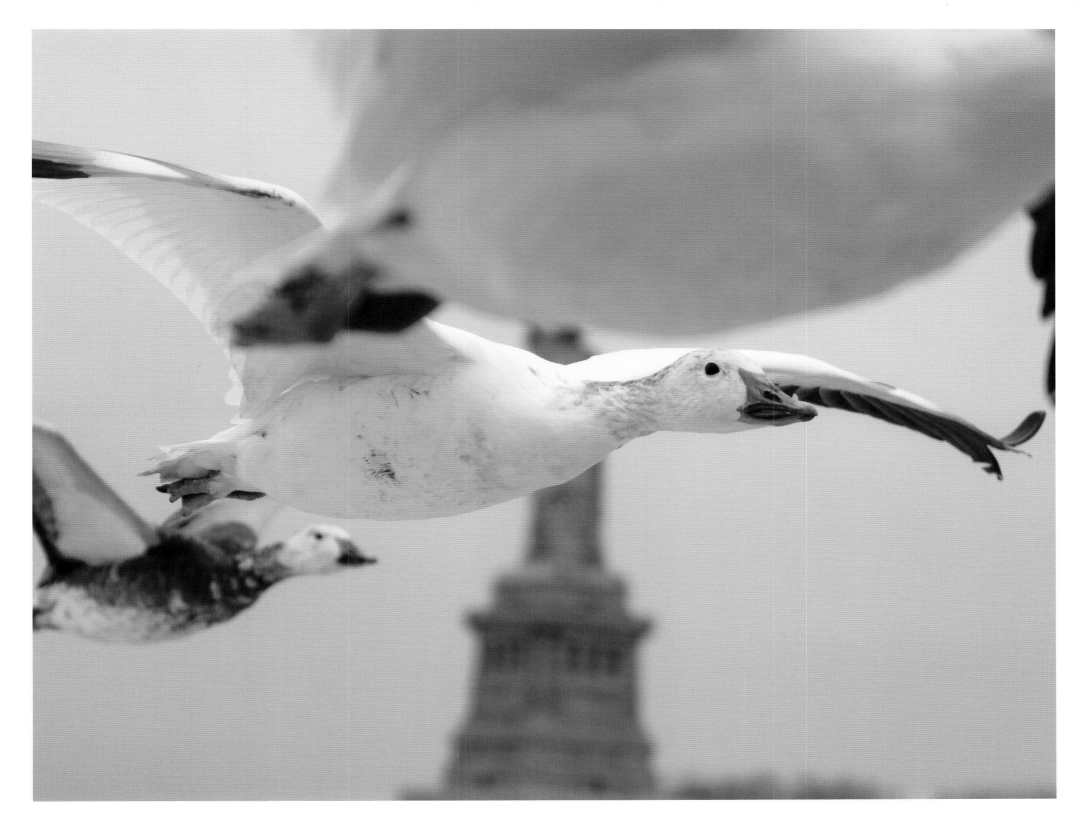

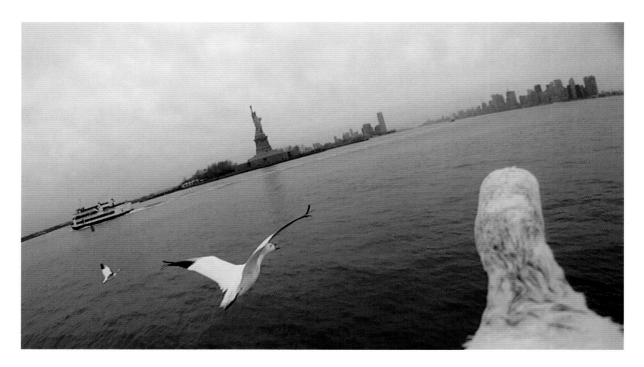

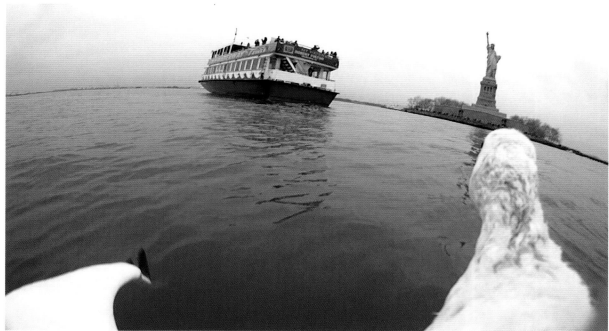

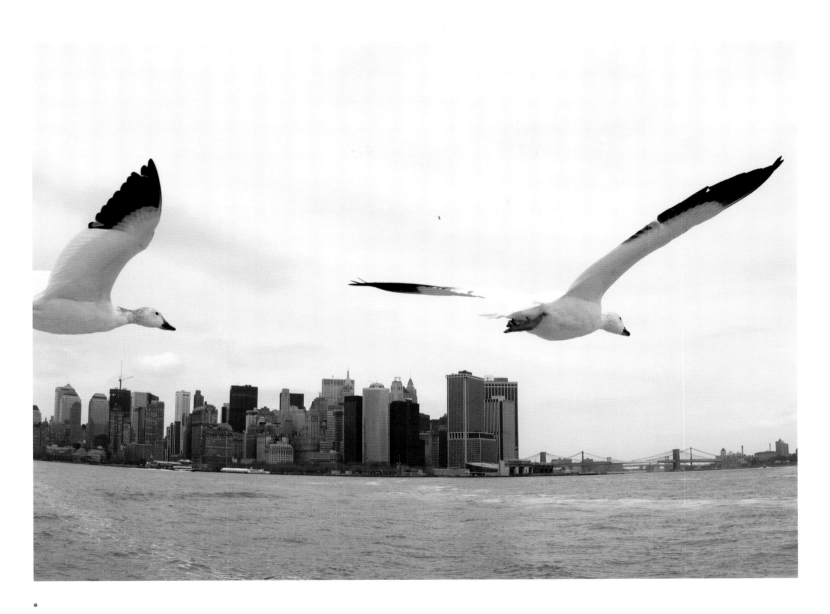

SNOW GOOSE, New York, New York, USA
Most of these geese are greater snow geese, and travel
so deep inside the Arctic Circle that they are the most
northerly breeding geese in the world.

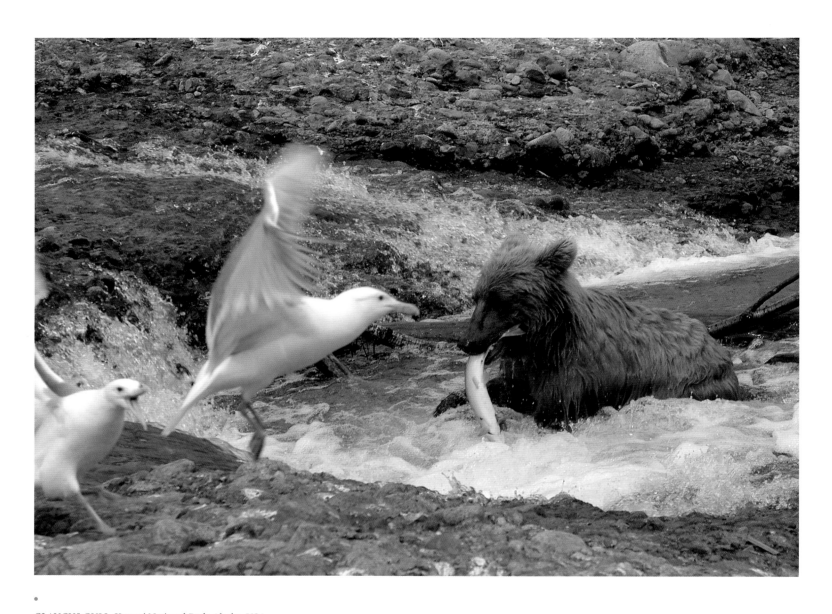

GLAUCUS GULL, Katmai National Park, Alaska, USA
Glaucus gulls and bald eagles (right) can be opportunist
scavengers, ready to poach salmon from hunting bears.

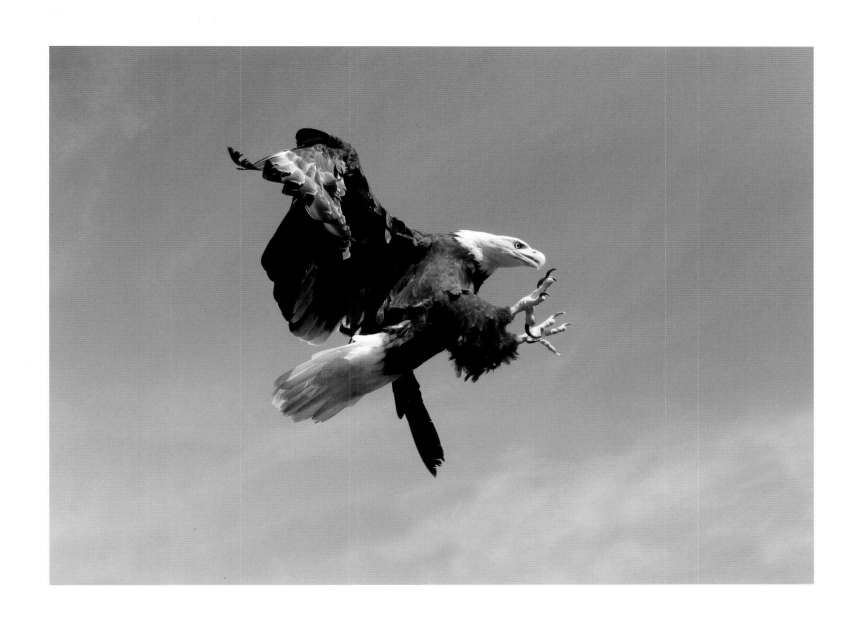

GRIZZLY BEAR, Katmai National Park, Alaska, USA
Grizzlies are normally solitary animals but will tolerate
other bears at fishing sites; and, wherever there are
fishermen – whether animal or human – there are sure
to be birds.

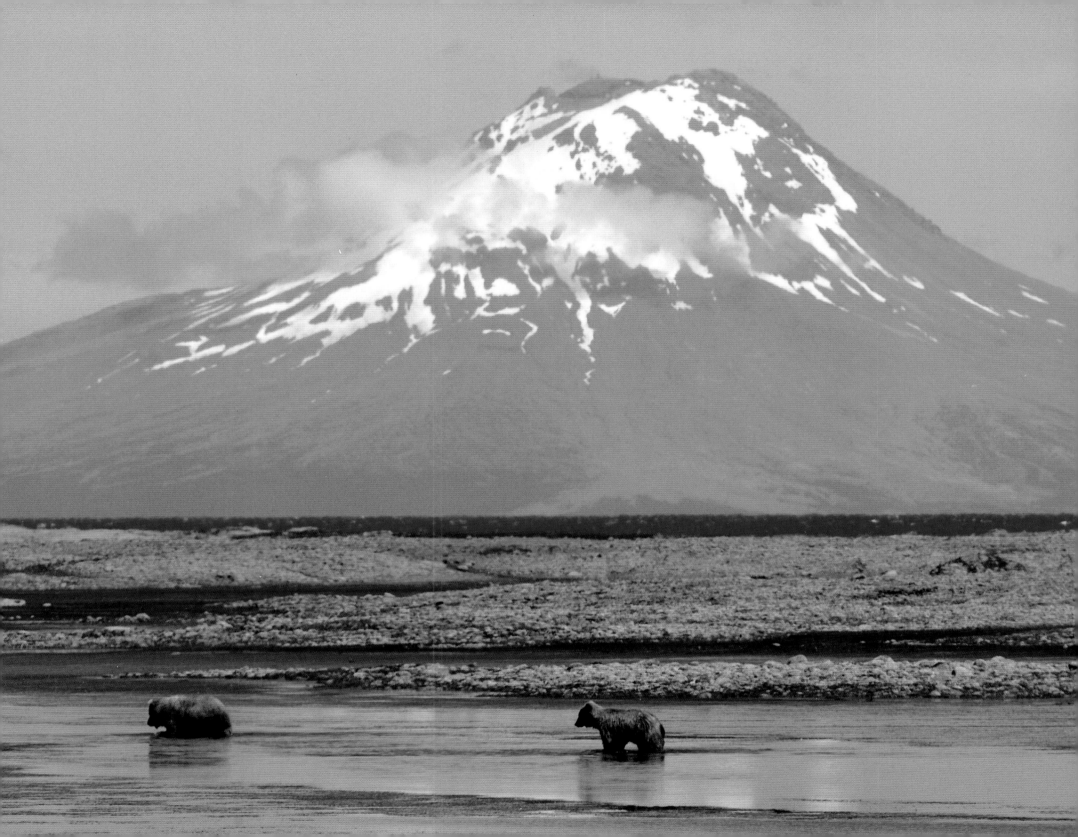

SOUTH AMERICA

**From the ugly functionality of the Andean condor
to the flamboyant beauty of the scarlet macaw,
South America's varied terrain provides
a home for an exotic array of species.**

The Andean condor is arguably South America's most iconic bird. It's a threatened species, yet if you're in the right place at the right time, you can still see groups of 50 or more soaring together over mountains, glaciers, ice fields and hot deserts from one end of the Andes mountain chain to the other. The birds are mainly scavengers, and from their vantage point high in the sky they quickly locate anything dying – say, a male guanaco seriously injured in a fight – or something already dead. On the outskirts of Santiago in Chile, condors have become urban birds for they join the gulls and other avian riffraff at the municipal garbage dump. One group in Peru even takes an annual trip to the seaside. At Paracas, condors soar high above the rocks and beaches when southern sea lions are breeding. They look for the bloody altercations between massive bull sea lions, for these heavy mammals are careless about where they fight: they squash pups, and the condors are there to clean up the mess.

It is a role more usually associated with giant petrels, and on the Atlantic coast of Argentina these birds do just that. The petrels are spectators to a dramatic natural event on the shores of Peninsula Valdés, where huge killer whales surf into the beach and pluck novice sea lions and elephant seals from the shallows. Unlike the kelp gulls in South Africa, which track the prey, here the petrels watch out for the tall, dark dorsal fin of the predator. And killer whales, like sharks, are messy eaters, so there are always plenty of leftovers for the birds to feast on.

Not one of the New World vultures (nor the giant petrels, if it comes to that) is renowned for its beauty, but another South American icon certainly is – the scarlet macaw. Unlike the vultures, scarlet macaws tend not to make lengthy journeys. One population in the Maya Mountains of Belize does make a migration from one side of the mountains to the other to breed, but those in the Amazon are stay-at-homes, although they do make daily flights to the 'colpas', or clay licks, along the riverbank which may provide a mineral supplement to these and other birds.

The scarlets, along with other macaws and smaller parrots, arrive at the exposed bank and mill about, waiting for more birds to arrive. They'll only drop down when there are enough birds present; if too few turn up, they disperse and return the following day, but if they deem enough birds have appeared then, one by one, they drop down to the lick. Blue-and-yellow macaws tend to dominate, and they bully the scarlets. The scarlet macaws, in turn, bully the mealy Amazon parrots.

The mealy Amazons, however, have a back-up plan. If they cannot get a look in at the riverbank, they

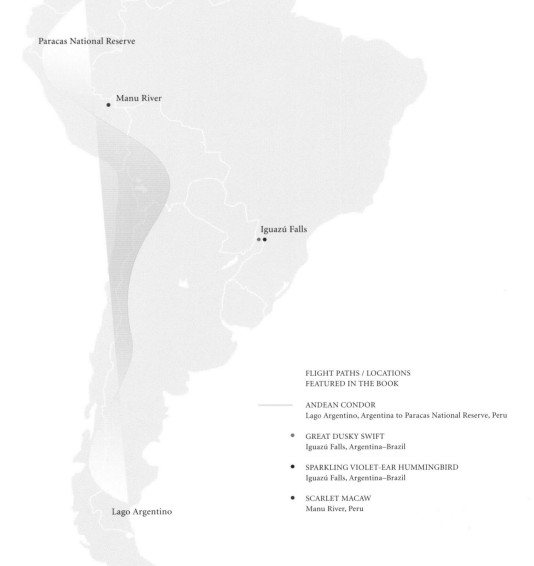

head into the forest where peccaries, tapirs and spider monkeys have their own clay licks. The parrots simply wait until the bigger animals have had their fill and then fly down to pick up the scraps. But they have to beware: all that activity might attract predators.

To the south, on the border between Brazil and Argentina, are the breathtaking Iguazú Falls, one of the world's great natural wonders. The word Iguazú translates as 'big water', and big it is – 2.7 km (1.7 miles) long with 275 separate waterfalls and cataracts. When the River Paraná is in full spate, water cascades down the 80 m (260 ft) drop, with half of it plunging into the aptly named Devil's Throat. Remarkably, on the basalt cliffs behind these walls of water are the roost and nest sites of great dusky swifts, one of a few species of swifts that regularly perches on exposed rock faces. They dart in through the waterfalls to their nests, turning on their side momentarily to offer less resistance as they pass through the water. To exit, they must drop vertically to pick up enough speed to punch their way out, then swoop up from the river to fly into the surrounding forest to feed before returning to the falls to roost or feed chicks. And, in the subtropical forest close to the falls, live hummingbirds, which feed on the nectar from plants kept moist by the mists from the falls.

Paracas National Reserve

Manu River

Iguazú Falls

Lago Argentino

FLIGHT PATHS / LOCATIONS
FEATURED IN THE BOOK

ANDEAN CONDOR
Lago Argentino, Argentina to Paracas National Reserve, Peru

GREAT DUSKY SWIFT
Iguazú Falls, Argentina–Brazil

SPARKLING VIOLET-EAR HUMMINGBIRD
Iguazú Falls, Argentina–Brazil

SCARLET MACAW
Manu River, Peru

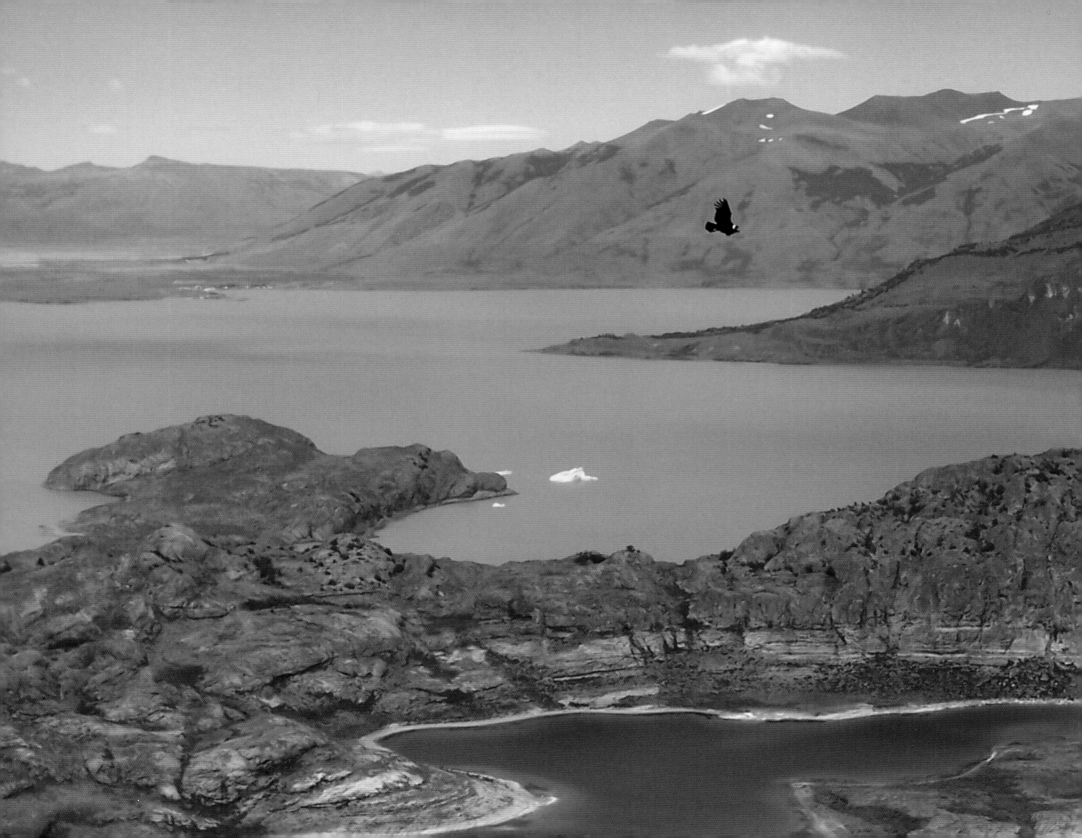

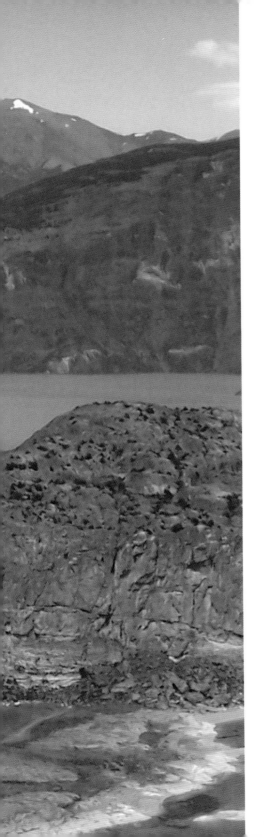

ANDEAN CONDOR, Lago Argentino, Argentina
The Andean condor lives mainly in the Andes and its foot hills from western Venezuela to Tierra del Fuego, especially where there is little tree cover.

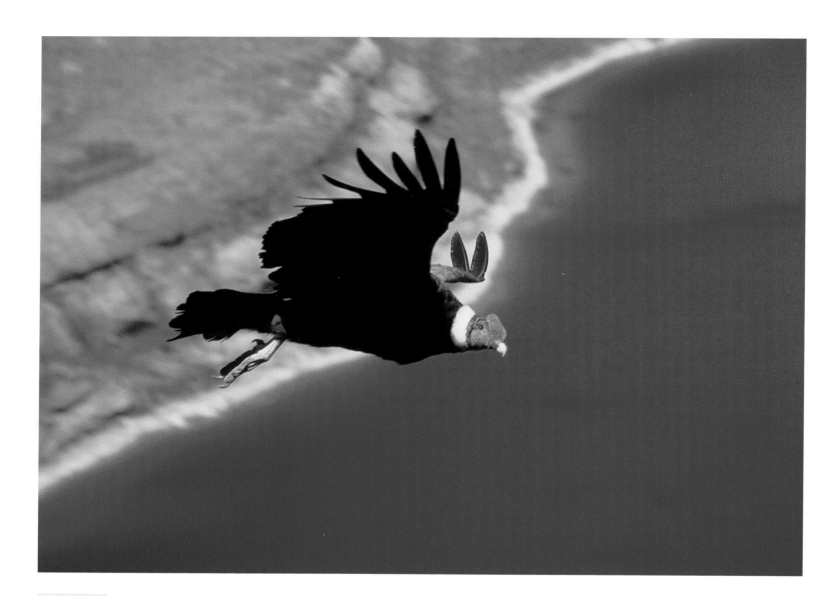

ANDEAN CONDOR, Lago Argentino, Argentina
With a wingspan of 3.2 m (10.5 ft), the largest of any land
bird, the Andean condor can soar on thermals and updrafts,
barely flapping its wings during its flight in search of food.

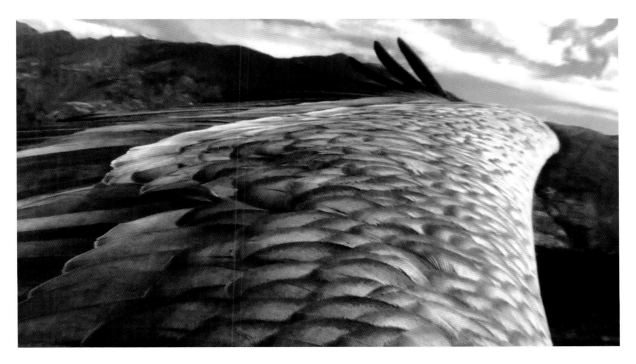

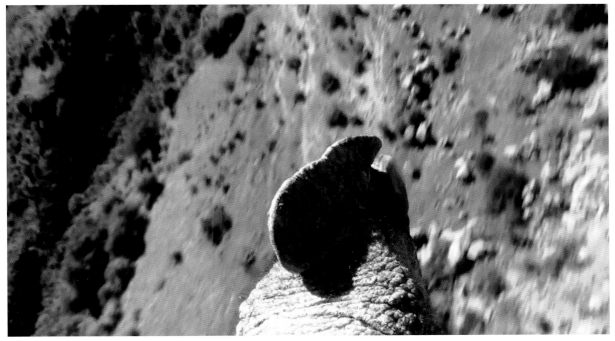

ANDEAN CONDOR, Andean foothills, Argentina
Condors might travel more than 200 km (125 miles) in a day
before they spot a carcass. They often have to go several days
without food, so when they find carrion they gorge themselves
with meat, making it difficult to take off again.

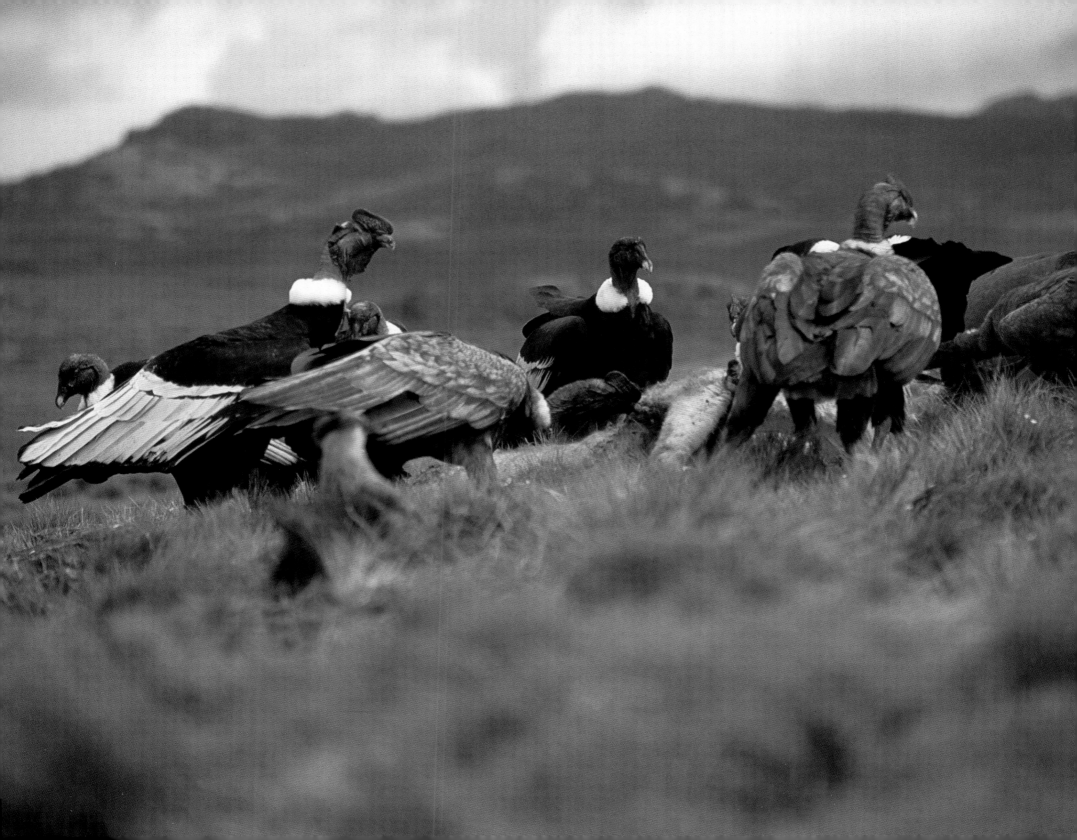

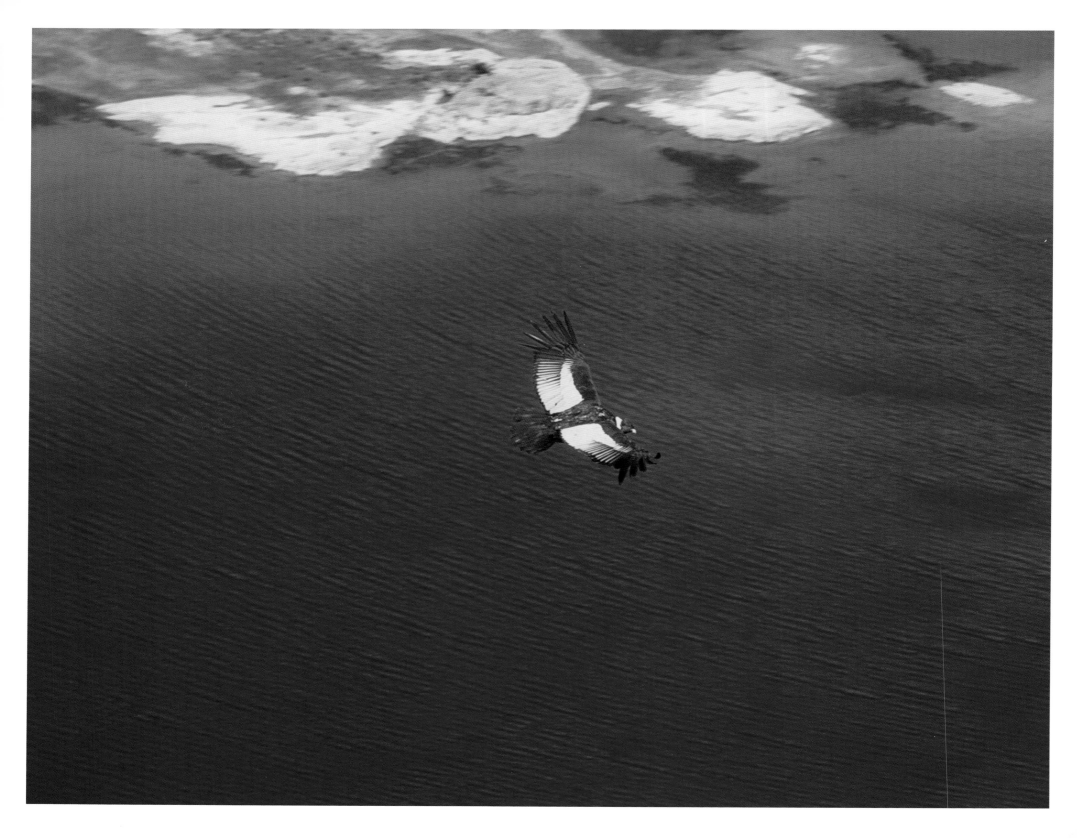

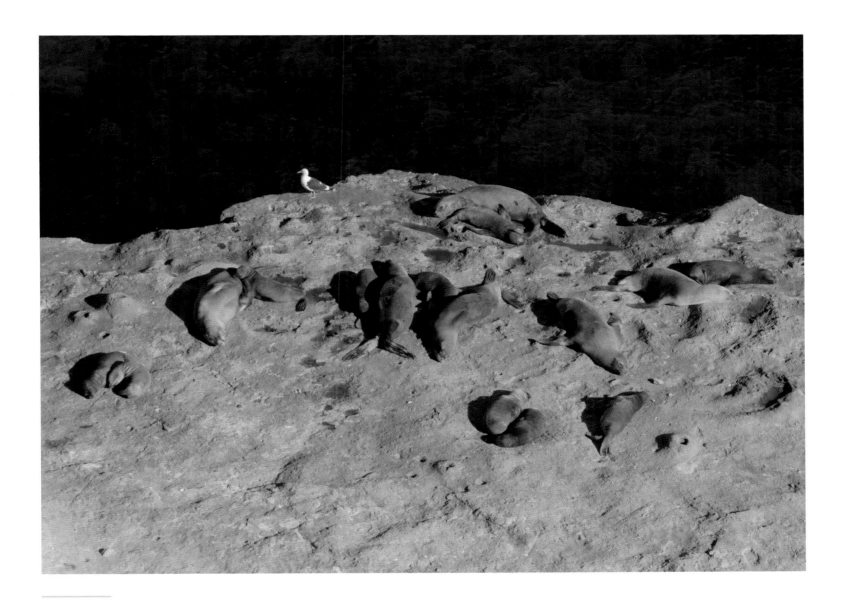

ANDEAN CONDOR, Paracas National Reserve, Peru
During December and January, condors migrate from the mountains
to Paracas on the coast of Peru, where they feed on dead sea lions,
including pups squashed by fighting males.

SALTO MBIGUA AND SALTO SAN MARTÍN, Iguazú Falls, Argentina–Brazil
The spectacular Iguazú Falls on the Argentina–Brazil border are formed of no
fewer than 275 separate waterfalls divided by rocky islands.

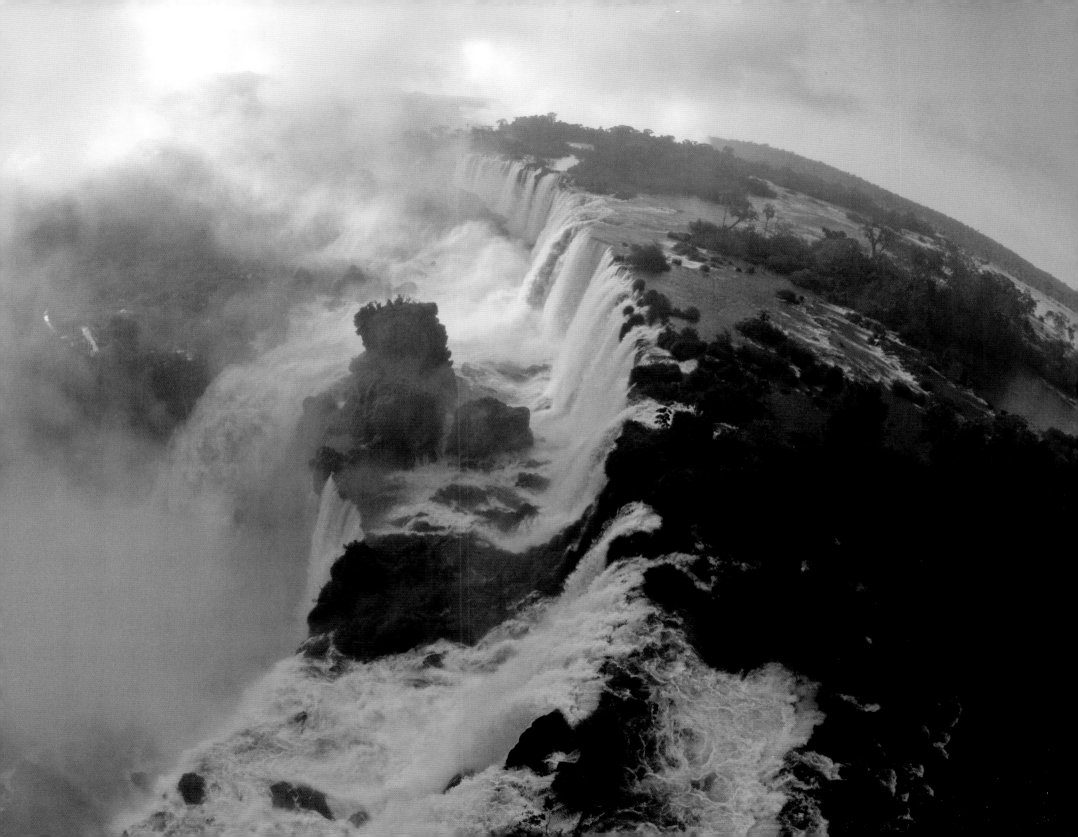

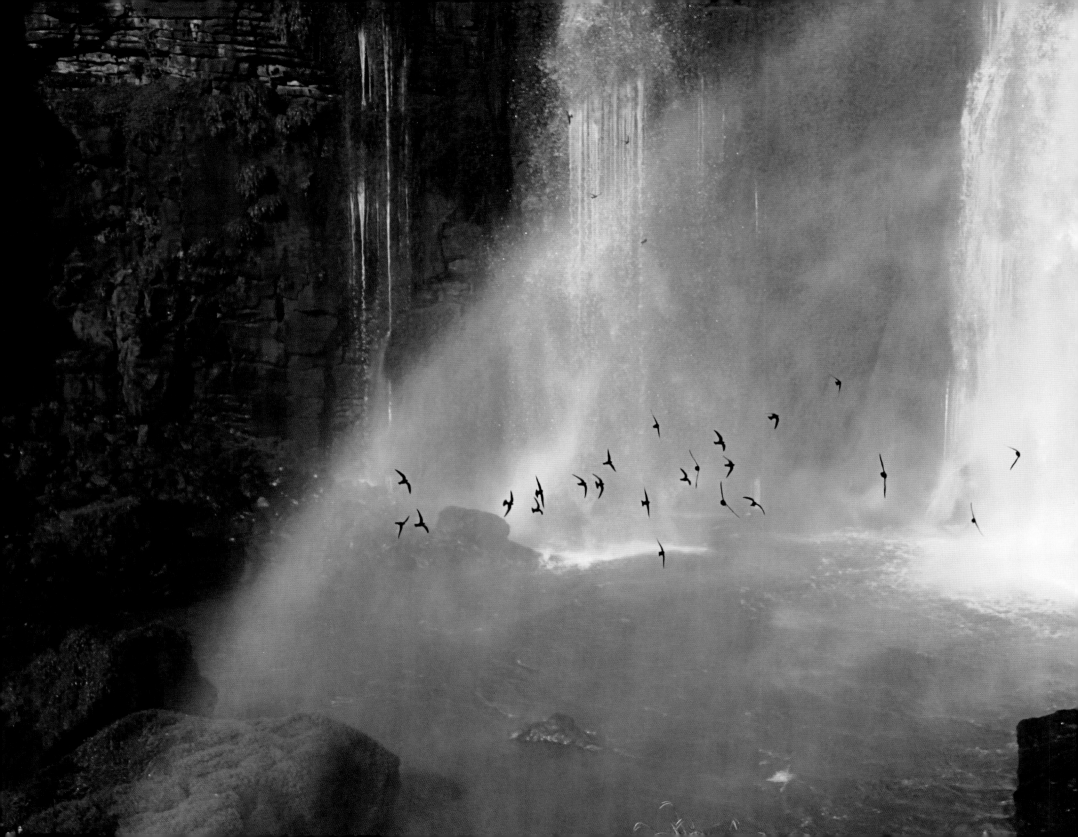

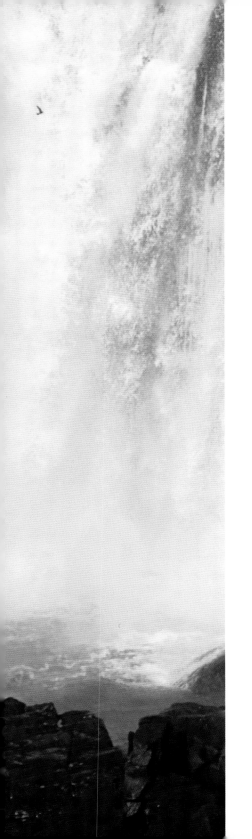

GREAT DUSKY SWIFT, Iguazú Falls, Argentina–Brazil
Thousands of great dusky swifts make the falls their
home, surviving by clinging to the rockface with sharp,
curved claws.

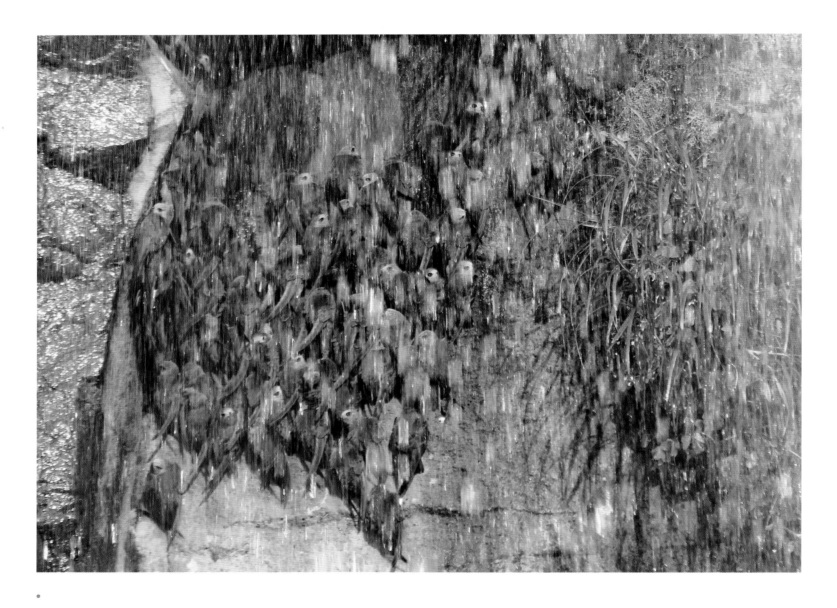

GREAT DUSKY SWIFT, Iguazú Falls, Argentina–Brazil
Disc-shaped nests of moss and stones, held together by mud
and saliva, are built directly behind the curtain of water, safe
from predators.

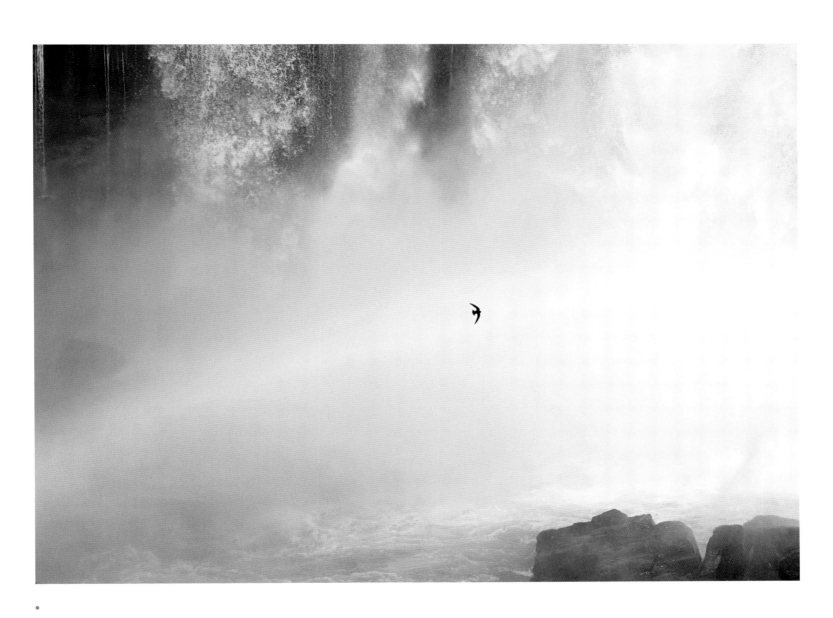

GREAT DUSKY SWIFT, Iguazú Falls, Argentina–Brazil
The swifts swoop low over the water at the base of the falls
and high over the canopy of the rich subtropical forests to
catch insects on the wing.

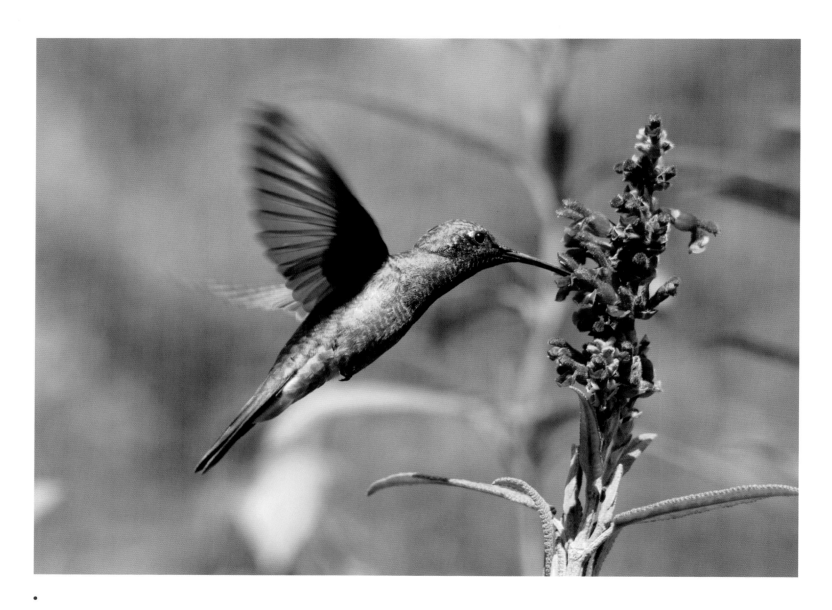

SPARKLING VIOLET-EAR HUMMINGBIRD, Iguazú Falls, Argentina–Brazil
Bejewelled hummingbirds flap their wings at 12–90 beats per second, depending
on the species, and hover in front of flowers to feed delicately on their nectar.

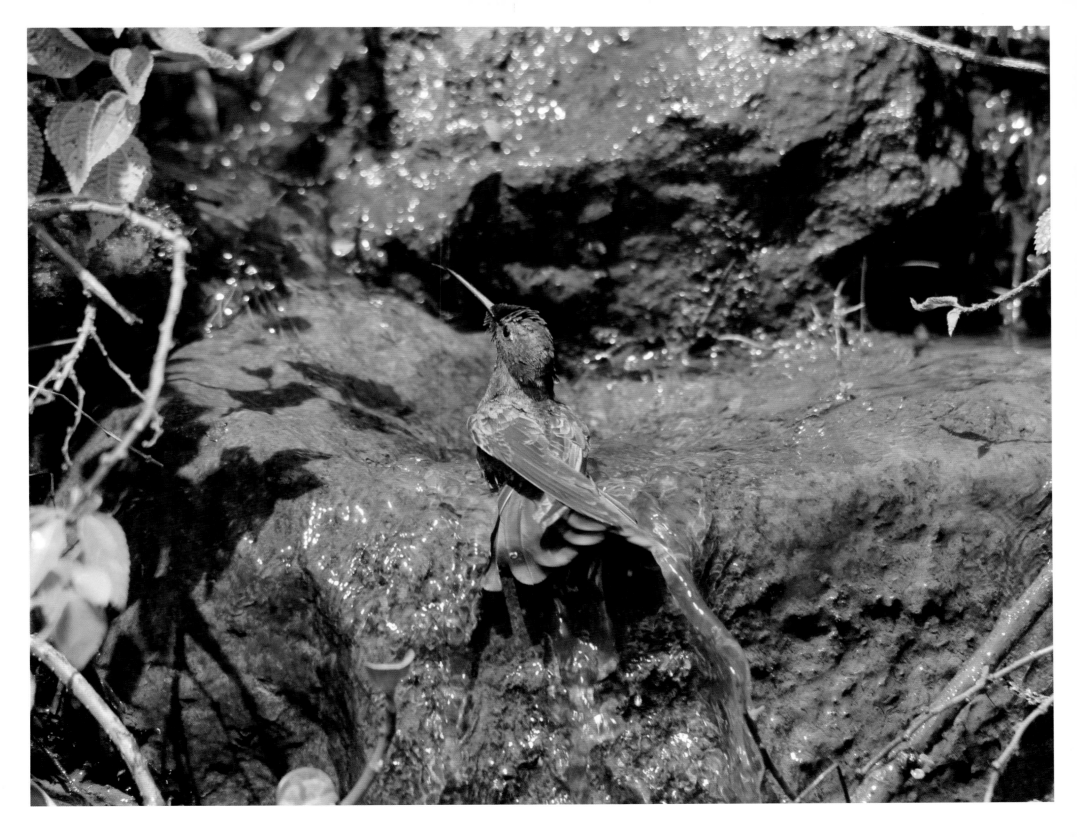

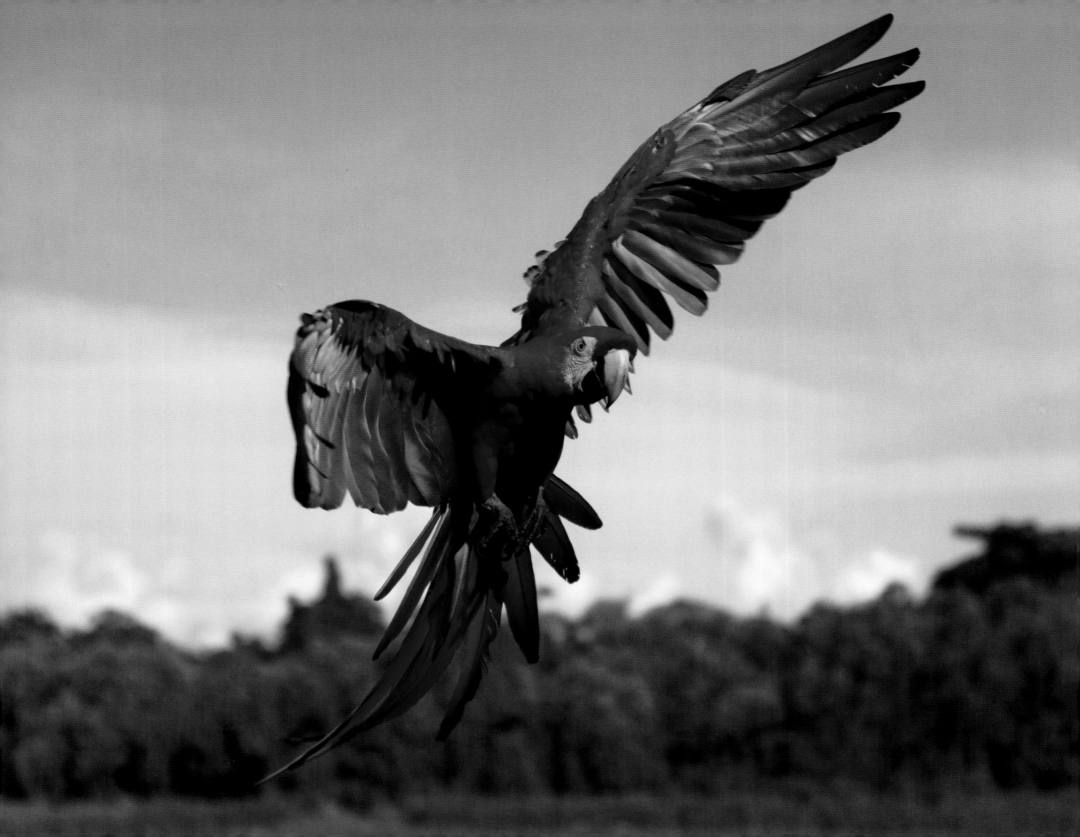

SCARLET MACAW, Manu River, Peru
Scarlet macaws are active at sunrise, as early as 5am.
They mate for life, and so a single macaw is usually sure
to be followed closely by a partner.

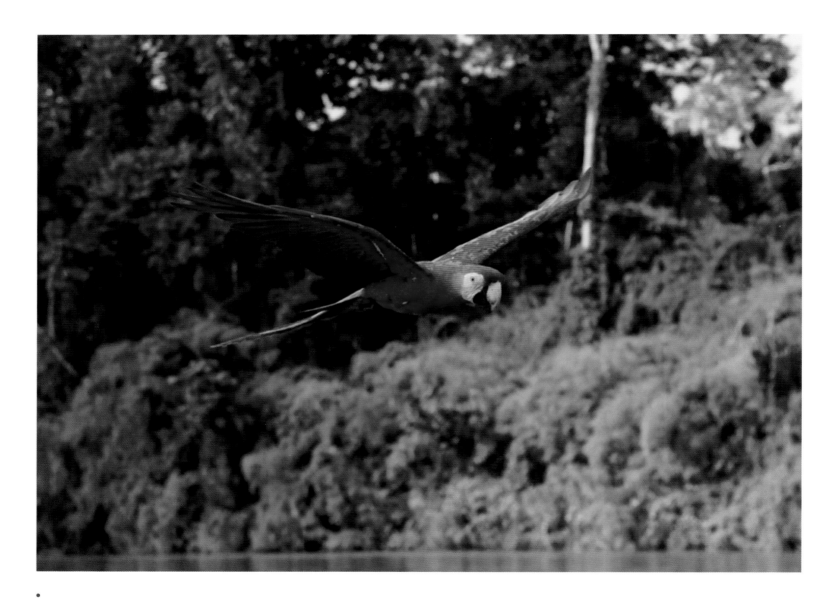

•

SCARLET MACAW, Manu River, Peru
These macaws travel regularly each day between nocturnal roosting sites and daytime feeding sites. They also stop off each morning to feed at clay licks, or 'colpas', on eroded riverbanks.

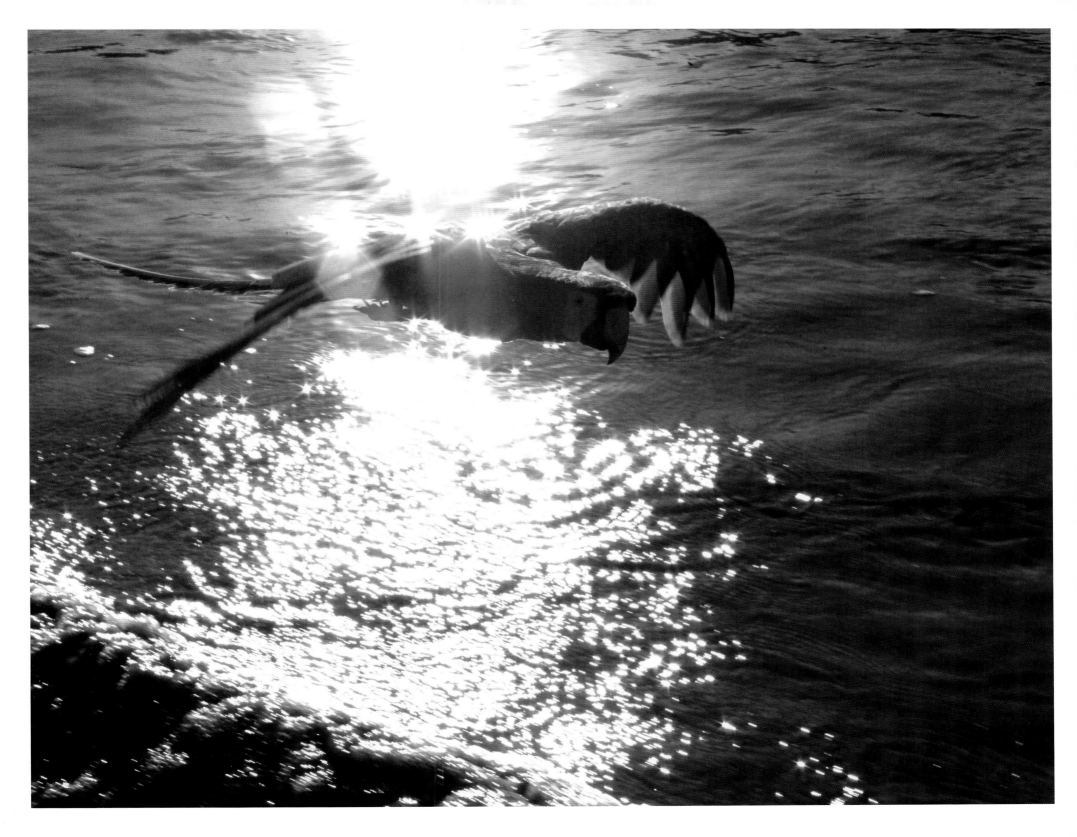

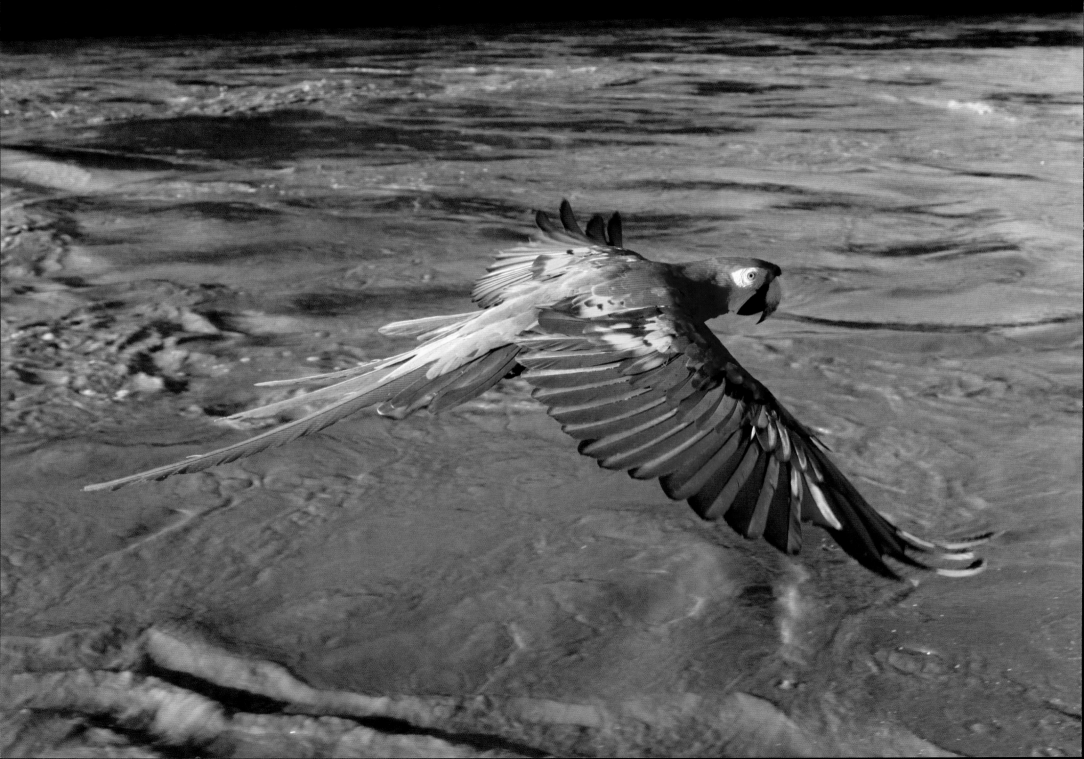

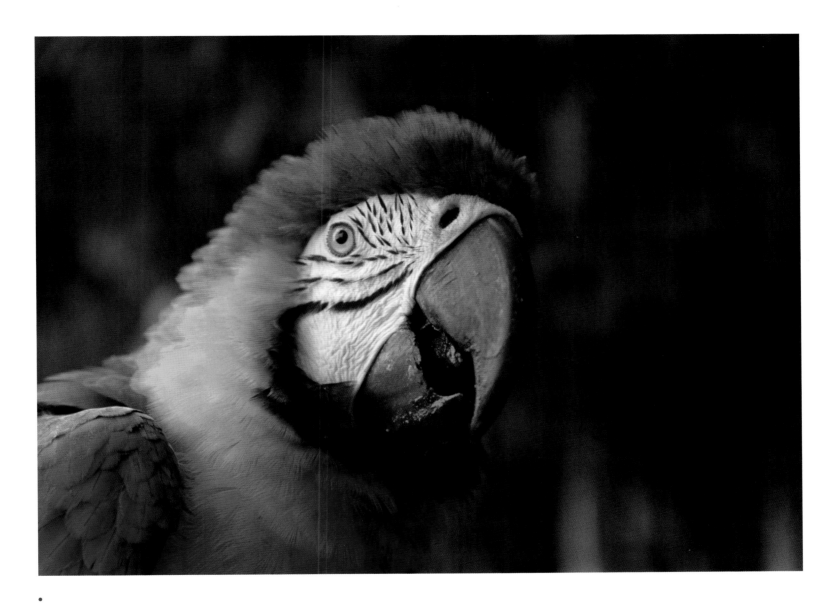

•

SCARLET MACAW AND BLUE-YELLOW MACAW, Manu River, Peru
Blue-yellow macaws (above) tend to dominate any activity at clay licks,
to the detriment of scarlet macaws.

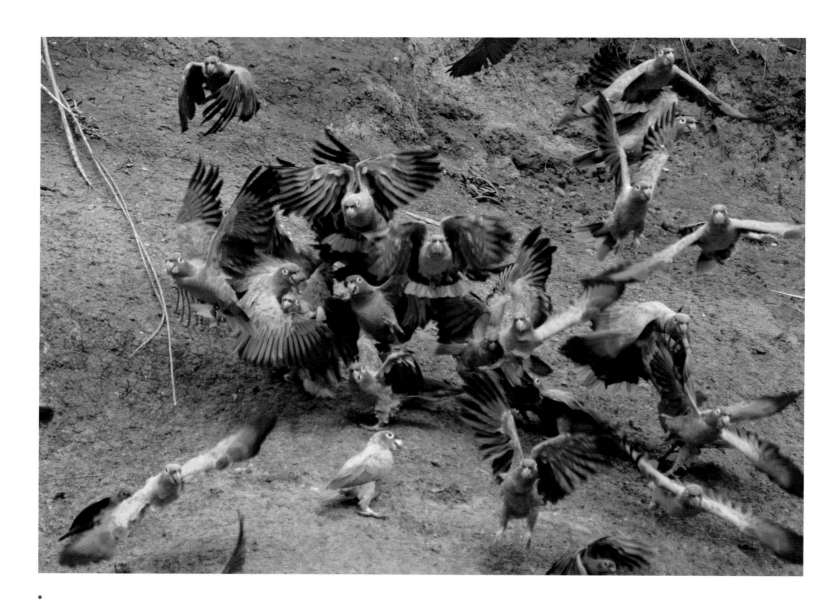

MEALY AMAZONS, Manu River, Peru
It is unclear why parrots and macaws eat the fine soil.
It may neutralise toxins from unripe fruit in the parrots'
diet, or it could be consumed as a sodium supplement.

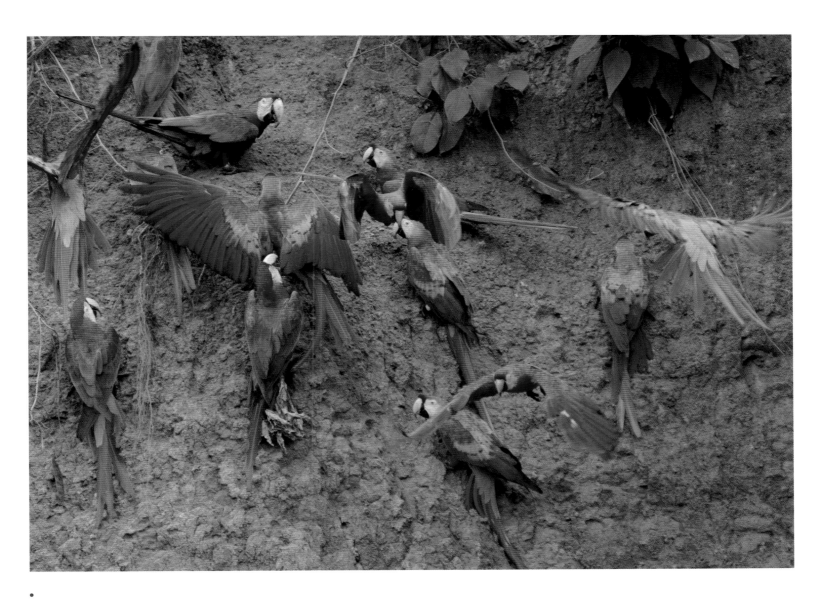

SCARLET MACAW, Manu River, Peru
Each macaw defends its patch at the clay lick. Any parents
present will take clay back to their nest for their chicks.

SCARLET MACAW, Manu River, Peru
Visits to the clay lick tend to be seasonal, with a peak
of activity from July to February, especially at the time
of maximum growth of chicks in the nest.

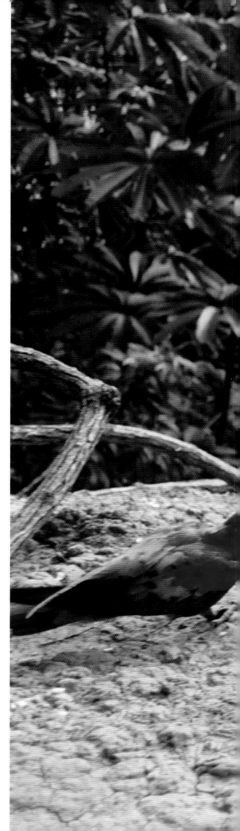

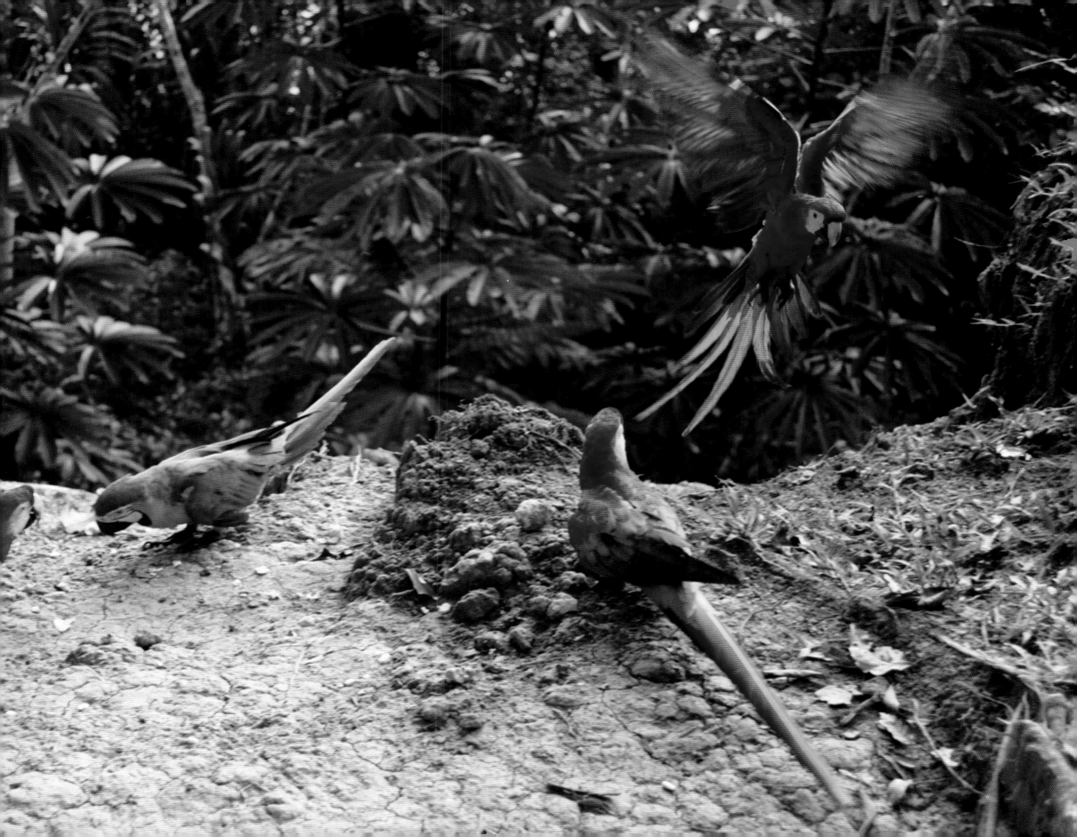

AUSTRALIA & ASIA

This vast region comes with an array of natural obstacles to birds – from epic mountain ranges to hot, arid desert landscapes. But through ingenuity, natural ability and a little help from the locals, a wide range of bird species find ways to survive.

In Australia – the hottest and driest continent on Earth – the availability of water tends to determine bird movements, and none more so than the familiar budgie. The budgerigar is a nomadic Australian parakeet that gathers in huge flocks – over a million strong – in times of drought. These flocks are an understandable magnet for bird predators, especially Australia's biggest falcon – the black falcon. Flying with rapid, powerful beats the falcon makes continuous raids on the flock, trying to separate an individual, which it then chases like a fighter aircraft in a dogfight. The budgies themselves are not slow when it comes to flying. They zigzag rapidly and drop like stones, almost falling into the water as they try to outmanoeuvre their pursuers.

Brightly coloured rainbow lorikeets tend to fly in pairs, but come together in flocks, much like the budgies, in response to the calls of others. They have a tongue adapted to collecting nectar from flowers, and in some parts of Australia, they're so tame that they'll gather in huge flocks at feeding stations where visitors can hand feed the birds with specially prepared nectar.

Across the water into Asia, that immense mountain chain – the Himalayas – separates the north from the south of Asia. With peaks of up to 8,848 m (29,000 ft) above sea level it should be a formidable barrier to birds but more than one species is able to overcome it.

Bar-headed geese go right over the top, some flying at 10,000 m (33,000 ft) – making them the world's highest actively flying birds. Surprisingly, they don't make use of upslope tail winds to gain height but power up the mountainside in the morning, when the air is still, maximising safety and control as they cross the highest parts of the range. In this way, they complete the trans-mountain part of their journey in just 7–8 hours. They make this extraordinary passage twice each year between breeding grounds in Central Asia and wintering sites across the Indian subcontinent.

Demoiselle cranes on a similar journey take a lower route. Although they seek out mountain passes the valleys they enter are at altitudes up to 8,000 m (26,000 ft). Buffeted by winds and attacked by golden eagles, those that make it through arrive in autumn in a desert – the great arid Thar Desert of Rajasthan on the India–Pakistan border. Here, the cranes get a helping hand for local people revere and worship them. In fact, the desire to protect and nurture these birds is so great that enormous enclosures, resembling prison courtyards, have been built to protect them. In the past, the cranes dropped in for short stopovers and handouts from the village before moving on, but now the winter living here is so good they have changed their migration pattern and stay put until spring.

Kushiro Marsh
Lake Kussharo

Himalayas

Deshnok • Jaipur
Keechen
Jodhpur • Pushkar

In many parts of Asia, many wild creatures are revered in a similar way, including an animal that attracts an otherwise almost universal loathing – the black rat. There are over 6,000 rats in the Kami Mata Temple in Deshnok, otherwise known as the 'rat temple'. The daily handouts of grain that the rats receive lure in the area's scavenging birds – the ubiquitous feral pigeon or blue rock dove. Elsewhere in India, those same pigeons duck and dive amongst the herdsmen and their charges at the Pushkar camel fair, and at the Palace of the Winds in Jaipur they have taken over every available niche in its substantial walls to roost or nest.

All this frantic activity contrasts with the reserved tranquility on the Japanese island of Hokkaido, where the Japanese or red-crowned crane is a resident rather than a migrant like its mainland relatives. It has little need to go far, for in winter the cranes are fed daily. They don't mind the cold, and it's often on crisp, frosty days that they perform a mesmerising dance in the snow: wing-flapping, bowing, jumping, running and tossing sticks and grass, in one of the most elegant displays in the entire animal kingdom. The cranes are not alone on the island, however, as grain is also put out for the equally graceful whooper swans that drop in while on their annual migration. The swans make for lakes fed by hot springs, so the water remains open all winter.

FLIGHT PATHS / LOCATIONS
FEATURED IN THE BOOK

DEMOISELLE CRANE
Himalayas, Nepal to Keechen, India

• RAINBOW LORIKEET
Sydney, Australia

• BUDGERIGAR
Outback, Australia

• BAR-HEADED GOOSE
Himalayas, Nepal

• ROCK DOVE
Pushkar / Jaipur / Deshnok, India

• INDIAN VULTURE
Jodhpur, India

• JAPANESE CRANE
Kushiro Marsh, Japan

• WHOOPER SWAN
Lake Kussharo, Japan

• Outback

Sydney •

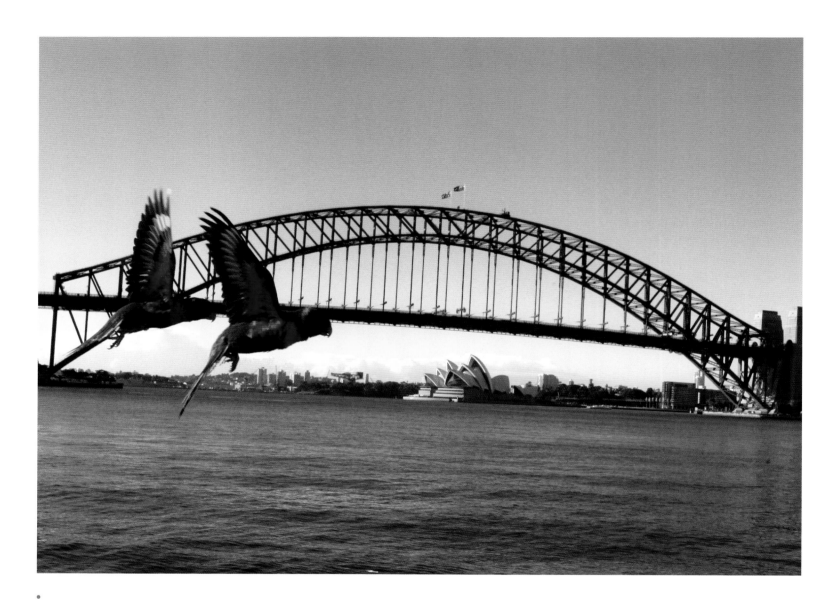

RAINBOW LORIKEET, Sydney Harbour, Australia
These vividly coloured parrots are found along the entire eastern
seaboard of Australia. They tend to fly in pairs, but may gather in
huge flocks, containing thousands of birds.

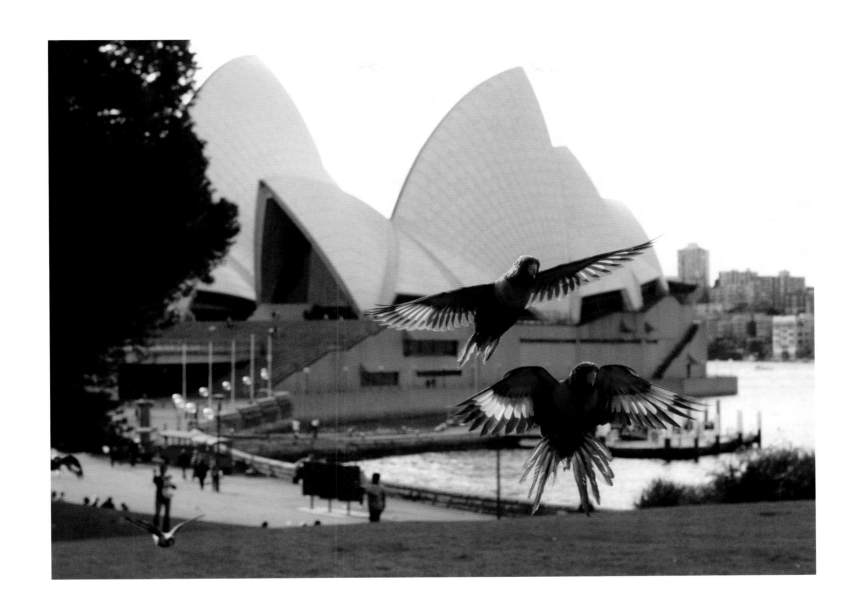

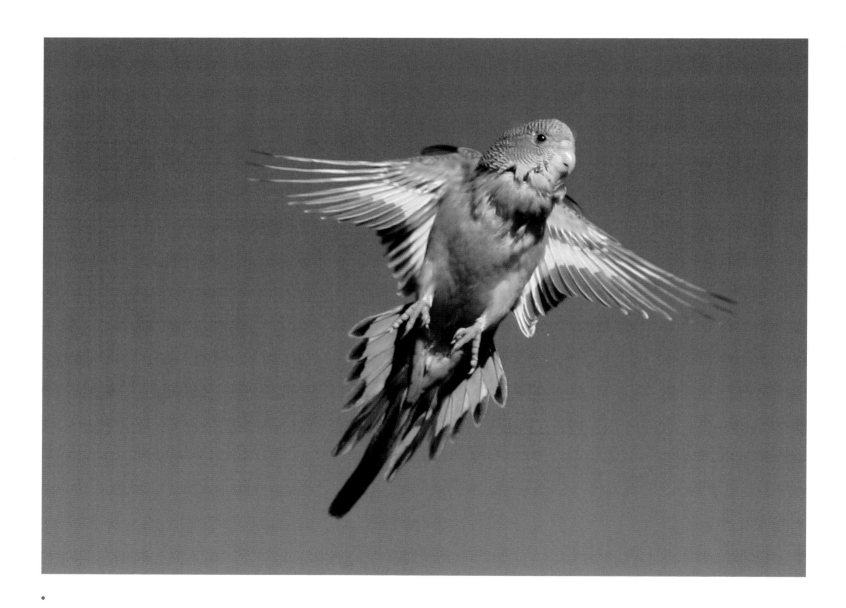

BUDGERIGAR, the Outback, Australia
Budgies are small nomadic parakeets adapted to live in the
dry areas of the Outback. They travel in huge flocks, or 'chatters',
which can be many thousands strong.

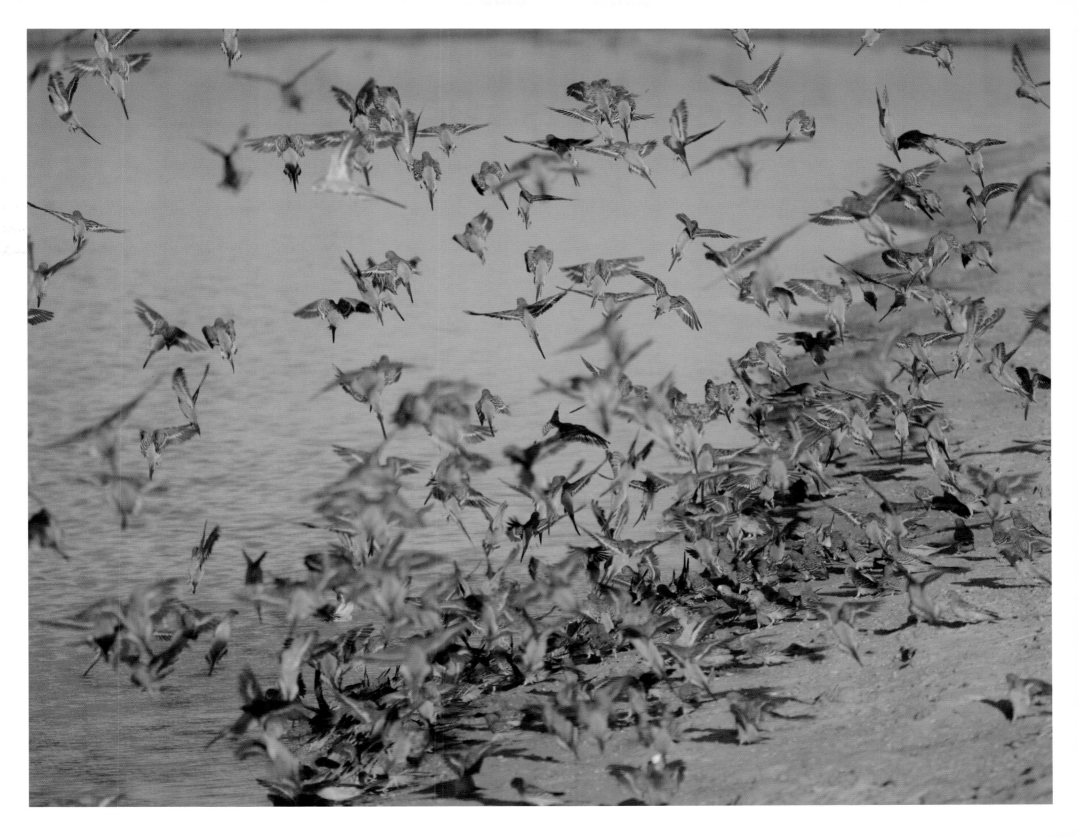

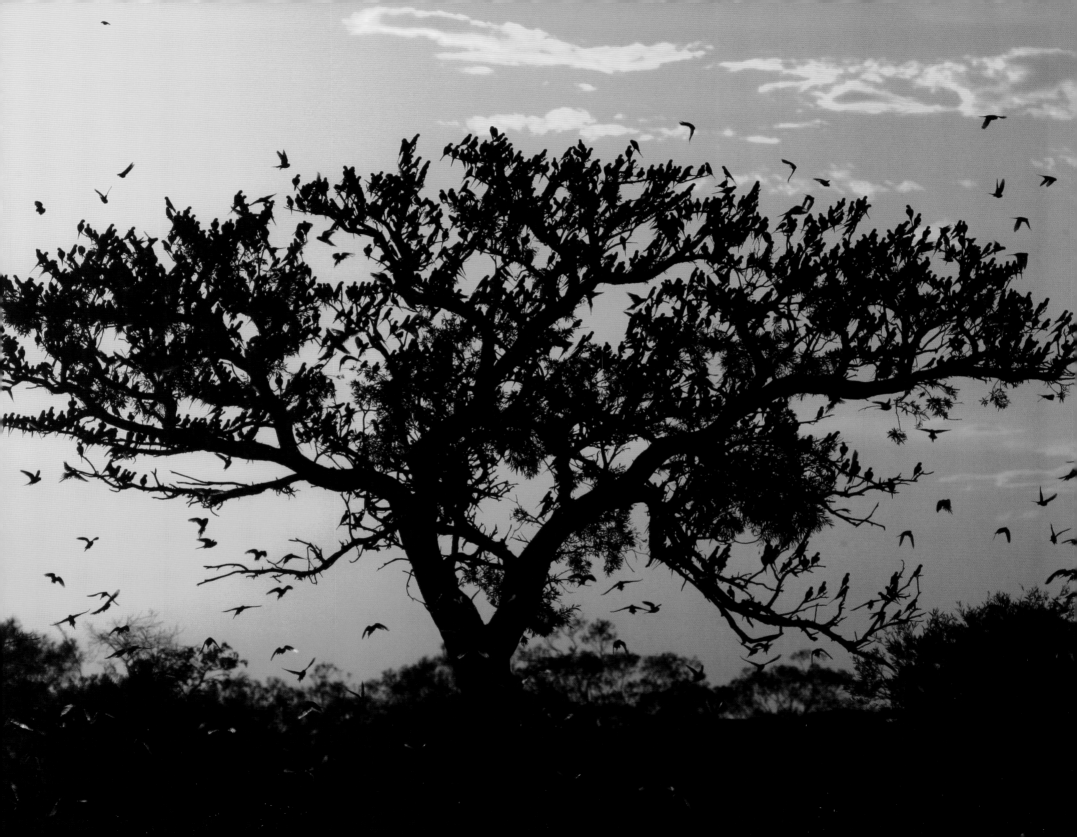

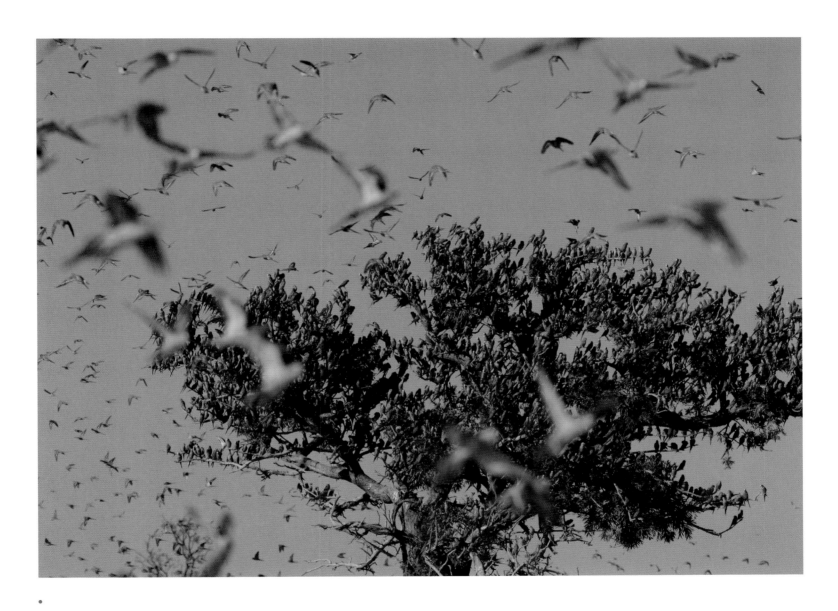

BUDGERIGAR, the Outback, Australia
Budgies can see at near-ultraviolet (UV) wavelengths and each bird
has its own unique UV identity, reflected by the spots and patterns
on their plumage. It's thought to be important in mate selection.

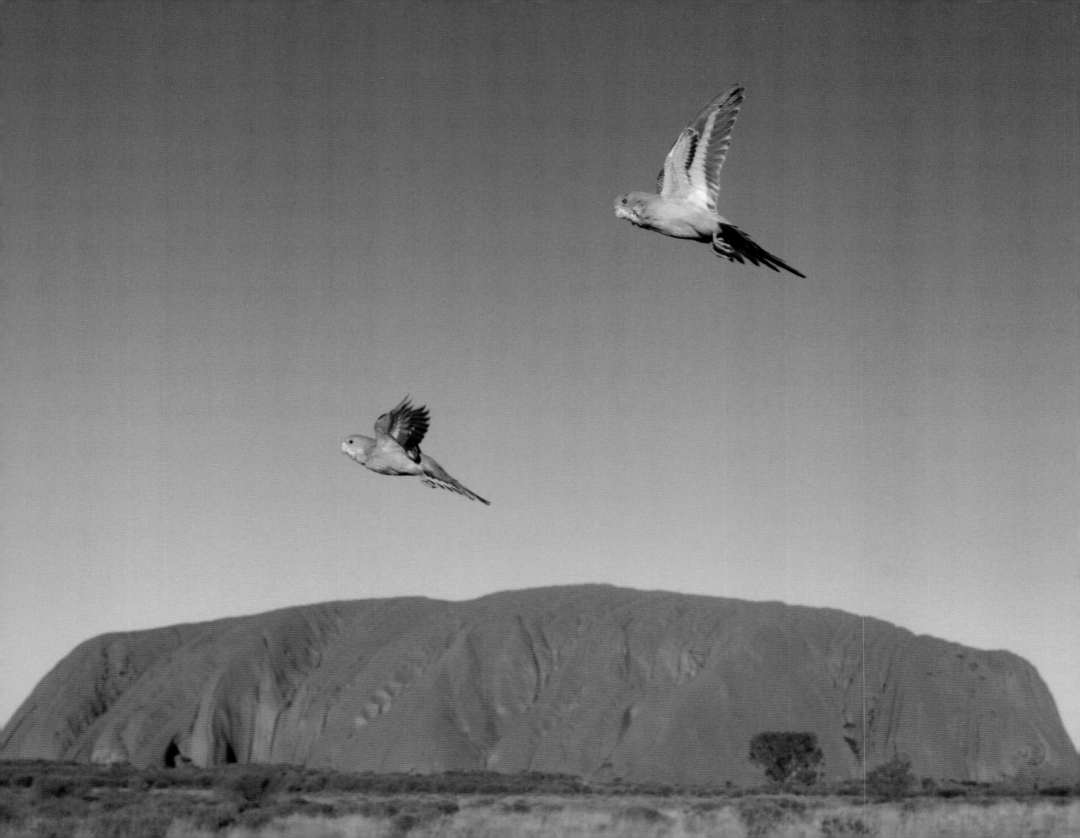

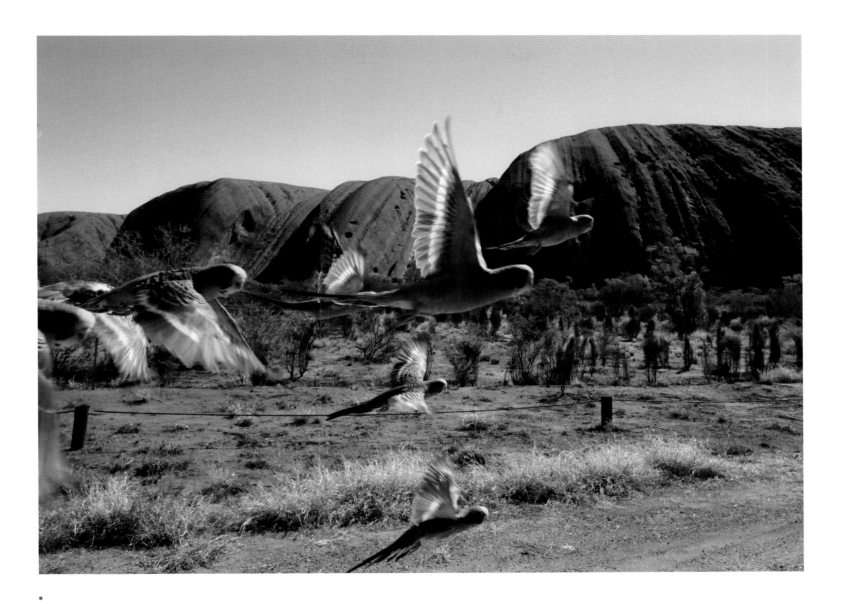

BUDGERIGAR, Uluru (Ayers Rock), Australia
The travel plans of budgerigars depend entirely on where widely
scattered supplies of food and water are located. The search can
mean birds flying for 400 km (250 miles) in a day.

DEMOISELLE CRANE, the Himalayas, Nepal
In late August and into September, demoiselles are on migration through the Himalayas in flocks of 400 or more.

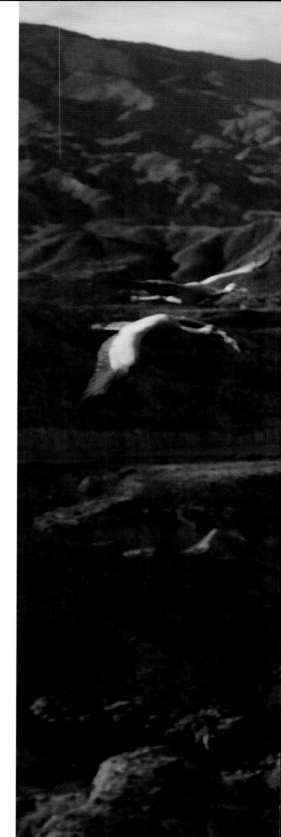

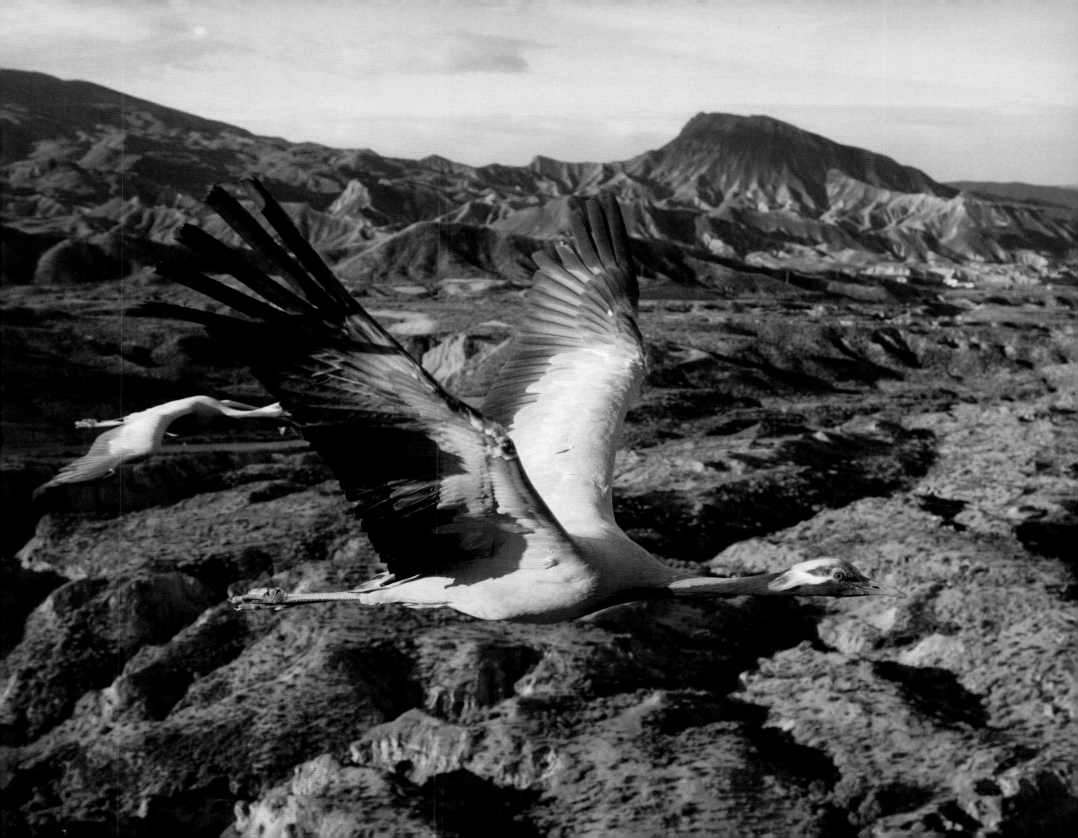

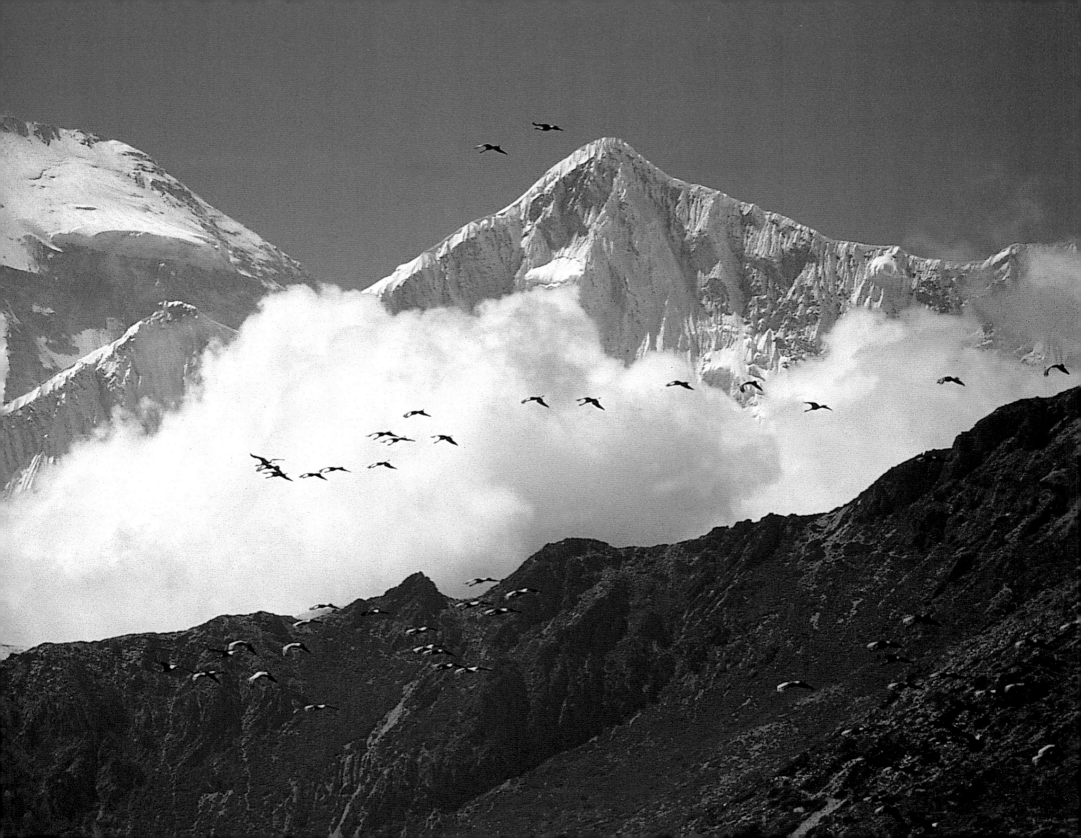

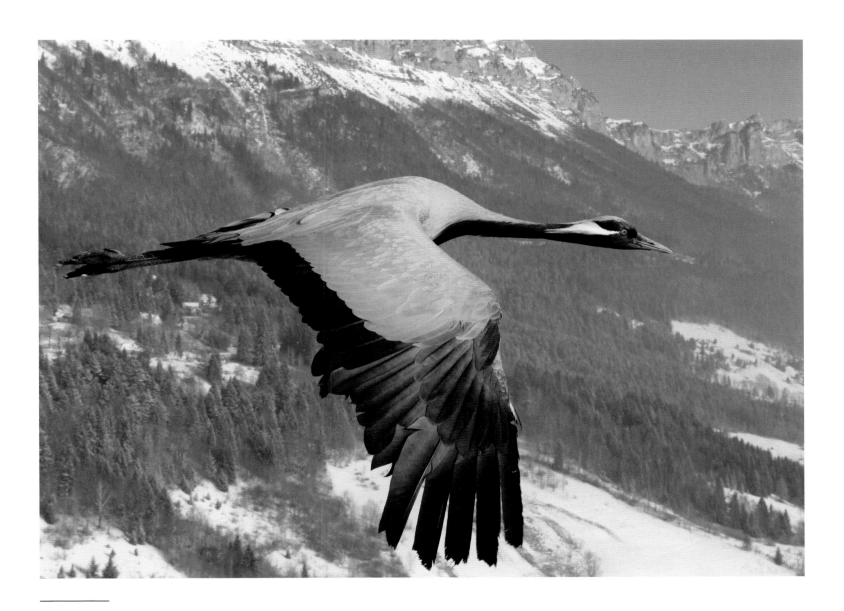

DEMOISELLE CRANE, the Himalayas, Nepal
The cranes fly to 2,000 m (6,500 ft), adopt the
classic V-formation and then soar. They must climb
to 8,000 m (26,000 ft) to negotiate the high passes
through the mountain range.

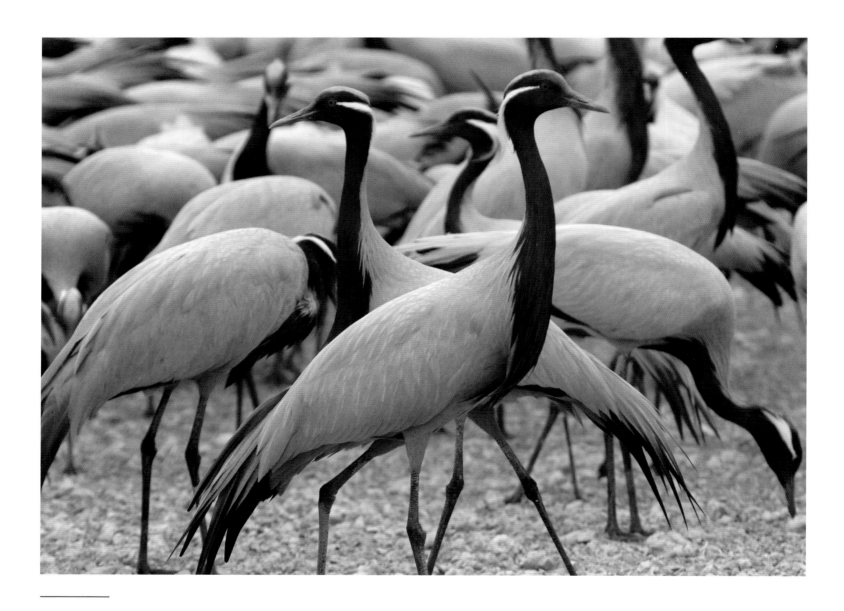

DEMOISELLE CRANE, Keechen, India
Many birds perish during the gruelling journey, but those
that reach the village of Keechen in Rajasthan are pampered
by the local community, which puts out grain for the birds
throughout the winter.

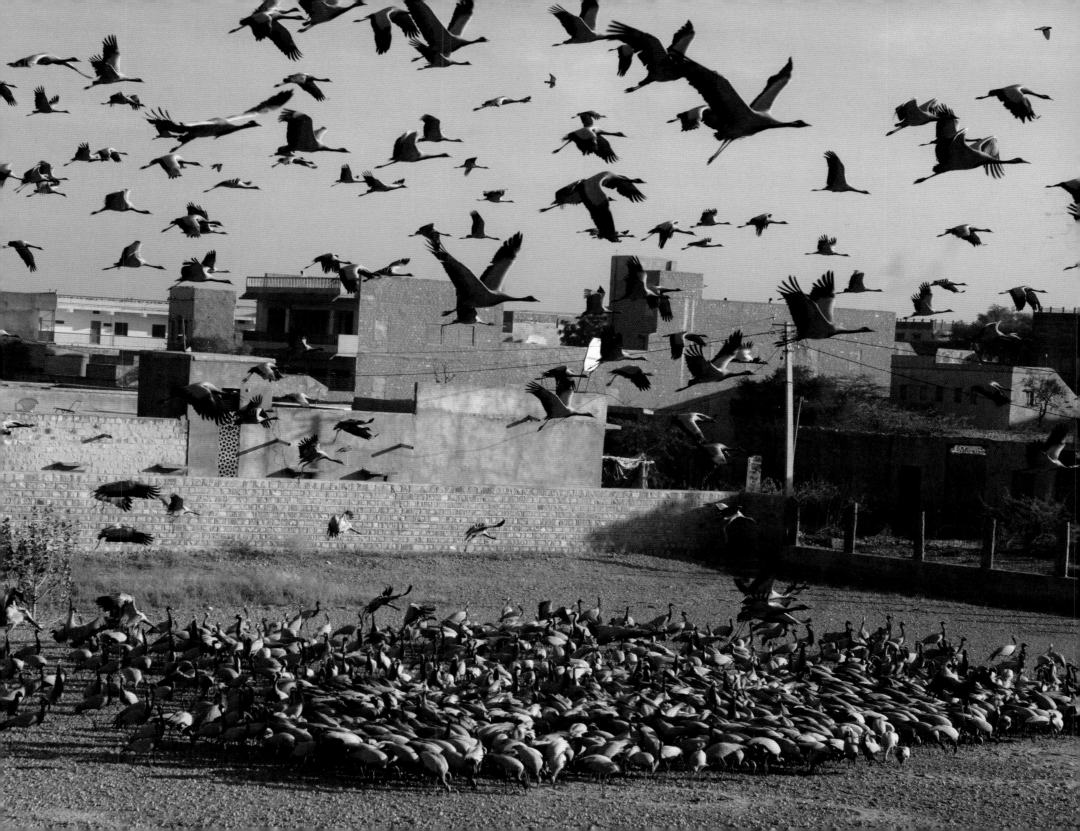

BAR-HEADED GOOSE, the Himalayas, Nepal
Rather than aim for mountain passes like the demoiselles, bar-heads
migrate right over the top of the mountains at altitudes of up to 10,000 m
(33,000 ft) – the highest migration of any bird. Heat generated by the body
helps keep their wings from icing up.

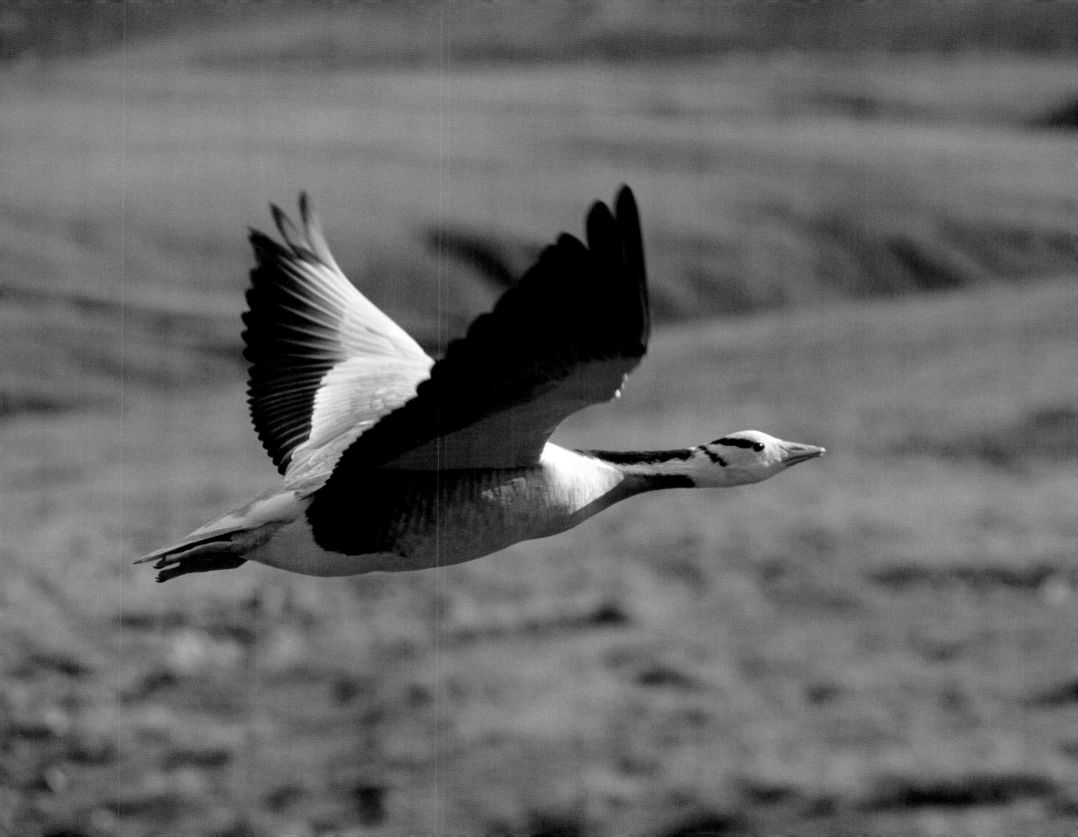

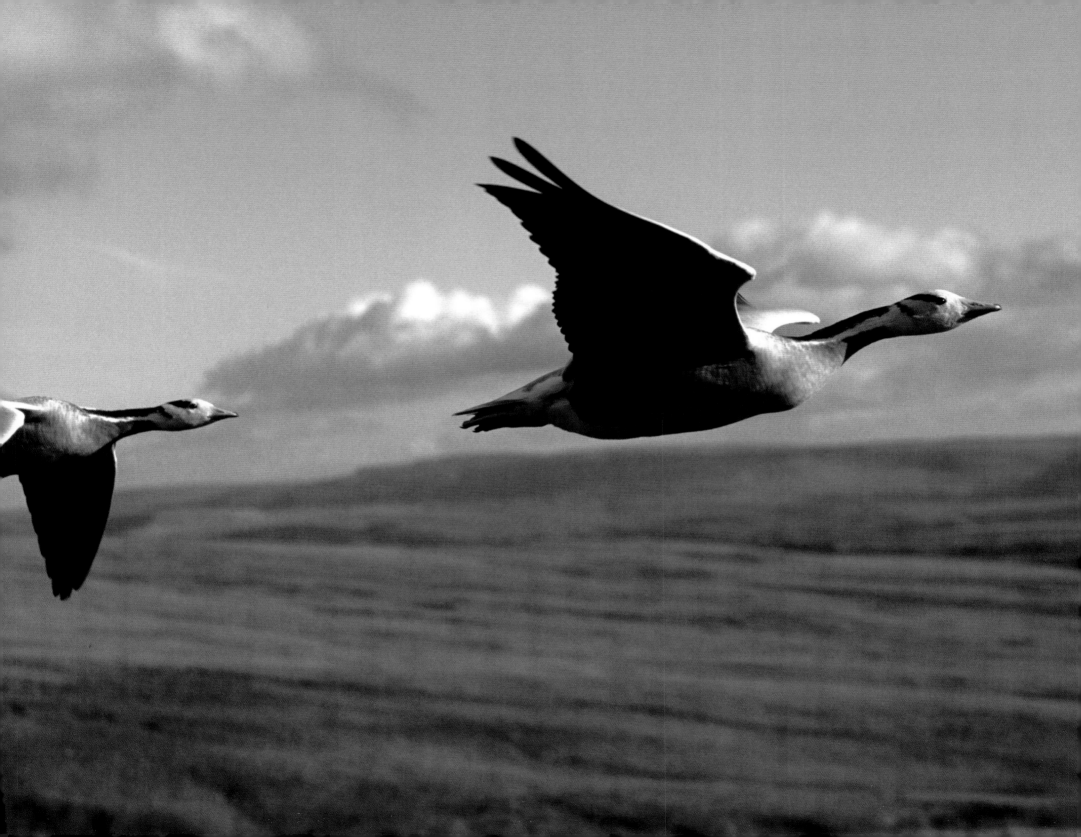

BAR-HEADED GOOSE, the Himalayas, Nepal
These geese have broad, powerful wings and are able to fly effectively even in thin air. They time their migration to beat the first of the winter storms.

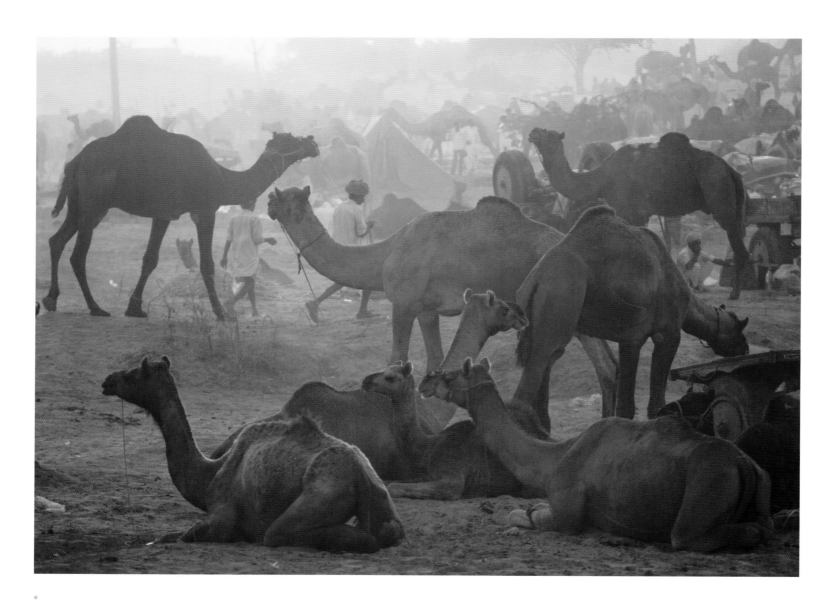

ROCK DOVE, Pushkar, India
The Pushkar camel fair attracts 300,000 people and 20,000
camels, cattle and horses, as well as countless feral pigeons
or rock doves that take full advantage of any spilled grain.

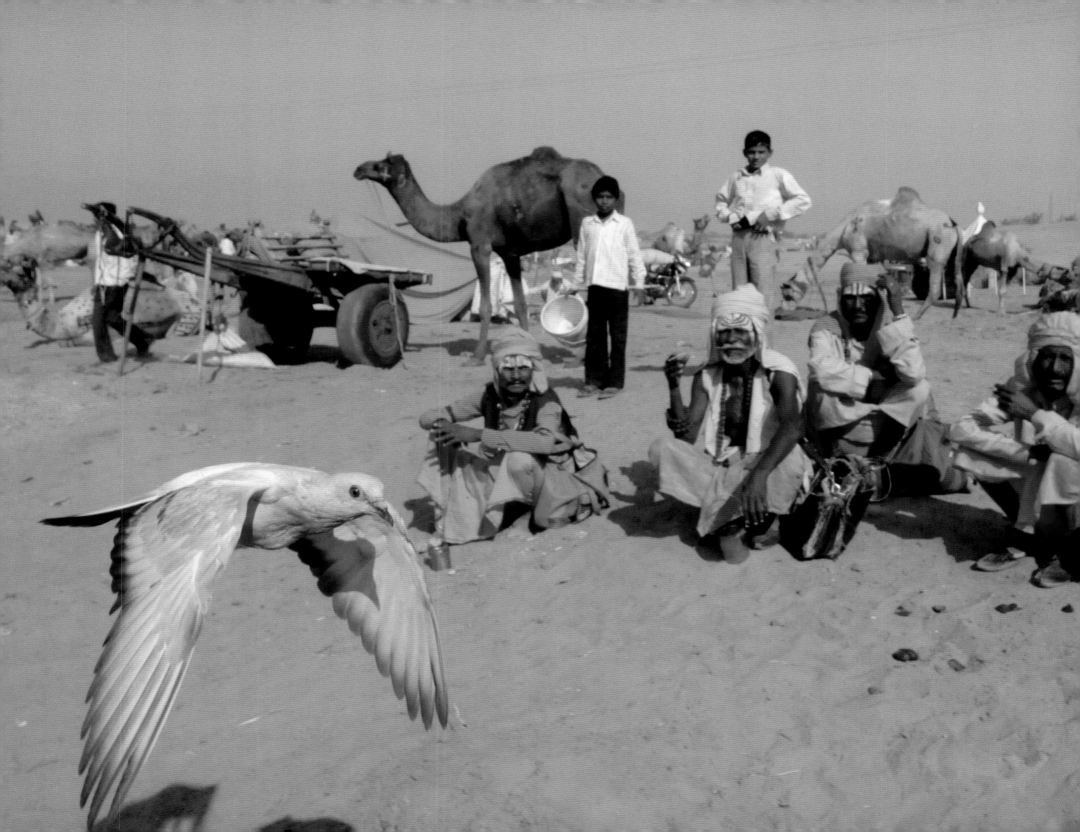

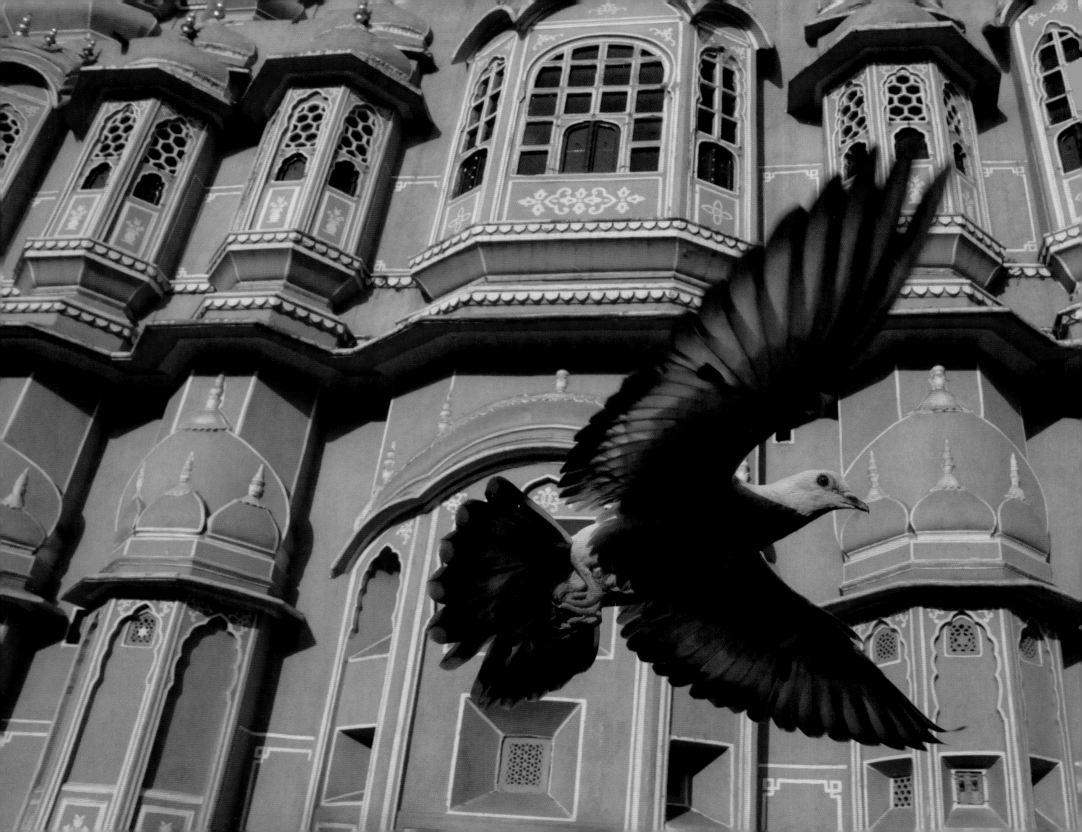

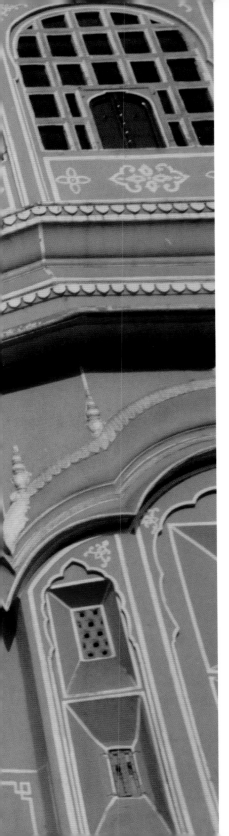

ROCK DOVE, Palace of the Winds, Jaipur, India
Hawks patrol the ramparts of this palace, reaching into the nesting alcoves with their talons to grab the hiding pigeons.

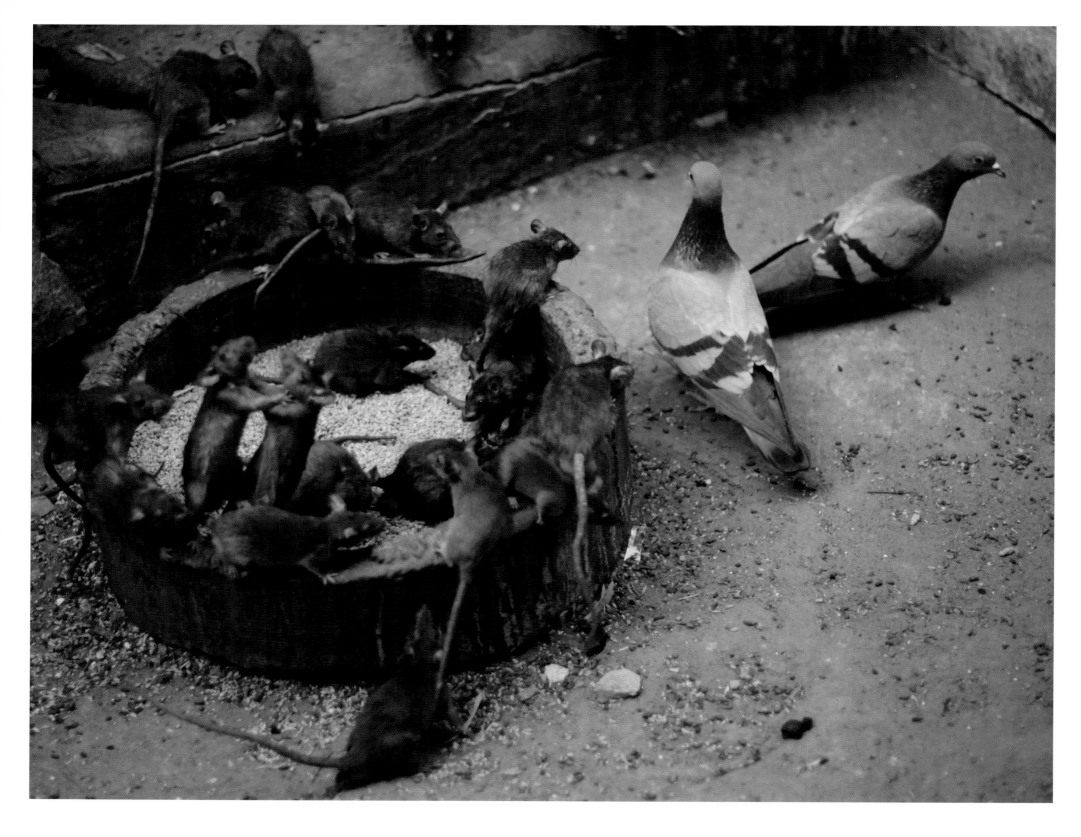

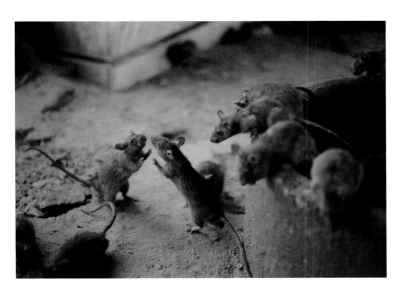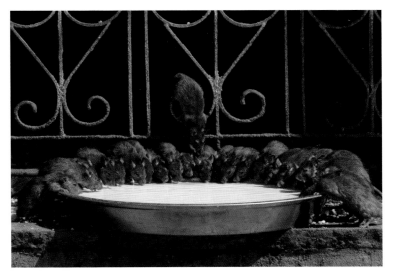

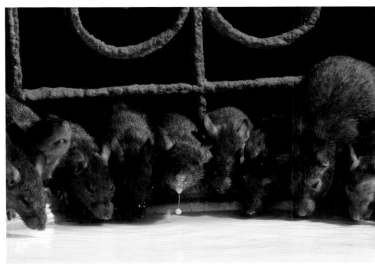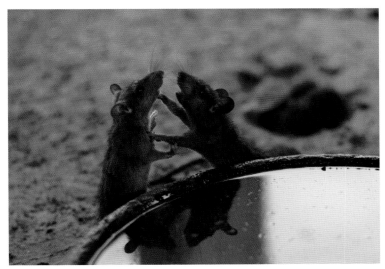

ROCK DOVE, Kami Mata Temple, Deshnok, India
The 'rat temple' is a paradise for pigeons as well as for black rats. Locals believe that their dead are reincarnated as rats, so they ensure that the animals are well looked after – meaning there is plenty of food on offer.

INDIAN VULTURE, Jodhpur, India
Scavenging vultures soar around human habitation,
such as Jodhpur's Blue City, and over the surrounding
countryside in search of carcasses.

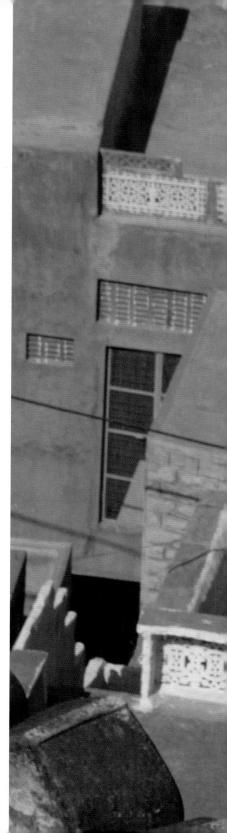

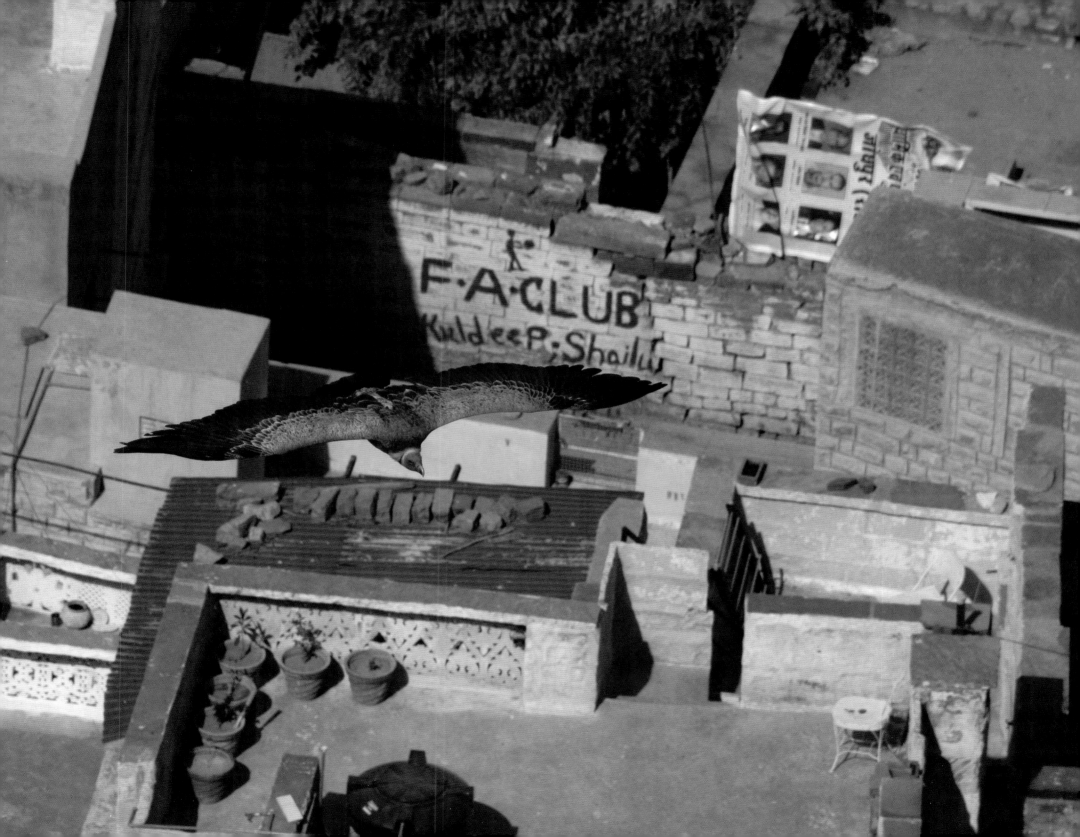

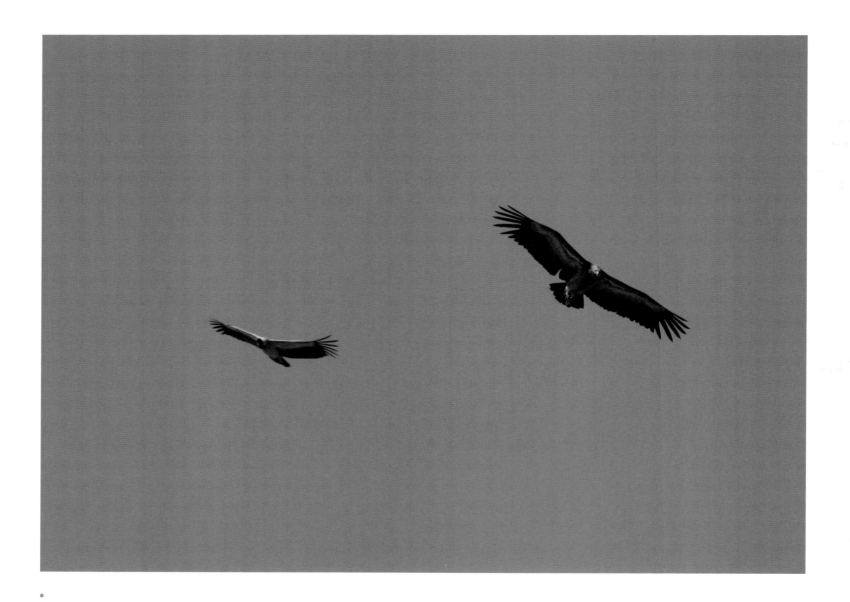

INDIAN VULTURE, Rajasthan, India
In the rural landscape, especially in tiger reserves, carcasses scavenged by
vultures include the victims of Bengal tiger attacks. But the birds must
be cautious, for tigers will charge and attack any caught stealing a kill.

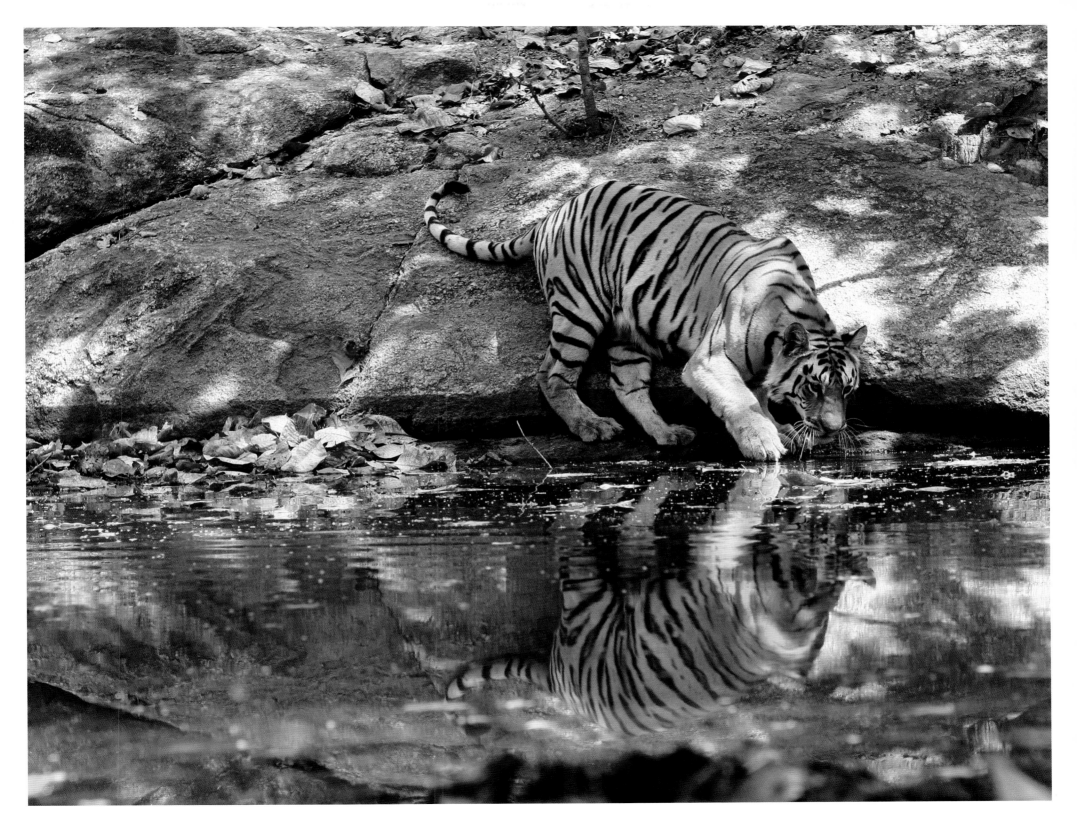

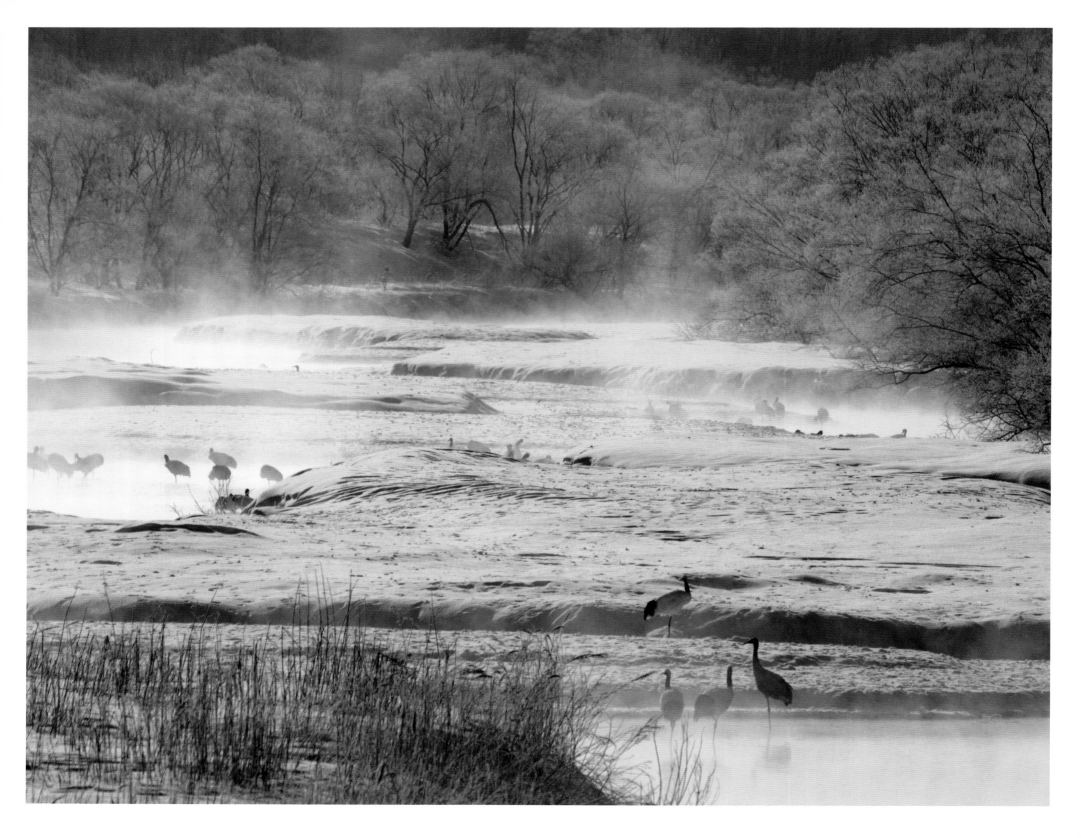

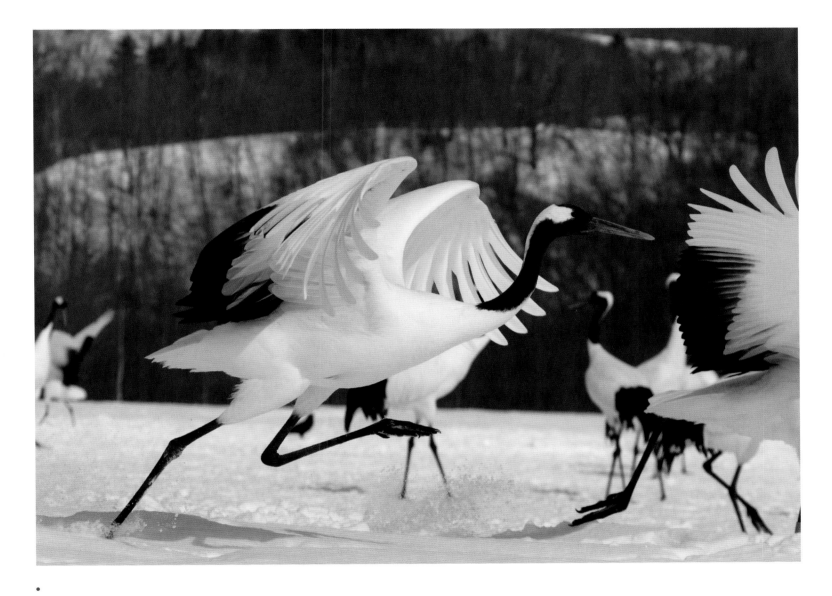

JAPANESE CRANE, Kushiro Marsh, Japan
Japan's 1,200 resident cranes represent about half the species'
world population. Most do not migrate far, and the Hokkaido
birds congregate at marshland sites for most of the winter.

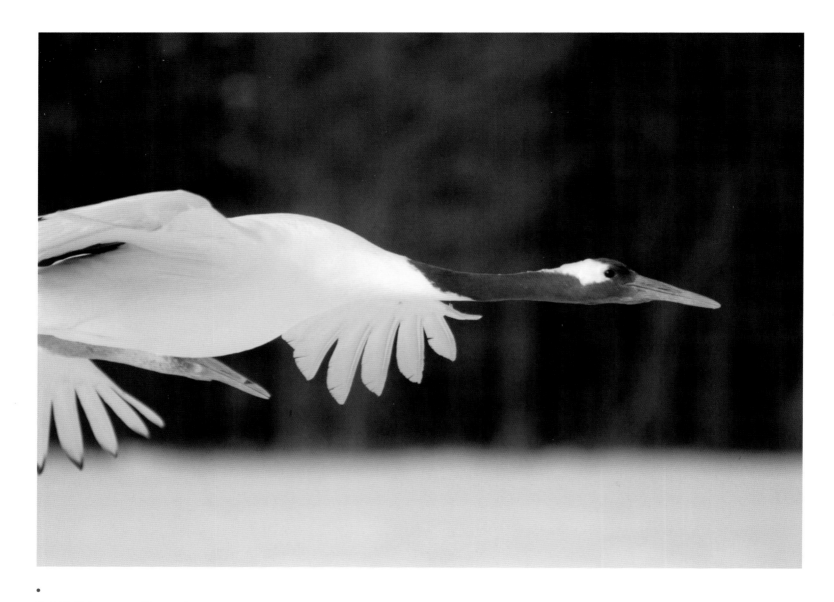

JAPANESE CRANE, Kushiro Marsh, Japan
Cranes pair off for life, but frequently reinforce their bond
with flamboyant dances.

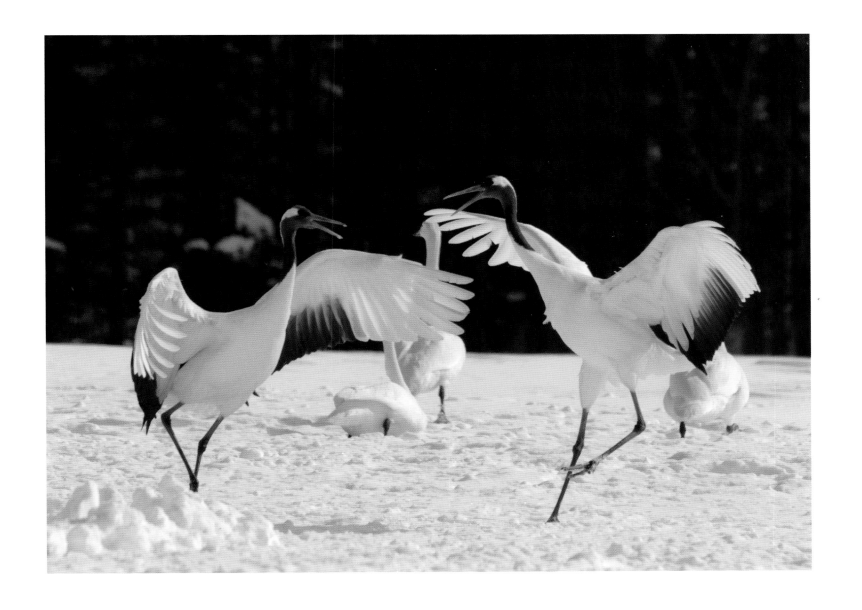

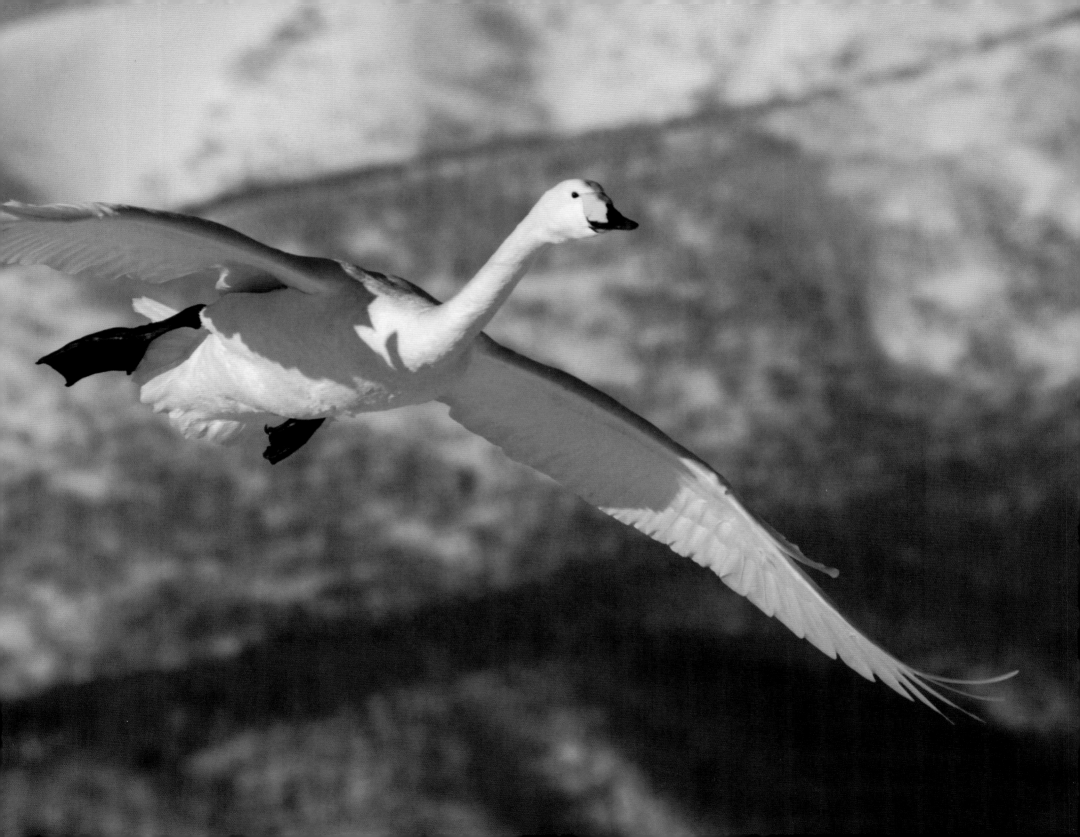

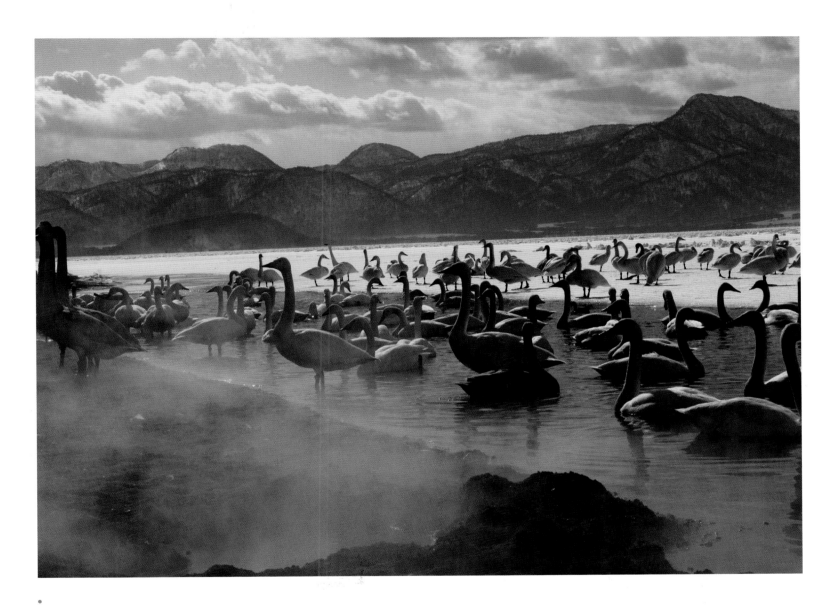

WHOOPER SWAN, Lake Kussharo, Japan
Each winter, 38,000 whooper swans arrive in Japan from
eastern Siberia. At Lake Kussharo, hot springs keep some
of its waters open even in the coldest weather.

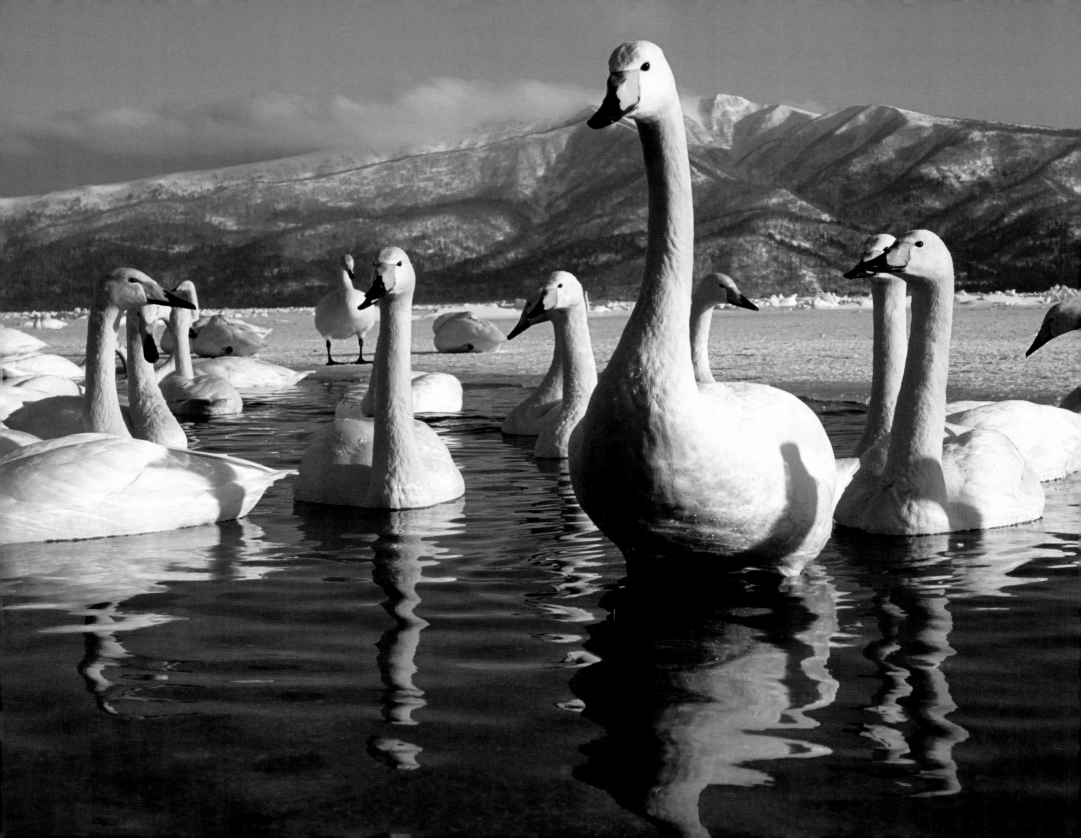

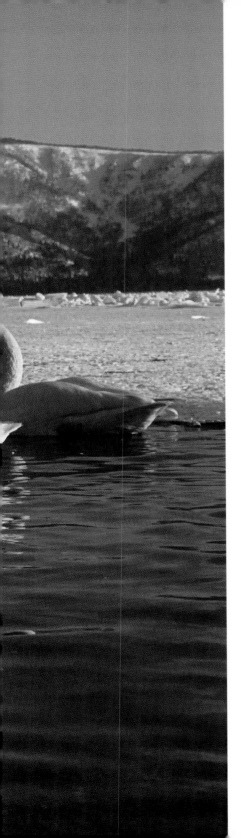

WHOOPER SWAN, Lake Kussharo, Japan
All may seem peaceful, but whooper swans can be aggressive,
and young males will fight fiercely over potential mates.

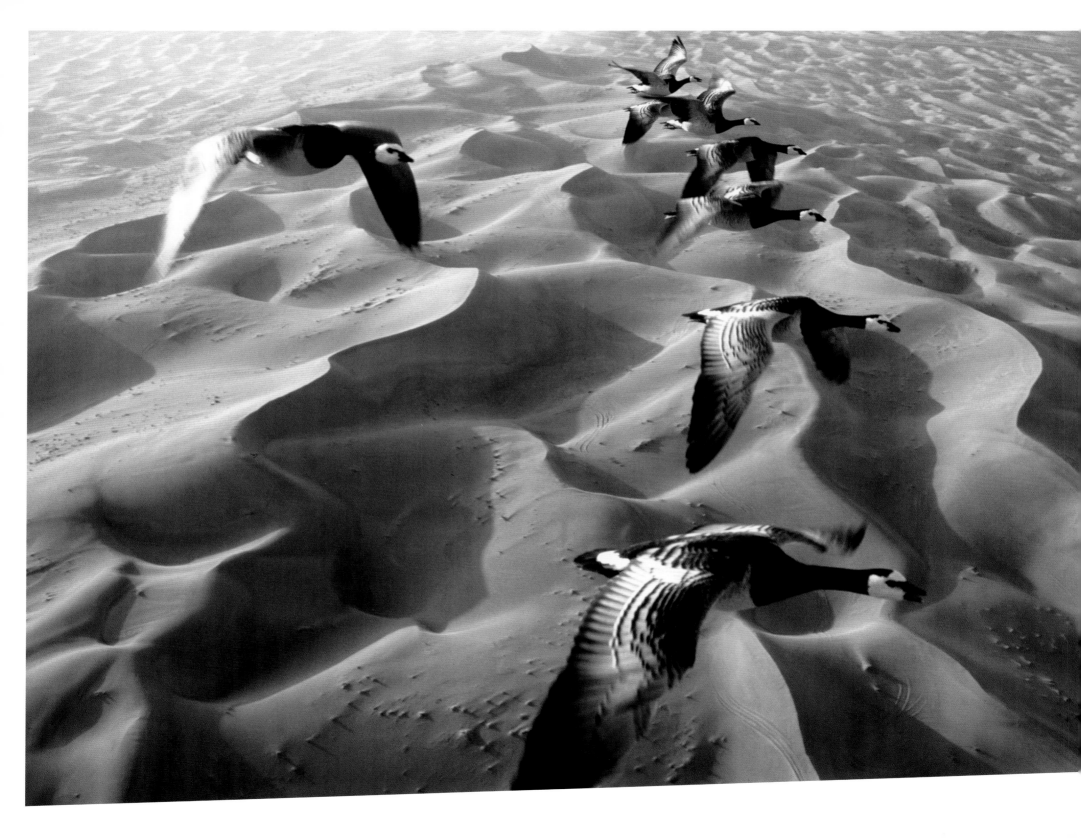

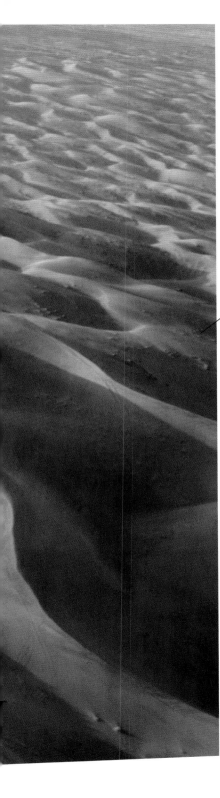

THE
MAKING
of

When we set out to make *Earthflight*, it became clear that studying the world through the eyes of birds would present us with a fresh way of looking at nature. Whenever and wherever one of nature's great spectacles unfolds, birds are always present, sometimes simply passive observers, but more often than not active participants. Watch the birds, we thought, and they'll lead us directly to the action – and so it proved. In fact, despite our painstaking research, birds seemed to know more about these natural events than we did. Birds would actually become our 'field biologists', and by seeing things from their perspective we observed spectacular events and fascinating behaviour that we otherwise would have missed. It meant that birds were our personal guides across and within continents. They would take us to where we wanted to be, and they ensured we were there at the right time. To be at one with the birds in this way, however, was a monumental challenge, for we didn't want gimmicky images but genuinely new observations. This was the ideal, but then came the practicalities.

Right from the start we realised that the success of *Earthflight* would depend on many different factors: wildlife cameramen who were willing to push techniques to the limit; camera technicians who could redesign and miniaturise equipment; modellers who could place our cameras into all kinds of flying machines; animal handlers who had a special kind of relationship with the birds we wanted to film; and zoologists and ethologists without whose work we would be flailing in the dark.

The people from all these backgrounds, we reasoned, would help us achieve our goal – to view the world from an animal's point of view. To do this we had to be that animal, to be a bird and take to the skies with them. So, as well as filming wild birds and their natural environment in the conventional way, we needed to explore novel filming techniques to get us up into the flocks and experiencing the miracle of flight at first-hand.

Building on the experience all those years ago on *In-flight Movie*, my directorial debut, we looked at ways in which we could apply the modern technology of High Definition (HD) and miniaturisation of cameras and employed a wide range of techniques to give us the best results possible. We experimented with ultra-lightweight on-board cameras with custom-built bird

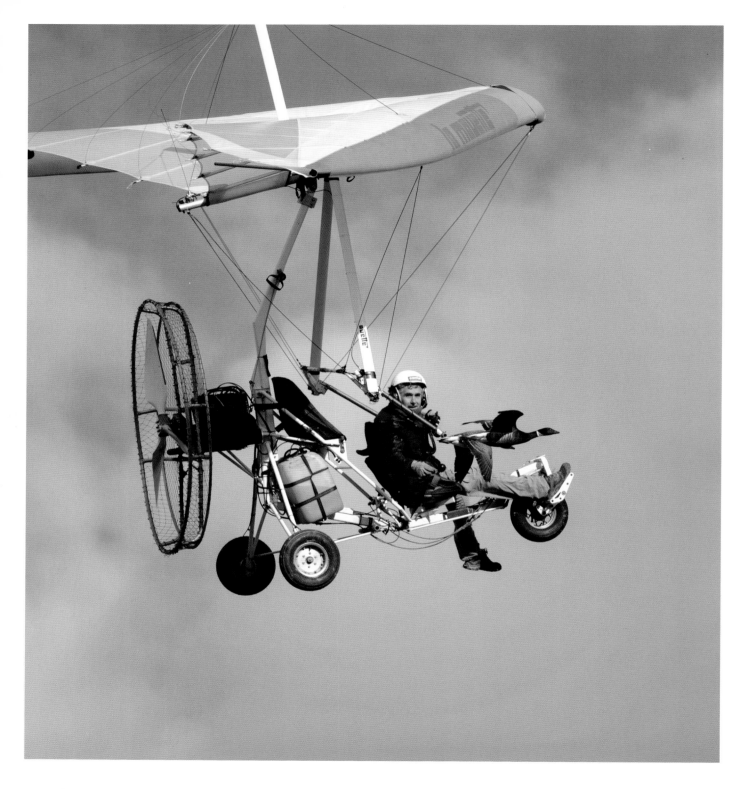

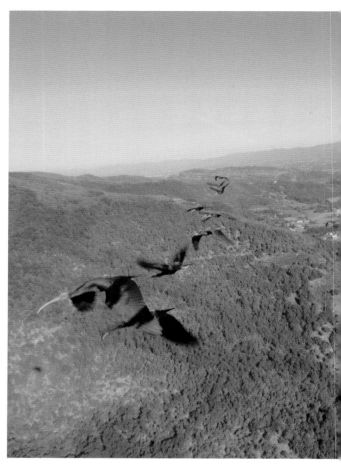

Up, up and away
Developing our microlight filming technique involved a number of teams working with a variety of imprinted birds, from storks and cranes to geese and ibis.

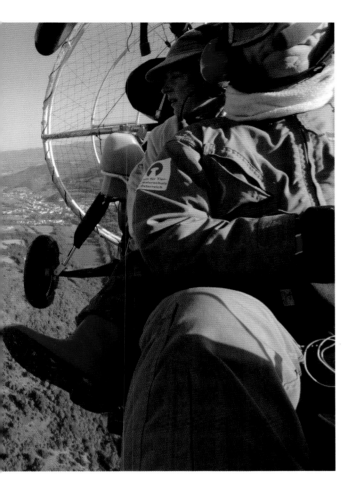

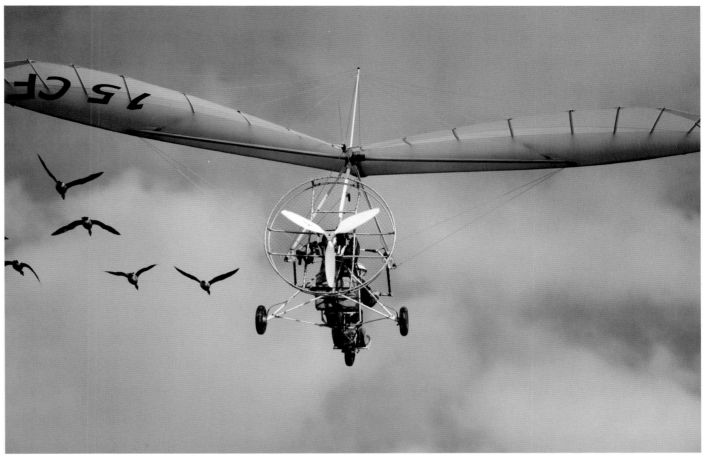

harnesses and camera mounts that reduced vibration to a minimum, which gave us a real bird's-eye view, and even showed us new and breathtaking details of how a bird actually flies. Working with trained, or 'imprinted', birds we were able to have them fly over, under and alongside microlights, paragliders, boats, trucks and cars and, in one case, a specially modified trailer. We developed novel camera platforms and associated kit – programmable model helicopters that were more like military drones, and model gliders designed to work like the birds themselves, flying in the thermals right in among the flocks. We had full-size helicopters with gyro-stabilised HD cameras and ultra-long zoom lenses

to capture the overall spectacle as well as full-size gliders that followed the birds along their migration path. We used specially designed camera dollies and cranes, and took into the field high-speed video cameras, operated more usually in a studio, that shot at a staggering 1,000 frames per second to slow down the action – and, of course, all this in fabulous HD. It was an enormous undertaking, which took years of careful planning, experimentation and ingenuity, with many unexpected setbacks and frustrations along the way. Above all, however, what remained key to this new approach were the heroic birds that would fly alongside the cameras and even carry them.

FLY WITH THE BIRDS

In the making of *Earthflight*, people who had very special relationships with birds were to play a major role. Some were professional falconers, familiar with the demands of wildlife cinematography, others spare-time bird enthusiasts or conservationists involved in reintroduction programmes. The most extraordinary relationships involved birds that were 'imprinted' on people from the moment they hatched. This meant that hatchlings would form an inseparable bond with a human surrogate 'mother', and so would follow in their footsteps wherever they went, which could mean

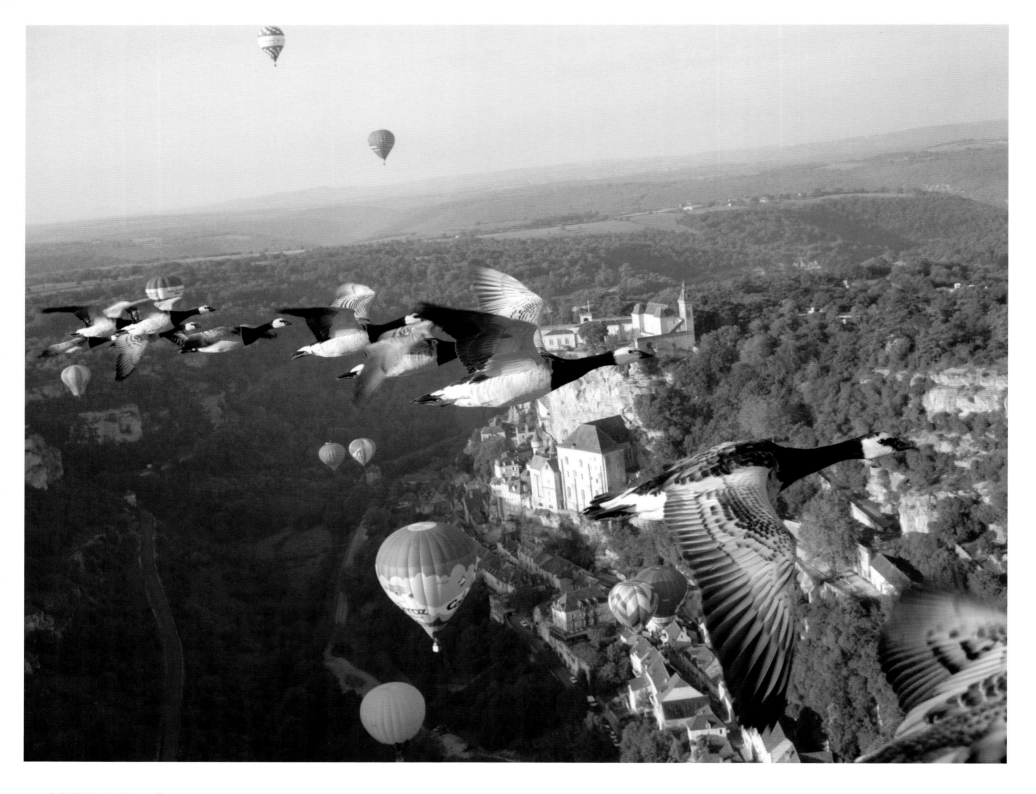

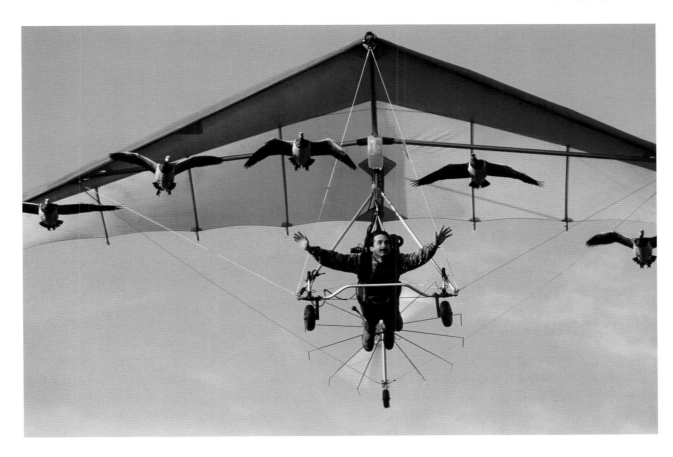

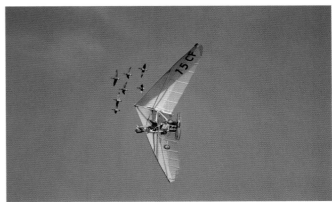

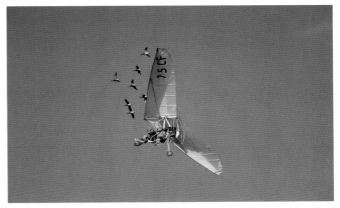

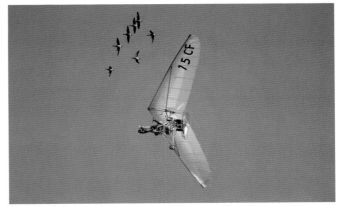

anything from travelling alongside a microlight high up in the air to a speed boat out at sea.

The technique of imprinting, and specifically the work of Christian Moullec, formed an integral part of many film shoots in Europe. Christian is a meteorologist with a passion for birds. His imprinting work was prompted by a concern, shared with Swedish ornithologists, for the future of the lesser white-fronted goose. The Swedes were having a problem returning captive-bred birds to the wild, for somehow the geese had to learn the migration route between southern and northern Europe. At first, barnacle geese were used as foster parents to teach the young white-fronts, but they

were working with far too few birds to make an impact. Christian reasoned that if he could encourage geese to follow him as he flew in a microlight, he could teach a sizeable flock to follow him along the migration route. Amazingly, it worked, and now Christian has taken his flying technique to another level. Living in an idyllic part of France – Aurillac in the Massif Central – he is so into the mindset of the birds with which he flies, he has almost come to live like a bird himself.

For our enterprise, however, Christian had to work with birds that are not usually imprinted or trained by falconers – such as common cranes, white storks and several different species of geese. It meant that we

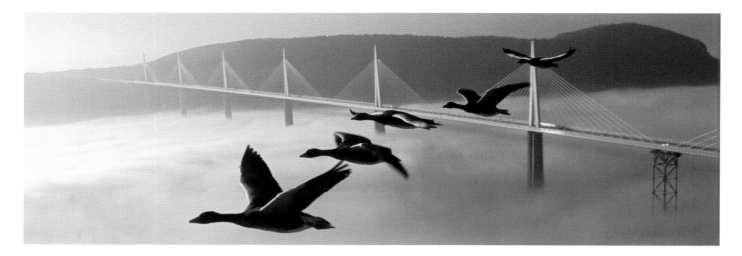

had to find eggs and get them to Christian just at the point of hatching. With storks, this involved somehow transporting the eggs from the UK, where they were being bred, to Christian's home in France at the right moment, just before they were about to hatch – ensuring they were well developed before making the journey, but not yet out of the egg. Flying with them on a commercial airline was not an option so they had to be driven to the cross-Channel ferry at Dover and carried by hand to Christian waiting in Boulogne. Four precious eggs were placed in an incubator, which had to be stabilised and kept at a constant temperature to minimise disruption. Travelling with them was *Earthflight* producer Tilly Parker.

'The first problem,' she remembers, 'was that the incubator was plugged into the car's cigarette lighter, and when the engine was switched off it stopped working – and we were facing a five-hour ferry crossing. The only option was to carry the incubator on board, but then I discovered that the incubator wouldn't work on the boat's electrical system. The only thing I could do was put the eggs under my clothes to keep them warm. Then came problem number three: one of the eggs started to hatch, and it was imperative that one of the first things it heard was an air horn, the main sound used in the imprinting process. I also had to talk to the eggs and the hatching chick in French to impersonate Christian, but without it seeing me, and sound the horn every couple of minutes. You can imagine the looks I got from the other passengers! Eventually we landed at Boulogne, and eggs and chick were fine. Christian then asked to hear my horn. "Disaster," he cried, "your English horn is different to my French one!"'

Fortunately, the birds were multilingual and took to the French horn just as well as the English one. By the time Tilly handed over the eggs, the first hatchling was out of its shell and rode all the way to Aurillac in Christian's shirt pocket. There, the four storks became honorary members of Christian's family, following him everywhere.

First, he had to get them used to the microlight, which he achieved by introducing a microlight wing to their pen. After some initial apprehension the birds took to the wing happily enough, even hiding under it for security. The next challenge was to get them used to the potentially frightening noise of the microlight engine, and so Christian turned to the best substitute he knew of: a chainsaw. He would walk around his farm followed by a bunch of chicks, all the while revving a chainsaw – a bizarre sight!

WAYWARD GOOSE

When working with the imprinted birds, there are always time factors and many other considerations to take into account before any filming can begin. There's the weather, especially wind speed and direction, and all manner of things that can spook birds – domestic dogs and cats, tall trees, helicopters, and on one occasion even a hot-air balloon. We could have everything in place and organised perfectly for a shoot, but there was always something for which we hadn't planned. Fortunately, Christian understands his birds so well he hasn't lost a single one. On one occasion, however, he nearly relinquished his unblemished record.

It was his very first shoot with greylag geese at the Millau Viaduct, France's longest and highest bridge. Fog filled the valley so the bridge looked as if it was floating on clouds, a magical sight. We had a big flock of 30 birds, and while doing a practice flight the lead goose, one of Christian's favourites, was upset by a gust of wind and flew away from the others. The rest of the flock became disorientated and Christian had to round them up and guide them to safety. He then went in search of his wayward greylag. Losing a goose to Christian was like losing a child: he simply had to find it. It was getting

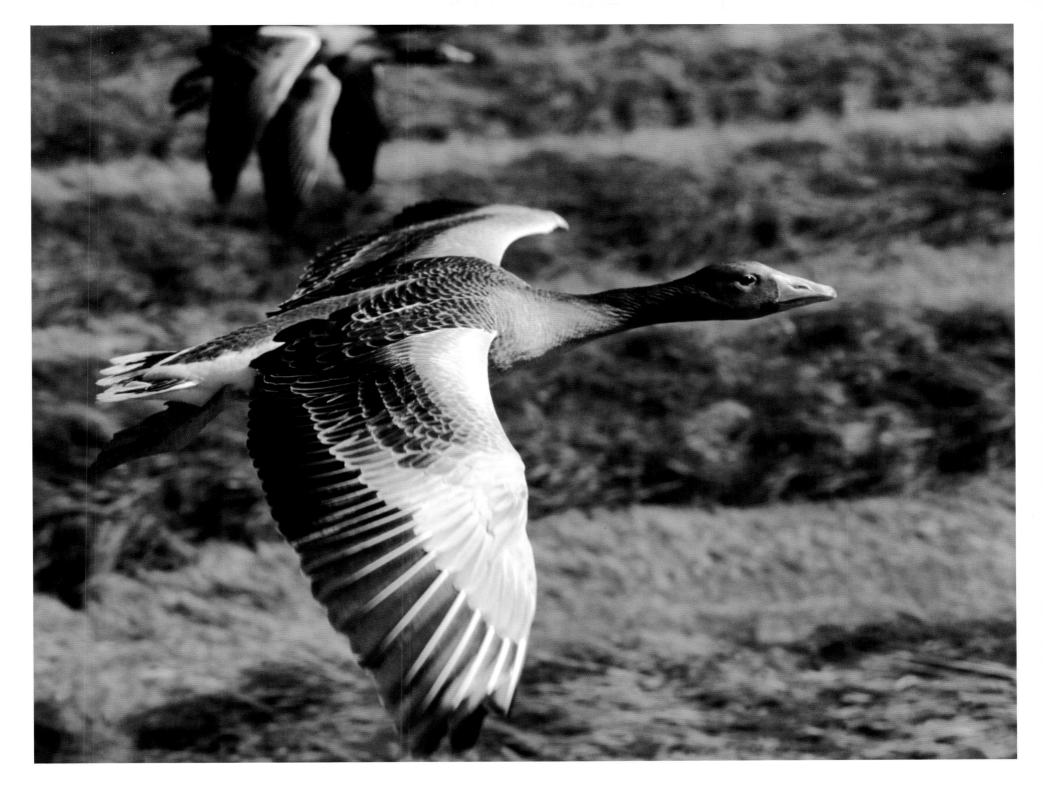

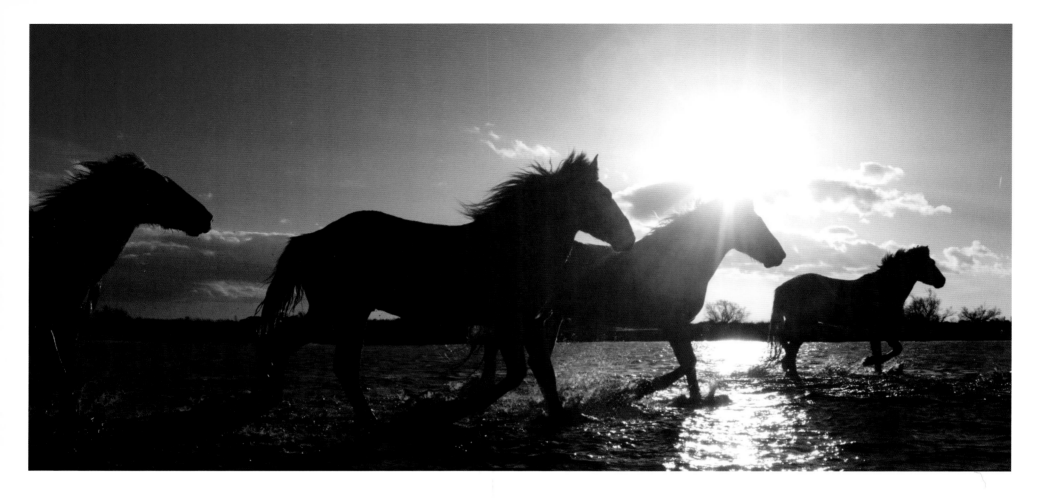

late and the sun was setting, but still he circled. The goose had vanished, but he didn't give up hope. He and producer Phil Dalton waited on the ground in the dark, but by 11pm Phil had to leave to look through the day's rushes. He started his car and as the headlights came on, the greylag goose came from nowhere and landed right in front of them. It had found its way back to a very happy and relieved Christian.

HANGING IN THE AIR

Christian's microlight has two seats, one for him and another for cameraman Richard Cook, also a microlight

pilot and instructor. The two men understood each other perfectly, with Richard knowing the limits of what Christian could do, and it was clear that much of what we achieved couldn't have been done without their partnership. However, despite the fundamental bond of understanding between the two men, neither actually spoke the other's language well, and so they communicated in a kind of technical 'franglais'.

This was tested to an extreme while filming cranes in the Camargue. Here, we had to manoeuvre the microlight and its entourage of birds to coordinate with a herd of galloping Camarguais, the famous white horses. While Christian called his obedient birds to

fly alongside, Richard was able to frame a shot of the cranes so that he could capture them against a backdrop of the horses crossing the marshes below. At the same time, cameraman Mike Richards was on the ground directly in the path of the thundering herd for the 'in the thick of it' close-ups. Despite the meticulous planning and expertise of those involved, it took five days to capture the moment when cranes and horses were perfectly aligned.

In the Netherlands we were faced with a very different scenario, that of filming the cranes flying over vast bulb fields, awash with colour. But we had only a very short window of opportunity to get the shots that

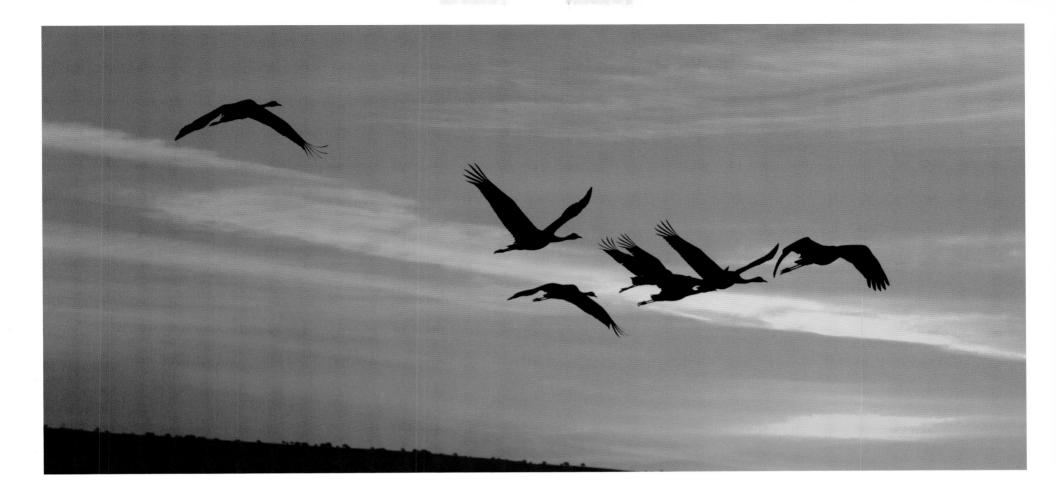

we wanted – first the birds had to have several days to get used to the new location, and then bad weather delayed filming. However, on the last day the weather was perfect and the birds were ready to fly. The crew was up at the crack of dawn, when the winds were slight and the light was good for filming. Then, Tilly heard something that could have scuppered her carefully laid filming plans: giant lawnmower-like machines had started to hack their way through the fields, pulping and discarding the beautiful flowers in order to harvest their bulbs for sale. Cue utter panic, as the stunning backdrop for our shoot vanished before our eyes. Tilly had to plead with the farmers to hold cutting for one more day so that

we could get the shots that we wanted. Thankfully, they agreed, resulting in stunning aerial shots of cranes flying over a wonderful patchwork of colour.

WILD BUDGIES

In Australia, assistant producer Matthew Gordon and cameraman Peter Nearhos were working with budgerigars, an altogether different experience to filming with the bigger birds. Budgies are small birds that fly in big flocks; in fact, the wild budgie flock the team encountered was one of the largest ever filmed, consisting of an estimated one million birds. They were

also working with a small flock of thirty imprinted birds trained by falconer Andy Payne and his colleagues from the Australian Raptor Centre in Queensland.

These colourful little birds are fast flyers that tire very quickly, so it was difficult to get long, sustained flights against iconic backdrops as we had with the geese, cranes and storks. Budgies are also exceptionally nervous birds, and so they behave differently from birds in smaller flocks, tending to react more to each other and less to the directions of their handlers. If one decided to fly off, for example, the others would follow, and Matthew would lose an enormous amount of time waiting for them to return.

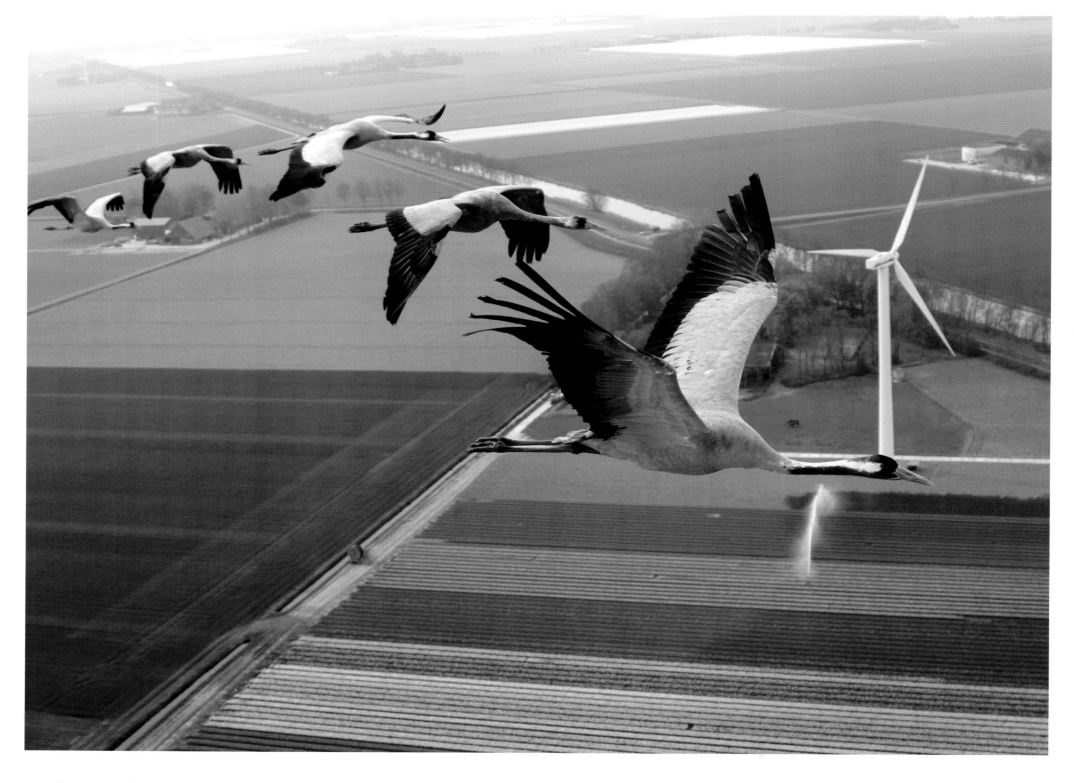

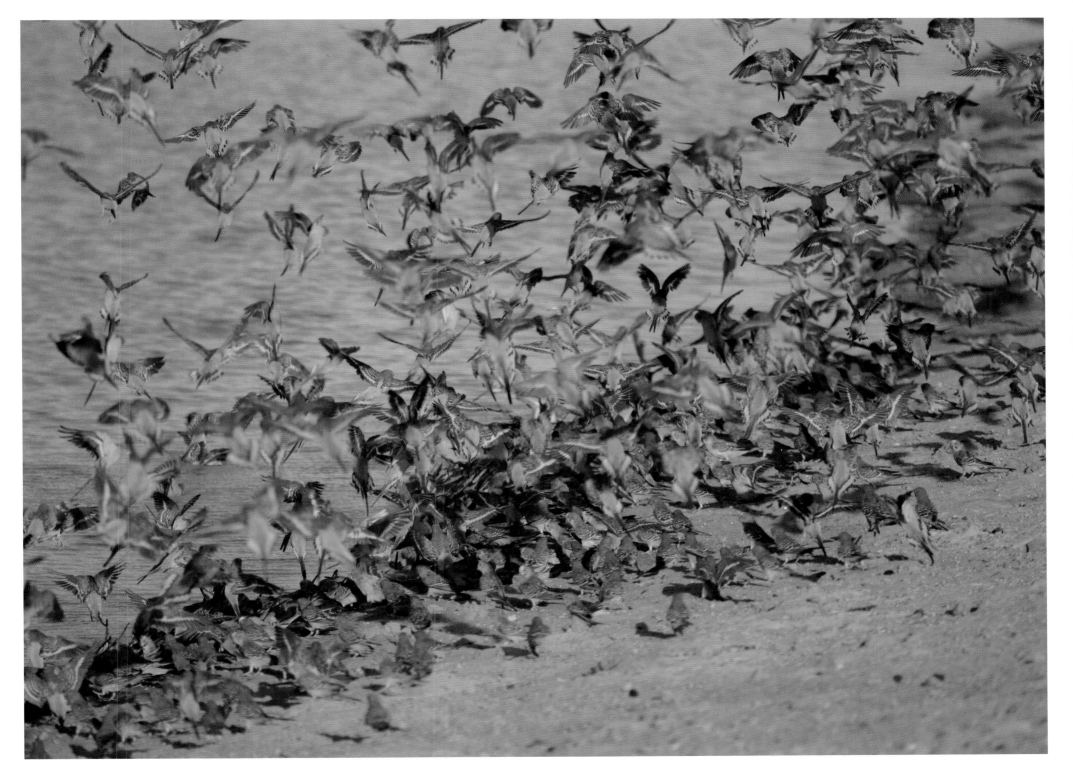

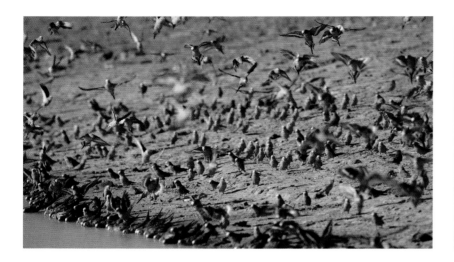

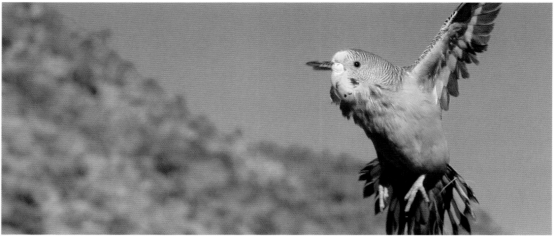

Despite these difficulties, we were determined to capture footage of the budgerigars flying past iconic Australian landmarks. As we had decided not to use computerised overlay techniques to capture our images (in which footage of birds in flight is placed on top of a previously filmed background), we were filming everything 'for real' – as it really appeared. This meant that we had to come up with a way of filming the nervous birds on their short flights. The solution was a rather novel rig, consisting of a long trailer pulled by a truck. At the back of the trailer was the release cage and at the front was the feeder cage. The birds were trained to fly from one to the other while the trailer was pulled along in front of an iconic landmark, such as Uluru (Ayers Rock) in the central Australian Outback. At first, in order to get the birds used to the rig without the risk of them flying away, the trailer had a Perspex screen along one side. This gave the birds the feeling that they were out in the open, but contained them just in case they wanted to veer off. When the time came to film, after six months of training, the screen was removed and the birds were flying free from one end of the trailer to the other.

There were still problems though – wind being a particular issue. If the budgies were hit by a gust, they'd fly off and it would take Andy a good three hours to get them all back. The birds that stayed were a great help to him, though. Their excited chirruping in the feeding cage encouraged their flock mates to return.

A HELPING HAND

Some of our animal handlers came from unexpected backgrounds, especially conservationists involved in captive breeding and reintroduction programmes with birds of prey. In the past people have tried unsuccessfully to reintroduce large birds, such as the white-tailed eagle, into many parts of Europe. Scientists eventually began to realise that they cannot just simply let the birds go, but must actually teach them exactly how they should behave – teach them how to be birds, in essence. They now train adult birds to fly and forage or hunt before their release, with the idea being that these birds will then go on to teach these skills to the next generation. It was some of those pioneering birds that were to feature in our films.

In the Peruvian Amazon, for instance, we wanted to film scarlet macaws visiting clay licks along the riverbank. Although we had already filmed some beautiful footage of wild birds attending these colourful gatherings, the scope of the concept behind *Earthflight* meant that we wanted to find some way of completely entering the birds' world rather than view it from afar, and so we were keen to fly alongside them. The problem of how to achieve this was solved when we found a rehabilitation centre that specialised in rearing young, abandoned nestlings and returning them to the wild. When the birds were released, they still retained a loose bond with the people who reared them. They lived like wild macaws but sometimes came when they were called, especially when offered a titbit or two – an ideal scenario for filming.

To film the birds we adopted a tried-and-tested method, opting for a boat as the camera platform and, armed with some tasty fruit and other treats, we soon had the reintroduced macaws eating, quite literally, out of our hands. But although they would come out of the forest to visit us, we were totally at the birds' beck and call. They would only come when they were in the mood and when the forest fruits weren't offering anything more tempting. Many days we simply never saw them at all, but when they did decide to arrive the results were simply magical. They would fly alongside the boat, often for a kilometre or more, allowing us to get spectacular shots of the macaw's colourful world.

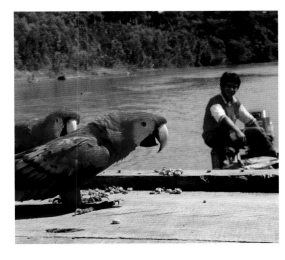

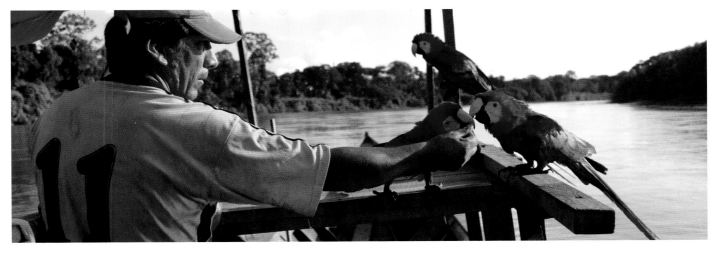

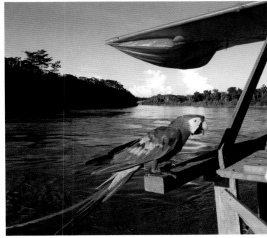

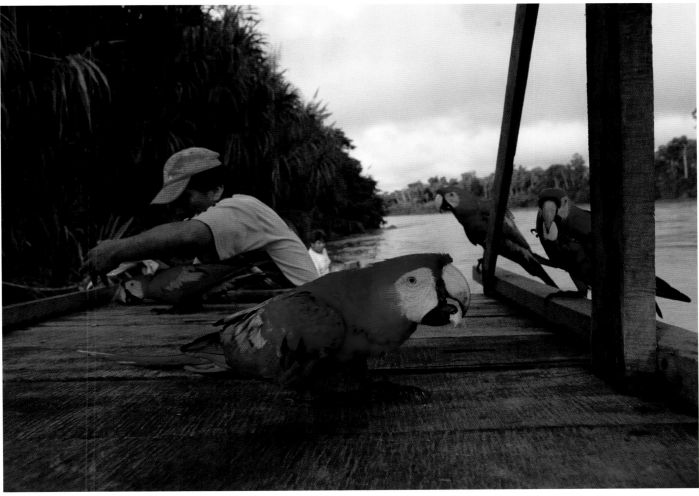

A chatter of budgies
The flock of budgerigars featured
in *Earthflight* (opposite page) was one
of the largest ever filmed.

Scarlet sparklers
Earthflight's scarlet macaws (this page)
had been reintroduced to the wild,
but still had a weakness for sweet biscuits.

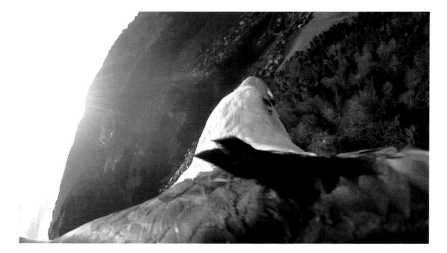

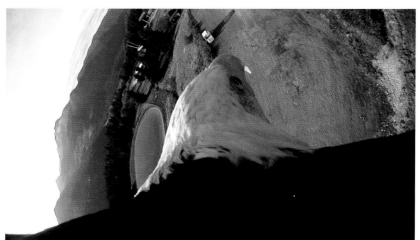

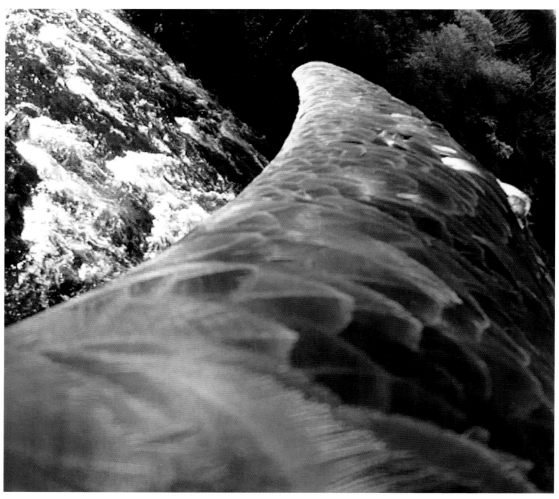

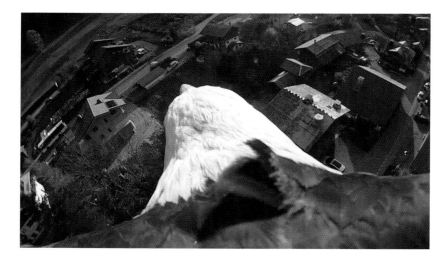

On-board cameras
Eagles, such as the North American bald eagle and the African fish eagle, are big and powerful enough to carry miniature High Definition cameras to give a real bird's-eye view.

PARAGLIDING WITH CONDORS

A reintroduction programme was at the centre of filming with another of South America's iconic birds – the Andean condor. Although we found Andean condors to be more numerous than expected, with sometimes 50 or more in the air at the same time, there were still many places where they're locally almost extinct and condor enthusiasts are reintroducing captive-bred birds to boost the wild populations. One of these locations is Cuzco in Peru, a country whose national bird is the condor, where birds bred from Peruvian stock but reared in Europe will be released into the wild through a collaboration between their Italian trainers and Peruvian biologists.

The aim is to ensure these birds eventually breed in the wild, but it's not simply a case of letting them go; as with similar programmes in Europe, the birds have to be taught basic skills such as flying and how to use thermals and updrafts to soar in the mountains and across the plains. To do this, the Italian team (who just happen to be extreme sports fanatics) have adopted paragliding as the preferred technique. This means jumping off a mountain with a highly manoeuvrable parachute, and gliding or soaring in the way of a wild condor. We had cameras on the Italians' helmets as well as on the birds themselves, and we followed them from the ground with long lenses, witnessing man and bird flying wing-to-wing, with birds and humans actually learning the techniques of flight from each other.

To help the process, the birds were kept in huge aviaries on a cliff side located in what used to be condor country. Huge barn doors to one side were closed initially while the birds became used to their new environment, but were then opened to give access to the outside world. The birds had the security of the enclosure and a regular supply of food, but they were free to explore if they wanted. At first, they would go a short distance and return, but then they would fly increasingly higher and further. The dream is that they never come back again, and go on to breed so once again there will be new generations of wild condors.

FEATHER CONTROL

When we set out on our remarkable journey, we had little idea about where our birds would take us scientifically – in particular, what they would reveal about themselves and the way they work. So it was especially exciting when we found that one of our filming techniques began to reveal things that we normally cannot see. The eye-opener was the way in which birds use their feathers during flight, and the key to this discovery was the development of ultra-lightweight, on-board cameras. It meant that the birds actually filmed themselves, and gave us intimate access to their airborne adventures.

The size of the camera depended on the size of the bird. Large birds, such as Rüppell's griffon vultures, were able to carry a specially adapted HD camera about the size of a matchbox, that weighed little more than 90 g (3 oz). It was attached to a carbon fibre and foam mount, designed specifically for each bird, which was strapped to its back like a tiny rucksack. The harness slipped over the shoulders and around the body, and was put in place very quickly with minimal handling of the bird. Within minutes the bird preened the harness into its feathers, so it was almost invisible, and it quickly seemed unaware that it was carrying anything at all.

Stability was an obvious problem, so we had to study carefully the bird's anatomy, placing the camera in such a way as to minimise it bouncing around when the bird flapped its wings, yet not interfere with normal flight. The camera position was also influenced by the way different birds hold their head while flying, as we wanted to see the bird's head in frame and therefore what it was looking at during the flight. We discovered that eagles, cranes and geese hold their heads out front, while vultures and condors take off with the heads in front at first, but then tuck them underneath when they are airborne.

We were able to vary the angle of view using a remotely controlled tilt-and-pan mechanism. A conventional shot would be with the head in the centre of frame, which is great for a pursuit by a bird of prey, but it could be less interesting when flying over a monotonous landscape. For a more exciting scene, such as flying over the African savannah, the camera could be tilted to one side, so the countryside below was framed by the head on one side and the wing on the other. The camera could also point directly to the side, so you could see along the wing and watch other birds flying alongside, say, in a V-formation or in a single line, and when it pointed backwards we could witness eagles being mobbed by other birds.

The pictures we obtained with these cameras produced a whole load of surprises. When you watch a bird from the ground, for example, you see it flying nonchalantly, looking occasionally from side to side, but the view from the camera on its back shows that it is constantly scanning the ground below, alert to anything significant. And, with a camera mounted on a Rüppell's griffon vulture, we could see the intricate way in which the feathers on its wings and body worked at take off, during flight and on landing.

These birds have a wingspan of 2.6 m (8.5 ft), and mainly ride on thermals. Their blood contains a special protein that makes it incredibly efficient at transferring oxygen to their muscles, and so they can breathe in

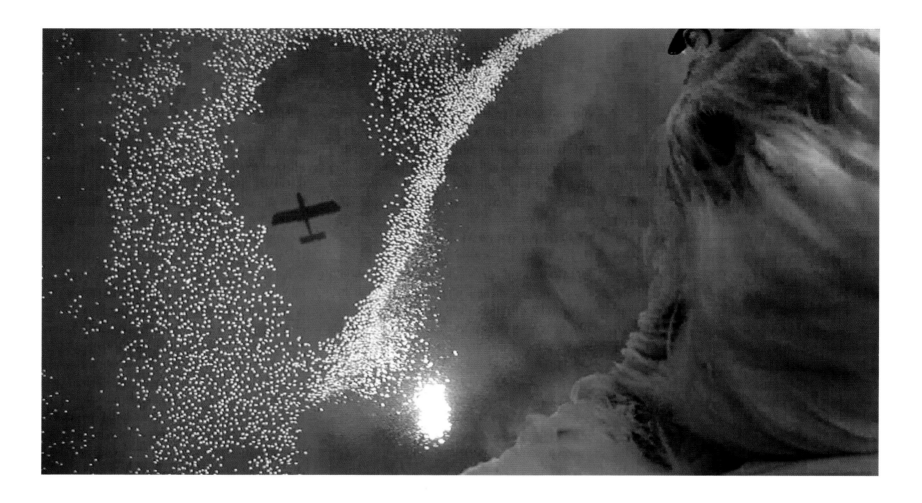

rarefied air and soar regularly at 6,000 m (19,600 ft); in fact, in 1973 a Rüppell's vulture collided with an airliner over Ivory Coast at 11,000 m (36,000 ft), making it the world's highest-flying bird, albeit while soaring rather than using wing power. The footage on our on-board cameras showed what extraordinary control the bird has over its wings and feathers on such an epic flight.

Every feather, we could see, is controlled by muscles and is constantly adjusted to maximise the airflow over the bird's body, thus ensuring maximum flight efficiency. Its tail is constantly moving, sometimes through 180°, a combined elevator and rudder system

that can also be fanned out and lowered to form an airbrake. On the wings, the primary feathers on the wing tip resemble fingers that seem to 'feel' the air as the bird soars, adjusting to the buffeting and turbulence in the columns of rising warm air, while the secondary feathers along the trailing edge of the wing adjust lift and drag.

When the bird came in to land, the on-board camera revealed how it slows to a stop. The secondaries drop like airbrakes, much like an aircraft's flaps, but the big surprise was on the wing's leading edge. All along this edge are what look like simple contour feathers, but as the bird slows down these flicked up, much like

the slats on an aircraft that increase lift at slow speeds. Scientists are now studying the pictures we obtained as part of their study of aerofoil performance to improve aircraft wings.

ABSENT WITHOUT LEAVE

'Patience' was a watchword for our film crews when working with either imprinted birds or those trained in the traditional way by falconers. These birds were flying free so the chances that one might be spooked by something and go AWOL were high, although throughout the filming of *Earthflight* we did not lose a

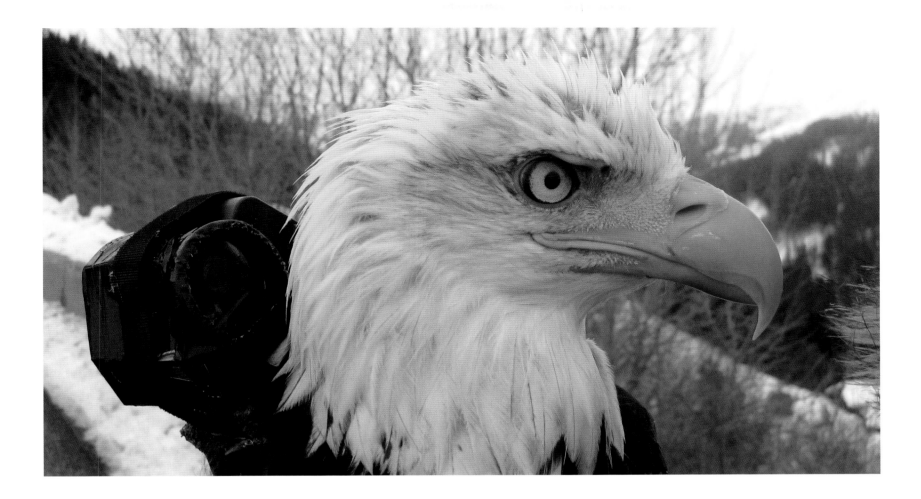

single bird. However, on another 'lost bird' occasion we came mighty close.

One of our camera birds was North America's most iconic – the bald eagle, national bird and symbol of the USA. Taxonomically, it's a sea eagle, but it's found close to large bodies of water right across the continent. It was to be one of our avian guides, so we approached Sutton Avian Research Center (SARC) in Bartlesville, Oklahoma, who were working on the natural history of bald eagles and their reintroduction to parts of America where they were once plentiful. So it was that our producer Rob Pilley found himself at the Grand Canyon with Steve Sherrod and Ryan Vanzant from SARC, together with two trained bald eagles called Bensar and Fiona.

The bald eagle can reach speeds up to 70 kph (40 mph) in powered flight, and dive at a staggering 160 kph (100 mph). On migration it soars on thermals or is carried on updrafts alongside mountains. However, captive-bred birds are unlikely to have experienced any of those effects, so they had to be eased gently into a flight that was to take Bensar and Fiona to one of the world's largest canyons.

At first they were flown from glove to glove over short distances to get them used to the new surroundings and what to them were novel wind and weather conditions created by the canyon; after all, the birds had never flown with 1,800 m (5,900 ft) of turbulent air beneath them. Practice over the canyon proper began with the birds attached to a long cord known as a creance, so that they could get used to updrafts and buffeting winds; but they quickly learned to fly in it.

On the second day, they were ready to fly free, and we could start filming. Fiona made her 300 m (985 ft) hop across the canyon, and Bensar flew along the rim, both birds little distracted by the immensity of the ravine below them. It was a good day. Day three started well, but on his fourth flight someone in the crowd of

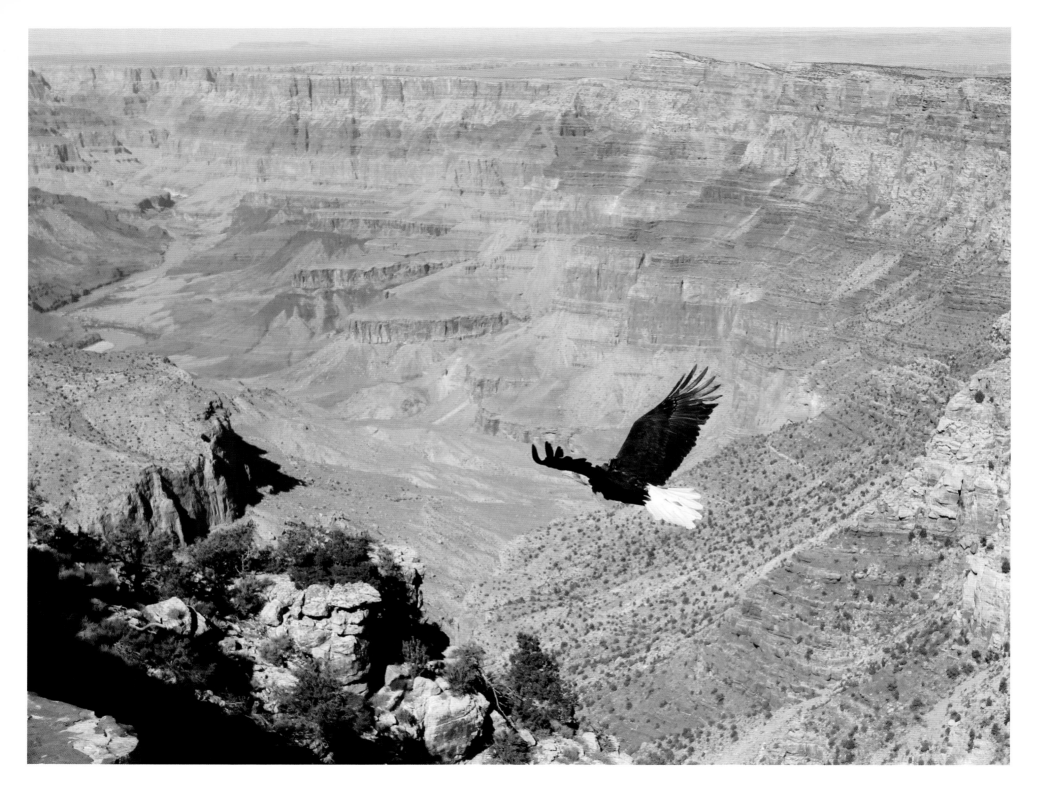

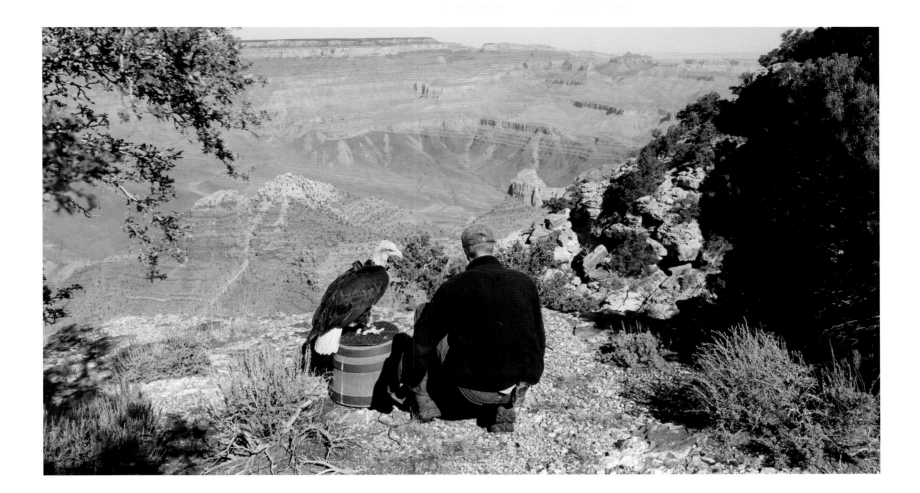

enthusiastic onlookers spooked Bensar and he took off in a wide arc. Under normal conditions, this wouldn't have been a problem. He would circle and return to the glove for a food reward, but conditions here were not what he was used to. Steve and Ryan tried to call him down, and he tried to return, but he was fighting the wind and blown increasingly further away, losing altitude all the time. He eventually disappeared deep into the canyon. Although he wasn't carrying a camera, so the team weren't able to see where he had gone, Bensar was still equipped with a radio tag, and the range finder indicated he was little over a kilometre away – albeit straight down!

With the help of the park ranger assigned to the project they found a precipitous trail that led to the area where the bird should be. About three kilometres (two miles) down the trail the radio signal was strong. Ryan climbed onto a boulder to get a better view and there was Bensar, about 200 m (650 ft) away, sitting in a juniper tree flapping his wings. Ryan put on the glove and called but Bensar's sojourn was not over yet. He flew on, moving into an area with no trail; access was so limited that not even the park rangers had been down there. So, the team went back for camping supplies and, the following day, trekked back into the canyon, making camp for the night with the aim of recovering Bensar the following day.

In the morning, they had the difficult task of clambering down the canyon, but just as things looked good, they clambered over a boulder and were confronted with a vertical drop of over 300 m (985 ft). There was only one thing for it: they had to trek out and find an alternative route. This involved a hike of 35 km (22 miles) over near-impassable terrain.

Ryan eventually found Bensar standing in a creek bed not more than six metres away. Bensar immediately came to the glove, and he was ravenous. It was at this point that Ryan was reminded why it's called the 'grand' canyon: he had to trek back out carrying an enormous eagle. The five-day ordeal was over, and Bensar was safe.

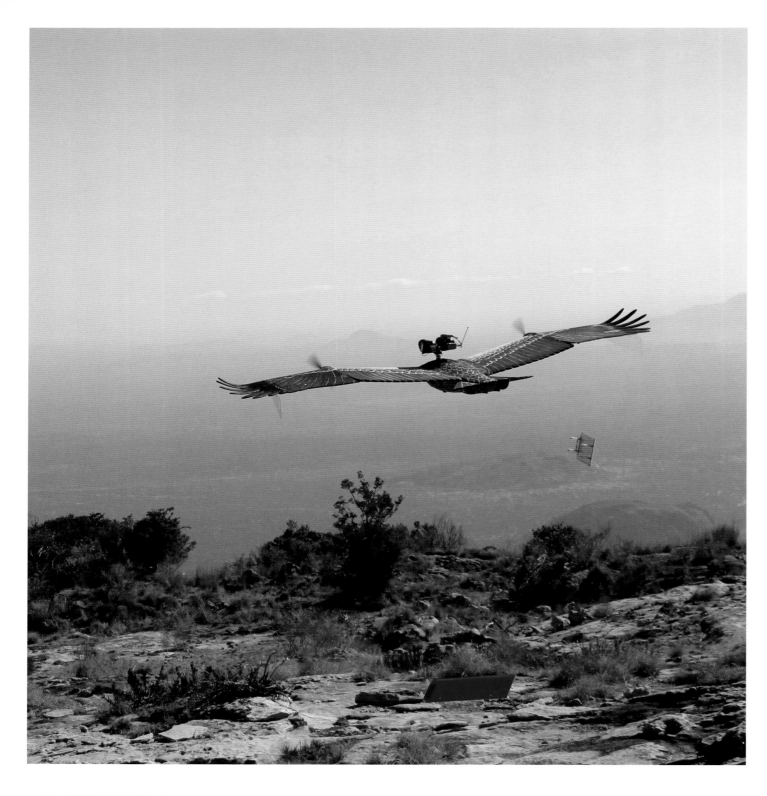

Vulturecam
Bird-shaped model gliders could carry a lightweight camera and be flown with wild bird flocks, giving a unique view of the behaviour of birds, such as white storks on their annual spring migration from Africa to Europe.

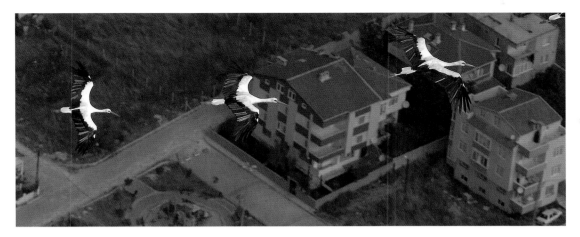
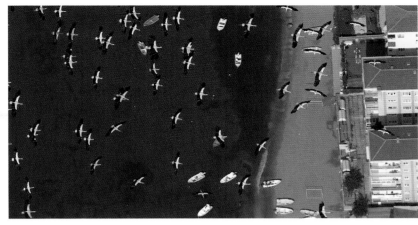

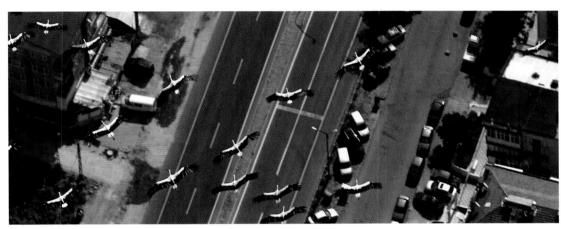
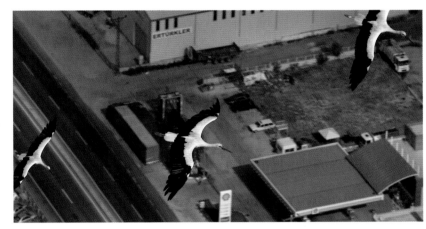

ARTIFICIAL BIRD

Flying with a trained camera bird to obtain a bird's-eye view of a continent was one challenge, quite another was soaring high in the sky with flocks of wild birds. To do this we brought in Malcolm Beard, a scale model-builing supremo. He built 'vulturecam', a vulture-shaped model glider made from strong but lightweight materials, such as carbon fibre, which would be able to fly with the birds. He was pushing the boundaries of what was possible with gliders, and such was the detail of his model that it even had a tail like a vulture and so, to some extent, it flew like the real thing.

These specialist gliders take a lot of time, money and ingenuity to build, so we drafted in another camera wizard, Geoff Bell, to create many of the other remote camera devices that we used. It was with some trepidation that Geoff took a remote-controlled glider to Israel to fly with the storks heading out of Africa and Asia, through the Middle East to Europe. Paperwork and permissions were understandably tough to obtain in such a volatile region, but Geoff's concerns were either the prospect of having his lovingly built kit blown out of the sky by a stray missile or being locked up as a spy – an airborne camera is, after all, a difficult thing to explain to the authorities. As it happens, neither occurred but while

the glider was airborne, unmanned military drones were passing overhead, a constant reminder that conflict was not far away.

Unfortunately, the glider was not in the air for long. It crashed on the first day. Normally this meant an EPH for Geoff – an 'early plane home' – for it's difficult to rebuild such a machine in the field, but on that particular excursion it was the only flying device that we had with us, so it would have meant abandoning the entire shoot. However, as chance would have it, there was a model aircraft enthusiast at the kibbutz in which he was staying, and he helped fix Geoff's plane with balsa wood, glue and the judicious use of gaffer tape.

It looked dreadful, but it flew and Geoff, together with producer Phil, was able to deliver amazing pictures, with the camera right in there among the flocks, with storks above, below and in front, giving us the feeling that we were actually one of the birds.

SNOW GEESE LAKE

The snow goose was another iconic bird that was to play a big role in the North America programme. They migrate each year between wintering sites around the Gulf of Mexico and summer breeding sites in the Arctic, travelling along the flyways than run north to south across the continent. One of their refuelling stops on the Central Flyway is the Platte River in Nebraska, where their arrival is an extraordinary natural spectacle.

It was March when Phil Dalton, Geoff Bell and cameraman Mike Richards arrived to start filming. Winter was still hanging on, with patches of snow and ice around, but when they reached a shallow lake, about three kilometres (two miles) long, it was white not with snow but with a sea of snow geese. The crew have seen some pretty dramatic natural events, but this was the first time they had seen so many birds in one place – it was estimated that there were about three million geese.

While Mike focused on the long lens shots, Geoff piloted his remote-controlled glider over the lake to see the birds from the air – a bald eagle's point of view, for eagles are a major predator. The glider is launched from a ramp and flies straight up, aided by a small motor and propeller, to about 300 m (985 ft), before the motor is cut and the glider sails back to earth. It has wide wings so it can fly slowly, and a camera mounted on the front that beams a guide video signal to the film crew below. Geoff flew the plane from the ground while Phil composed the shots, and they captured some amazing aerials not only of the snowy-white carpet of birds, but also flying within the arriving or departing flocks. However, things were soon, quite literally, to take a dive.

A passing truck spooked the birds and they all flew up together, creating an enormous white wall of snow geese. Geoff lost sight of the glider and was flying blind. Phil tried to guide him using the on-board camera but, by the time the birds cleared, the glider was out of range of the transmitter so Geoff lost control. The glider nose-dived into the lake, with the unique HD pictures the camera had taken stored electronically in the camera. It had to be recovered.

Fortunately the lake was very shallow, and the glider's tail plane could be seen sticking out of the surface of the water. The team moved out gingerly onto the ice, breaking through when it became too thin and wading through the freezing water to the stricken glider. The nose and camera were embedded in soft mud, but Phil was determined to recover the pictures. The video card was extracted and put in another camera, but the pictures were still in the original camera's memory. There was only one thing for it: the camera had to be dried out and reactivated. As luck would have it, the download was successful, but only just: a few seconds later the camera shorted out and that was that. During the three years of production there were many moments like that, obtaining shots by the skin of our teeth, because the devices we've been using are cutting edge. It was the price we sometimes had to pay for pushing technological boundaries to capture the breathtaking shots that we so desperately wanted.

BATTLING BUREAUCRACY

We visited every continent in the world except Antarctica, and were three-and-a-half years in the field. With such an undertaking, planning by the production team based in Bristol – Anna Thomas, Margaret Pitt and Emma Ballinger – was paramount. It meant mountains of paperwork and hard-to-obtain permissions. We flew trained birds over London, New York, Paris and Venice, as well as many other well-known landmarks – cranes over the châteaux of the Loire Valley, brent geese over Mont-Saint-Michel, and barnacle geese over Edinburgh. We were breaking new ground, using techniques that were hard for a layperson to comprehend and a challenge for any bureaucracy we encountered. Our determination could also lead to some bizarre situations.

In New York, for example, Rob Pilley and cameraman Neil Rettig were on the Hudson River filming imprinted snow geese flying in front of the Manhattan skyline, when the bird with the on-board camera lost sight momentarily of the camera boat. It spotted a tourist boat and flew down, but realising its mistake it made for some rocks to rest. However, these were not ordinary rocks: the bird had landed on Liberty Island, right next to the Statue of Liberty.

Rob soon discovered that retrieving the bird from this security hotspot would not be as easy as it seemed. When he went to the police station on the island to ask permission to land, the welcome was decidedly frosty. Rob was given a telephone number to ring and ordered to move his boat at least 45 m (150 ft) away before dialling it. When he finally rang the number the same policeman answered. Rob again asked for permission to land, which was abruptly denied.

Eventually, the police decided they would retrieve the goose themselves and a huge police cutter was called into action. The goose, meanwhile, had left the rocks and was under the pier. At this point, common sense prevailed and the police cutter hove to and, realising

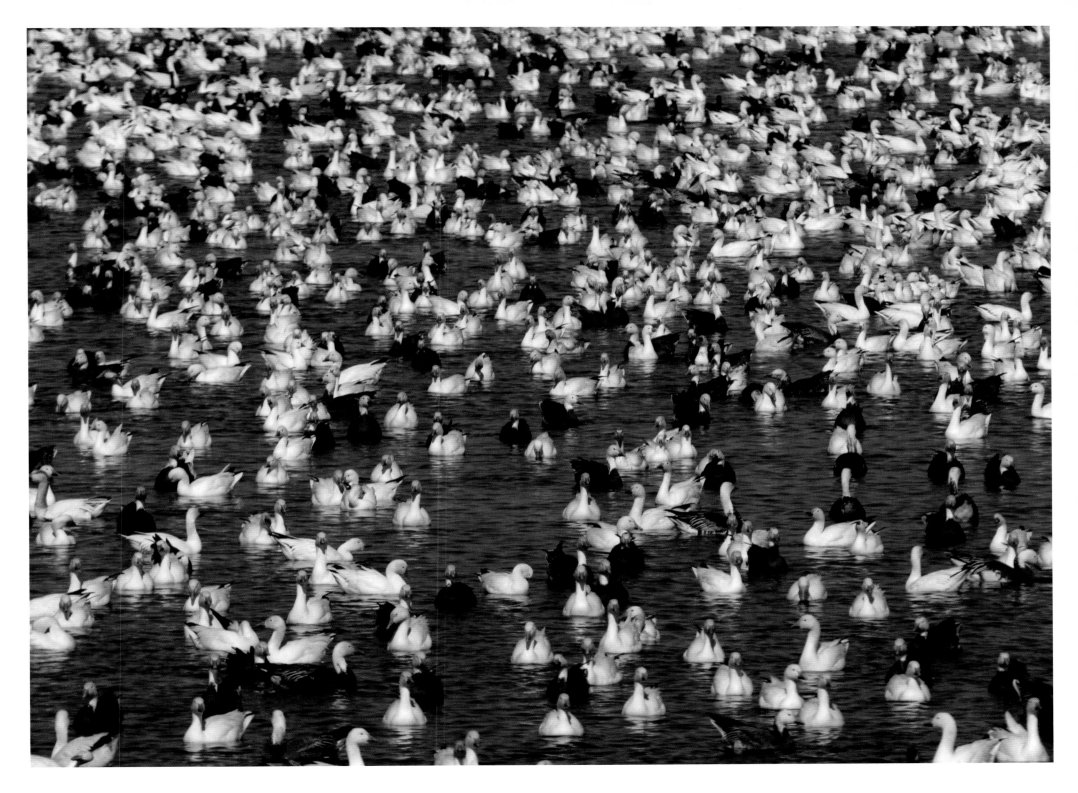

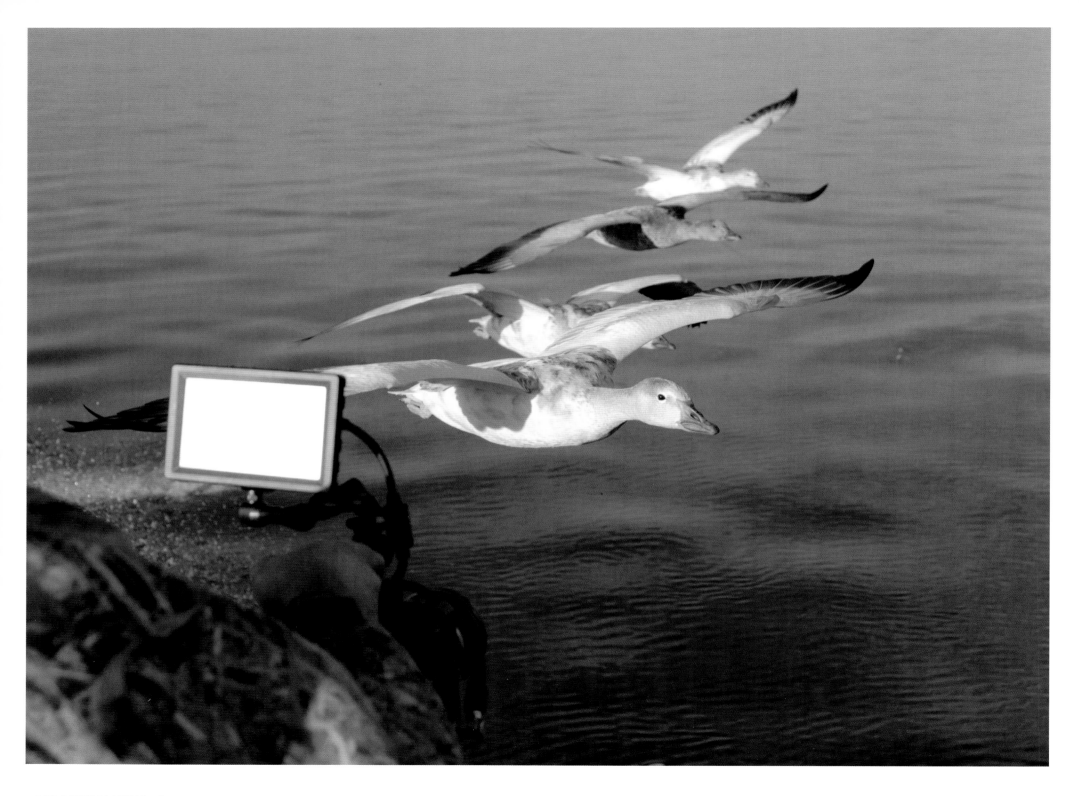

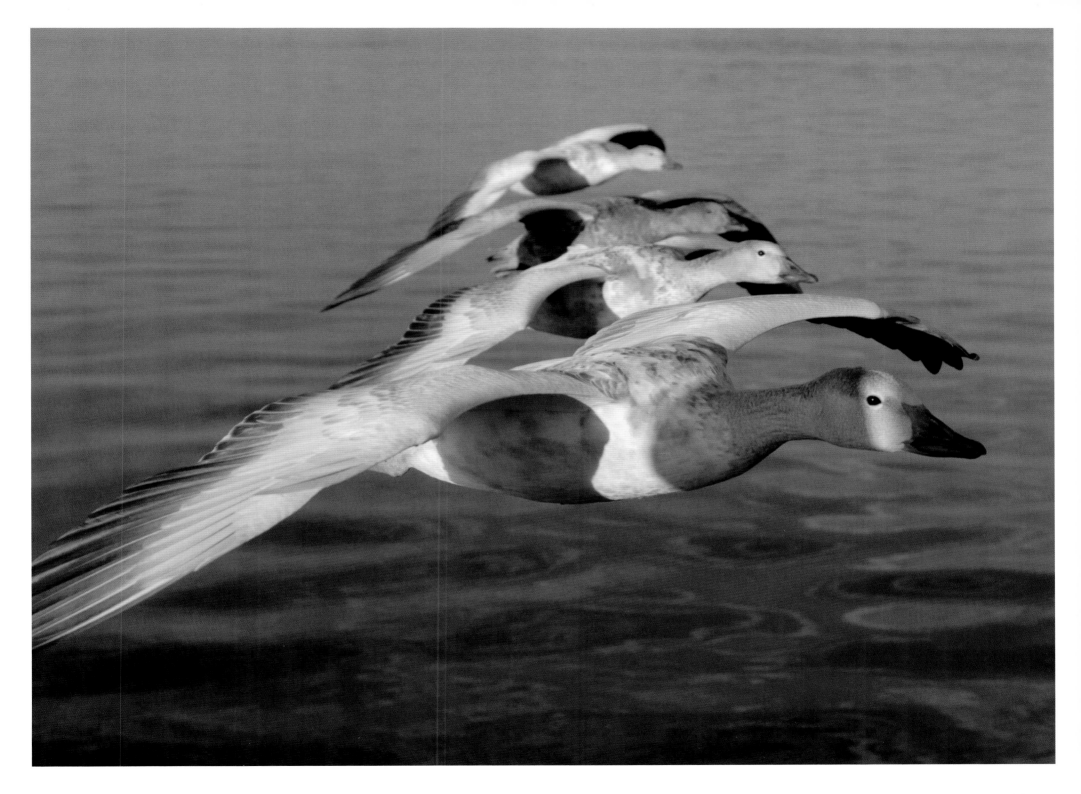

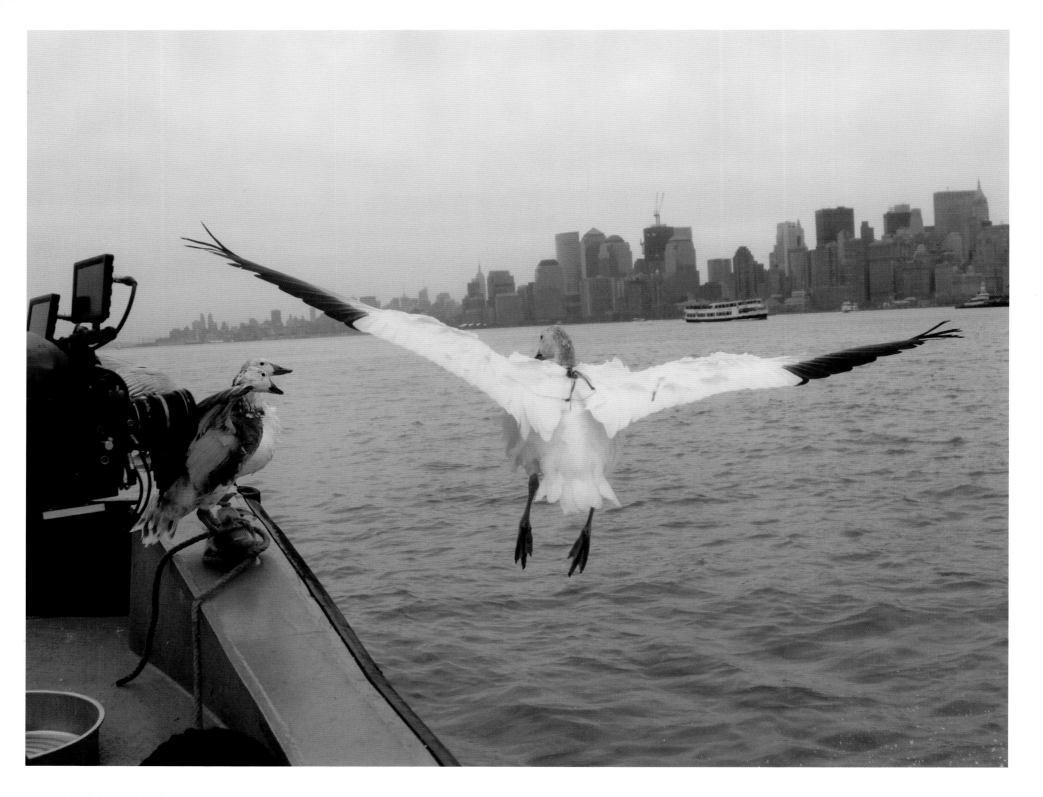

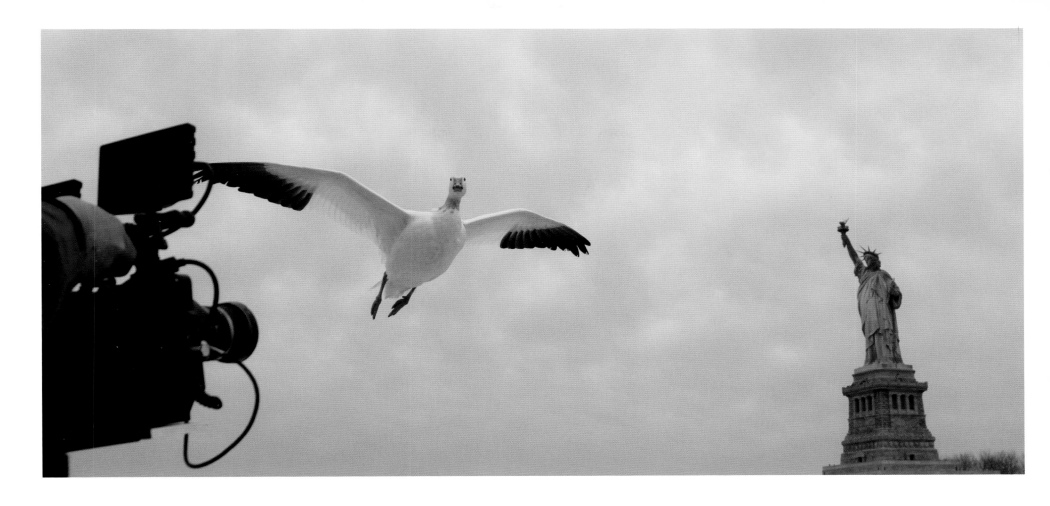

they didn't have the expertise to capture the bird, took Rob to collect the valuable goose, which he did with due ceremony and to a standing ovation from watching tourists, while the on-board birdcam caught most of the action – all from the goose's point of view.

H5N1

Restrictions of a different kind hit us unexpectedly when embarking on another shoot with trained birds, this time in the Himalayas. We wanted to be in Nepal to document the migration of demoiselle cranes through high mountain passes. We had already filmed spectacular material of wild flocks being attacked by golden eagles and peregrines as the cranes struggled against the weather to make it to the other side. But we also wanted to supplement this material with intimate shots obtained with our own imprinted birds. All the paperwork had been completed and permissions obtained – months of work – but it all came to nothing. We were victims of the dreaded bird flu. There was a spontaneous outbreak in Nepal a few days before we were due to set off. Even if we'd been allowed to take our birds in, restrictions meant that we would not have been able to take them out again, so Nepal was suddenly not an option for filming.

Bird flu was to curtail work several times during the filming period, and we had to be clear where we could go and when. Even though we might have all the relevant paperwork – export and import permits and veterinary certificates – each country has its own rules. So, if we had been filming in a country in which bird flu had been declared, no camera bird would have been able to leave, even though it was in full health and didn't have the disease. The border would be effectively closed. And, even if the restrictions were raised, the original country might not want to take the risk and would prevent the birds from returning home. It meant that we either switched locations, or waited for everything

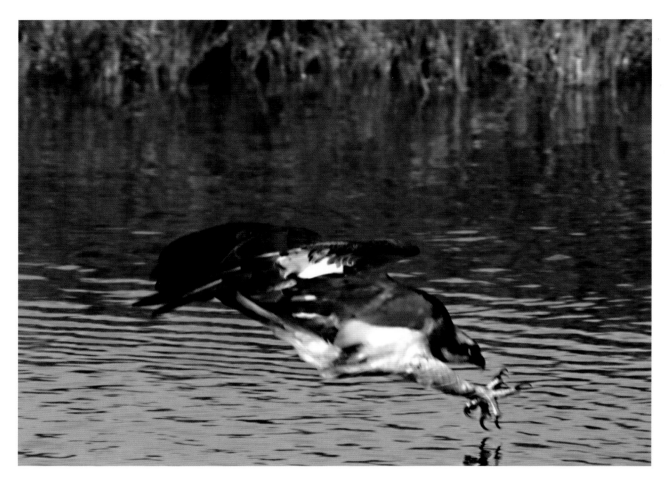

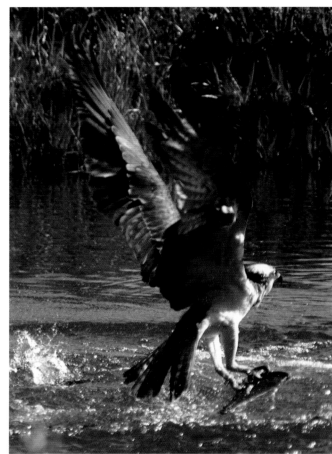

to die down, which could take months. It was a very frustrating scenario and one that was completely beyond our control.

OSPREY FARM

Thankfully, the filming process wasn't always this trying, and we occasionally came across some unexpected places that made our lives easier rather than more difficult. Filming wild ospreys catching fish is difficult at the best of times, but we wanted to film them from many different angles in ultra-slow-motion in order to capture the action in as much detail as possible. A fish farm

in Finland was to be our salvation. Wild ospreys had become such regular visitors here that the management had decided that, rather than try to scare them away or discourage them from coming, they would set aside one of their ponds for them to use. It meant that there were more pairs of ospreys nesting in the area than in the rest of Finland. At breeding time, when they were feeding young, upwards of 80 ospreys visited during a single day, with well over 100 fish catches in a morning. Our high-speed cameras captured mesmeric images as the birds almost submerged to pluck fish from the water. Sometimes they'd reappear with not one fish but two, one in each talon.

RESEARCH SUCCESS

Filming ospreys catching fish was one of those rare moments when difficult behaviour suddenly became easy to capture, but usually being in the right place at the right time requires considerable research. When Rob Pilley sent cameraman Mike Richards to film the mass emergence of mayfly on the Tisza River, a tributary of the Danube in Hungary, success would be totally dependent on the quality of the information he had unearthed. Mike was there to film slow-motion footage of sand martins catching the mayflies, but his biggest problem was one of timing. The mayflies spend

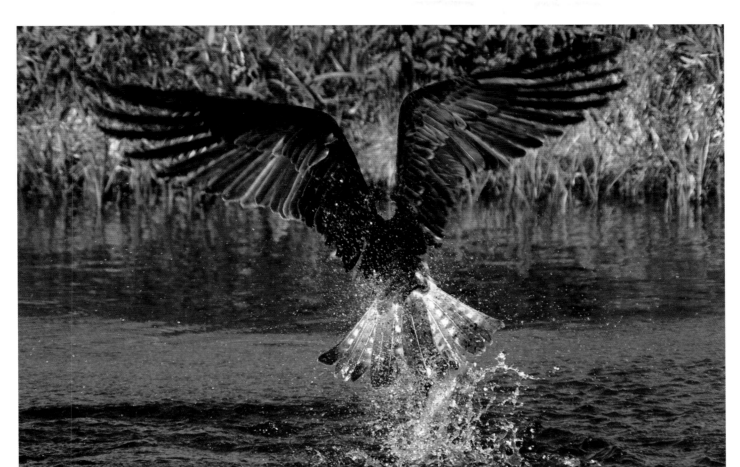

most of the year as aquatic larvae that live in the fine silt on the riverbed, but, come spring, they emerge in huge clouds as adult flies that swarm over the water, a fleeting natural event that occurs over just a few hours in late spring. Until now, there was no way of knowing when the mayflies would appear, but research by Dr Bela Kiss of BioAqua in Hungary showed that the mass emergence depended on the temperature of the water. It has to be precisely 21.5°C (70.7°F), so, instead of waiting around for days or even weeks as other film crews have done in the past, by monitoring the water temperature we were able to predict exactly when and where the mayflies would appear.

We also found that the water warmed progressively upstream, so instead of just a single emergence, by tracking the temperature, we were able to predict at least ten mass emergences at various points along the river. It meant that cameraman Mike Richards filmed over 40 perfect catches, all shot with high-speed cameras; a neat solution to what should have been a very challenging shoot.

UP TO HIS NECK

On many occasions – and it goes with the patch – our production teams have found themselves in uncomfortable situations, and none more so than when producer Phil Dalton was at Bracken Cave in Texas, with cameramen Neil Rettig and Mike Richards. They had taken the trip to film the huge numbers of bats that fly out each night, and the predators that catch them. Peregrines, red-tailed and Swainson's hawks were captured on high-speed cameras. The crew saw the bats drop like stones as the raptors attacked, but many were caught. Swainson's hawks were the most successful, sometimes grabbing a bat in each talon, and even transferring one to its beak and catching a third.

Towards the end of the shoot Phil and Neil were able to enter the main roosting chamber, where a shaft

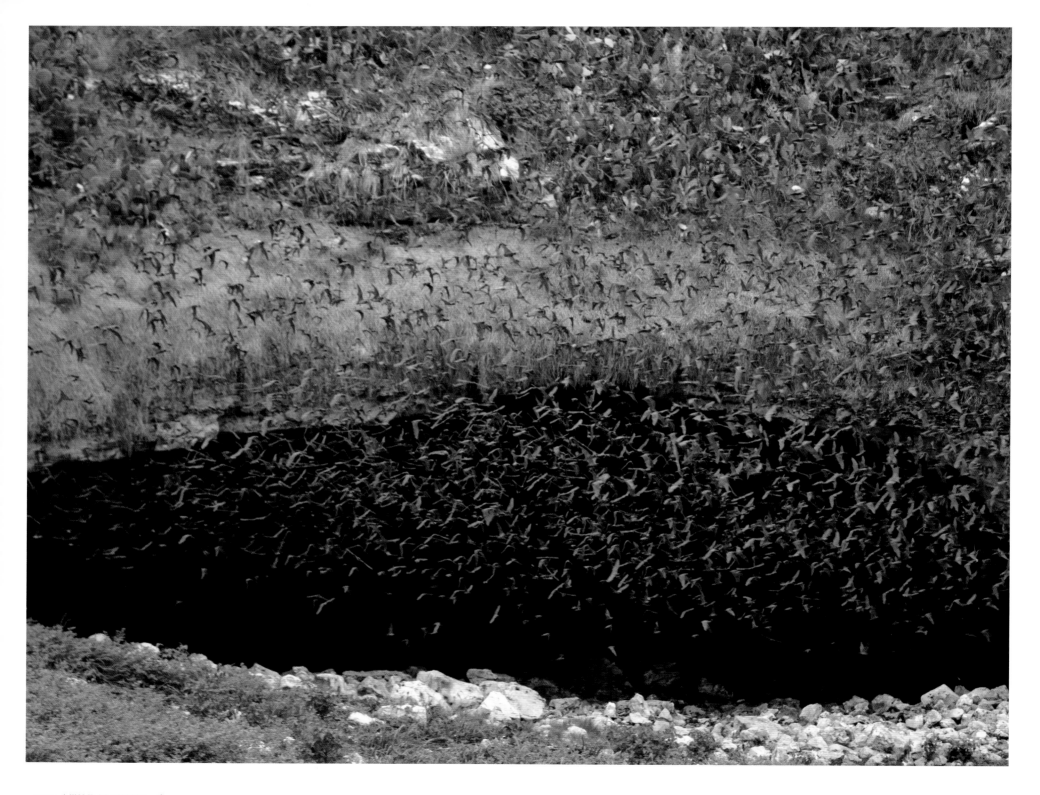

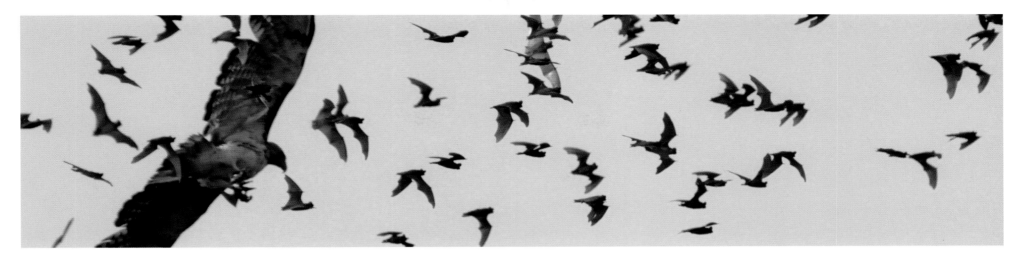

drilled through the roof once enabled miners to haul up guano – bat excrement – traditionally used as a fertiliser. The old shaft brought a beam of light into the cave, which was just enough to film with light-sensitive cameras. So, accompanied by a guide, they made their way into the passageways that led to the main chamber at the back of the cave system. They each wore a paper suit, tall rubber boots and a facemask with filters to screen out the ammonia, bat urine and other nasty odours in the cave. However, the filters lasted about 40 minutes, and then needed to be replaced to prevent suffocation.

Inside it was very hot and humid, and the trio had to wade through first ankle-deep and then almost knee-deep semi-liquid guano on which lived flesh-eating beetles that devoured any dead bats that dropped from above. There was a cloud of urine in the air and it rained mites, which got everywhere. The noise was deafening, and shining a torch at the roof revealed bats packed into every available space. It was not a place for the faint-hearted.

They got their shots, while beetles nipped at any bare skin, and by the time they were preparing to leave the filters of both Phil and Neil were beginning to clog and breathing was becoming difficult.

'I began to feel dehydrated and dizzy,' remembers Phil, 'but when we'd walked about 20 m (65 ft), I turned and noticed our guide wasn't with us. He was stuck in the guano, and couldn't get out. It was like quicksand, and he was sinking fast. We had to go back and help, by which time my ears were ringing and my fear was that I'd pass out and fall into the guano, where I vividly imagined I'd be consumed alive by flesh-eating beetles. The more we pulled, the deeper he got, but eventually we pulled him out minus his boots. I had to use all my willpower to get to the cave entrance, but when we were out I ripped off my mask and took in the most beautiful lungful of air ever.'

PURE LUCK

It's not unusual for wildlife camera-people and their production teams to work in hazardous situations, sometimes with dangerous animals and in unforgiving terrain. However, knowing the biology and behaviour of the subject helps keep people safe, and being with the right guides means that we know how to behave. Good planning and risk assessment ensure that measures are in place if something should go wrong. Despite all this, the weather, floods, droughts, and animals not

appearing when they should can scupper the best-laid plans. Budgets these days are so tight that there's no chance of going back, and it's not unusual for a shoot to yield less than has been hoped for. Nevertheless, there are just a few occasions when luck is on your side.

Wildlife cameraman Alastair MacEwen went to Svalbard to film polar bears raiding the nests of barnacle geese. It was a long boat ride to the nesting islands and, knowing the behaviour would be difficult to film (as far as we know, it hasn't been filmed for television before), he was to stay there for three weeks in order to stand a chance of capturing the shots that we wanted of this amazing spectacle.

He arrived late afternoon and was unloading the boat, when he spotted a polar bear swimming out to an island with nesting geese and other birds. He grabbed his tripod, quickly set up the camera and, surrounded by mobbing terns and skuas, he filmed the bear raiding the nests. The very thing he'd come to film was completed that afternoon, in less than an hour, and he phoned in to an incredulous production office with the immortal words, 'it's in the can!'

Alastair stayed on to get more shots – close-ups of the birds, and their eggs and chicks – and although he saw a couple more bears, he didn't even catch a glimpse

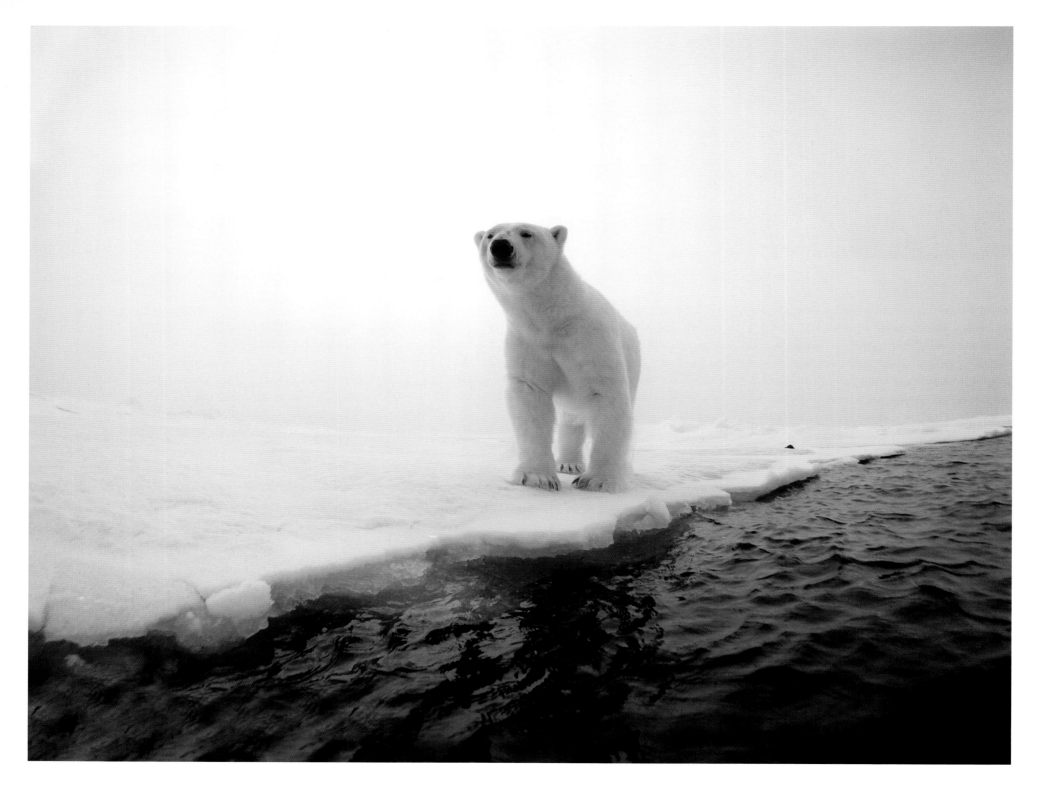

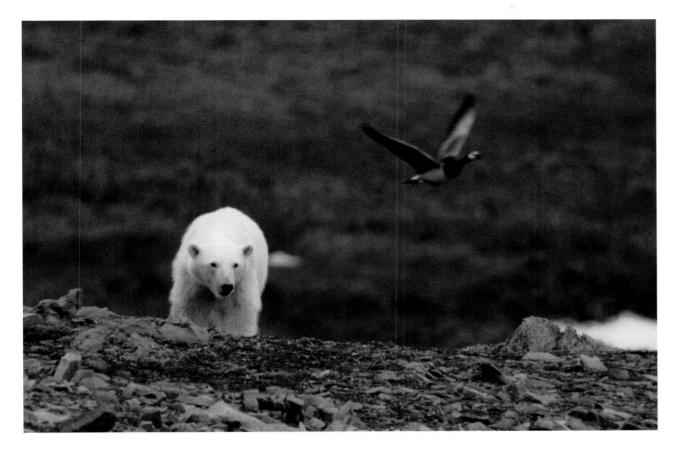

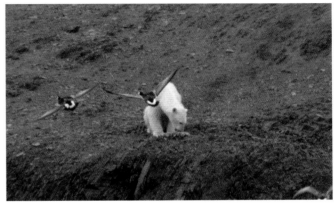

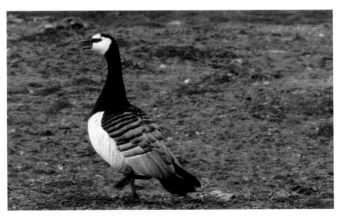

Nest robbers
Polar bears in the Svalbard Archipelago have taken to raiding the nests of geese, terns and gulls. For the geese, it means that an entire year's breeding can be wiped out.

of any more raiding for the rest of the time he was there. Now that really is luck.

All in all, the making of *Earthflight* has been a monumental undertaking – nearly five years from beginning to end. Here, we've only been able to touch on some of the breathtaking experiences that came and went over those years. We haven't mentioned, for example, how California gulls forsake the Pacific coast and head inland to Mono Lake in the middle of the desert to feed their chicks on flies, or how African fish eagles gather over the drying Okavango to catch flapping catfish concentrated in receding waterholes, or how millions of waders time their arrival at Delaware

Bay on America's Atlantic coast to coincide with the emergence of horseshoe crabs that lay their eggs in the sand. All amazing spectacles, and just a few examples of the ingenious survival techniques practised by a huge variety of birds, across the world.

To fly with birds has squeezed every ounce of ingenuity from our teams, no matter their task, and along the way we discovered not only how remarkable birds really are, but also how dedicated people are trying to keep them that way. From sailing over the Himalayas with bar-headed geese to plunging into the sea with hungry gannets off the coast of South Africa, it has been a privilege to enter the world of birds, and in doing so to view the world in a totally new way.

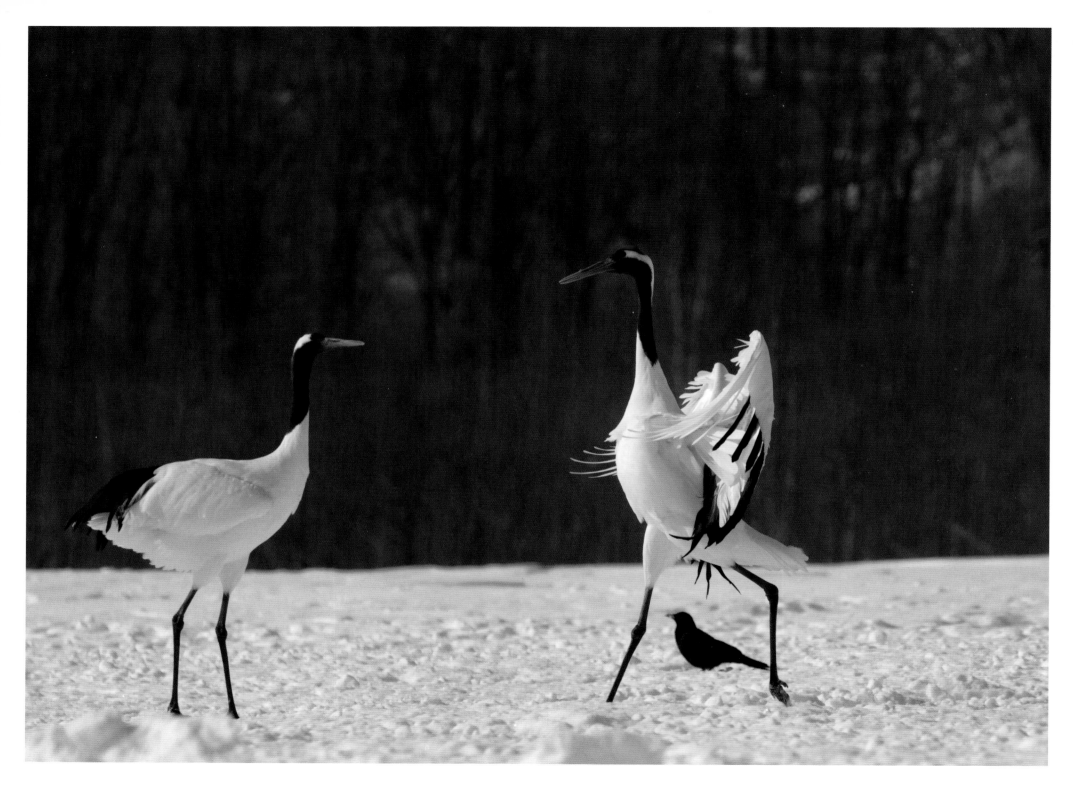

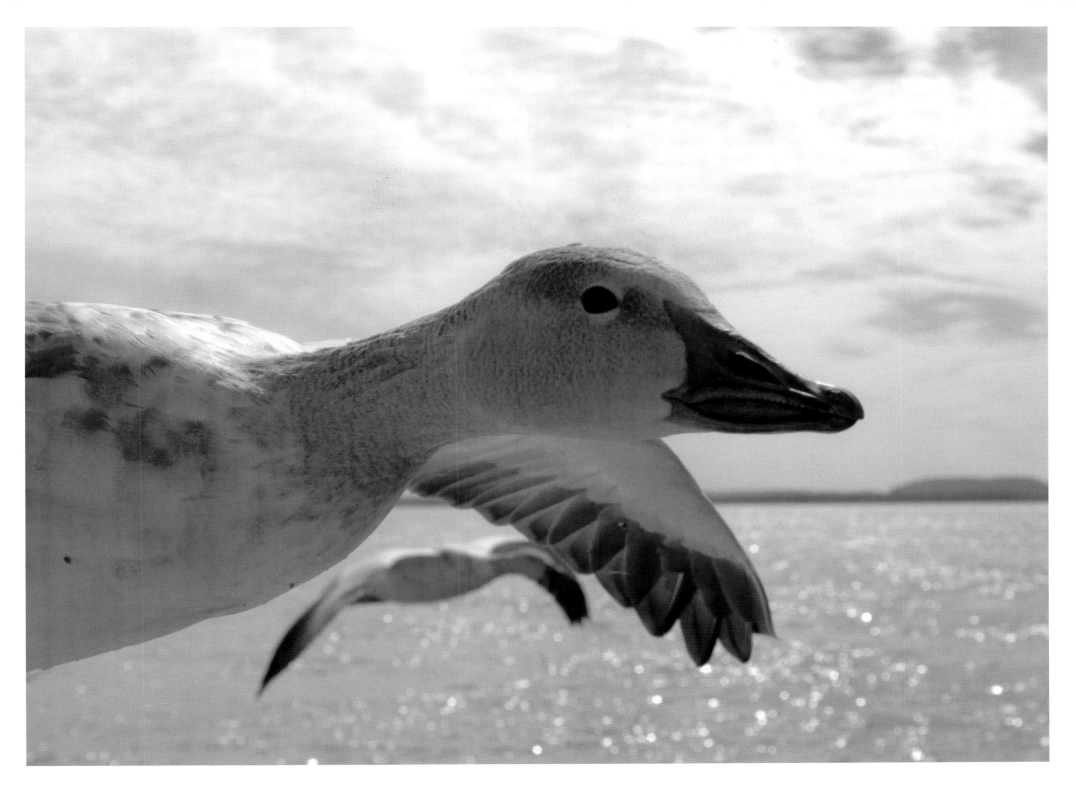

INDEX / ACKNOWLEDGEMENTS

ACKNOWLEDGEMENTS

Earthflight could not have been made without the contribution of many talented individuals. Some are acknowledged within the text or in the picture credits but on almost every shoot we have been given help and guidance from many different people. It would be impossible to thank them all but I would like to mention William Kimosop for his help filming flamingos, Laura Rettig, Keith and Sue Beseke for rearing snow geese. Andy Payne for his work with budgies and lorikeets. Suhail Gupta for arranging all our shoots in India and Paul Firetto for his wonderful work there with pigeons.

Of the camera team, Michael Richards deserves special thanks as he has been the mainstay cameraman across the whole project. Geoffrey Bell and his son Martyn have created many of the specialist camera devices. Microlight cameraman Richard Cook deserves praise for taking aerial filming to new heights. Richard Jones filmed many of the important sequences in Africa. Alfredo Barroso helped capture some extraordinary behaviour in Mexico. Neil Rettig made a big contribution to North America and Jim Clare took care of much of South America. The film Editors, Stuart Napier and Imogen Pollard are also due a special mention and Anna Fuller and Sam Taylor have dealt with the technical challenges of extracting and processing the digital files.

I would like to reserve special thanks for my own team who were responsible for the success of the completed project. Producers Philip Dalton, Rob Pilley, Tilly Parker and Assistant Producer Matthew Gordon have worked tirelessly to capture the remarkable imagery and it would be impossible to overestimate their contribution. Philip in particular has spent many hours sorting through the many thousands of pictures we have captured and has been instrumental in many of decisions made on the book's layout and design.

This core team has been supported by some of the best production staff imaginable. Head of Production Anna Thomas, Production Managers Margaret Pitt and Emma Ballinger, and Researcher Huw Williams have worked many long hours, often at short notice, to keep the show on the road. Despite all the pressure they never let us down and we truly couldn't have done it without them.

Lastly, I would like to thank my wife Sara and my son Rory for their tolerance of the times either my body or my mind was absent while working on this project.

John Downer

PICTURE CREDITS

2 © Christian Moullec
4 © Christian Moullec
7 © Christian Moullec
10 Matthew Gordon
14 Philip Dalton
17 Christian Moullec
18 Michael W. Richards
19 Richard Cook
20-21 Christian Moullec
22 Christian Moullec
24 Philip Dalton
25 Michael W. Richards
27 Christian Moullec
28 John Downer
29 © Christian Moullec
30 Richard Cook
32 Michael W. Richards
33 © Michael W. Richards
34 Michael W. Richards
35 (top left, top right, bottom right) Michael W. Richards
35 (bottom left) Neil Rettig
36-37 Christian Moullec
38-39 Christian Moullec
41 Christian Moullec
42 Michael W. Richards
43 Philip Dalton
44 Richard Cook
45 Christian Moullec
46 Richard Cook
47 John Downer
48 © Christian Moullec
49 Christian Moullec
50 Christian Moullec
52 Philip Dalton
54-55 © Philip Dalton
58 Mark Payne-Gill
59 Michael W. Richards
60 Richard Matthews
61 Michael W. Richards
62 Richard Jones
64 Geoffrey Bell
65 Richard Jones
66-67 Philip Dalton
68-69: Philip Dalton
71 Philip Dalton
72-73 Rob Pilley

75 Rob Pilley
76-80: Rob Pilley
81 Michael W. Richards
83 Rob Pilley
84-85 © Angie Wilken
86-87 Michael W. Richards
88 Michael W. Richards
89 © Lloyd Edwards
90 Gordon Hiles
91 Michael W. Richards
92-93 © Alexander Safonov
94-95 Rob Pilley
96-97 Richard Jones
101 Mark Payne-Gill
102-103 © Mark Payne-Gill
104-105 Marcus Hunter
106 Marcus Hunter
107 Marcus Hunter
108 Michael W. Richards
109 John Downer
110-111 Philip Dalton
113 Philip Dalton
114-115 Adam Fox
116 Rob Pilley
118-119 Rob Pilley
121-123 Rob Pilley
124 Michael W. Richards
125 Philip Dalton
126-127 Sam Taylor
128-131 Rob Pilley
132-133 Philip Dalton
135 Philip Dalton
138-140 Jim Clare
141 Rob Pilley
143-144 Jim Clare
145 Michael W. Richards
147 Philip Dalton
148 Jim Clare
150-151 Jim Clare
152 Jim Clare
153 Philip Dalton
154 John Downer
156-159 John Downer
160-161 Philip Dalton
162 John Downer
166-168 John Napper
169-171 © Lindsay Cupper

172 John Napper
173 Matthew Gordon
175 Christian Moullec
176 © Rajendra Suwal
177 Christian Moullec
178-179 Michael W. Richards
181-182: John Downer
184 John Downer
185 Geoffrey Bell
186 Geoffrey Bell
188 John Downer
189 (top left, bottom right) John Downer
189 (top right, bottom left) Philip Dalton
191 © Dr Anil Kumar Chhangani
192 © Dr Anil Kumar Chhangani
193 John Downer
194-200 Michael W. Richards
202 © Christian Moullec
204 (left) Richard Cook
204 (centre) Andy Kemp
204 (right) Philip Dalton
206 © Christian Moullec
207 (left) © Christian Moullec
207 (right) Philip Dalton
208 © Christian Moullec
209 John Downer
210-211 Michael W. Richards
212 Christian Moullec
213 © Lindsay Cupper
214 (left) © Lindsay Cupper
214 (right) John Napper
215 John Downer
216-221 Rob Pilley
222 Rob Pilley
223 Richard Cook
225 Michael W. Richards
226-227 Matthew Gordon
228-229 Rob Pilley
230-231 Michael W. Richards
232-233 Philip Dalton
234 Philip Dalton
235 Alistair MacEwen
236 Michael W. Richards
237 Neil Rettig
240 © Philip Dalton

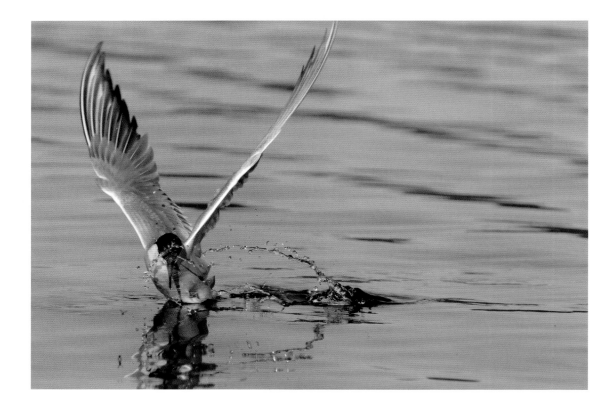

This book is published to accompany the TV series *Earthflight*, produced for the BBC by John Downer Productions Ltd and first broadcast on BBC1 in 2012. Executive producer: Cassian Harrison.

Producers: Philip Dalton, Rob Pilley, Tilly Parker and Matthew Gordon
Series producer: John Downer

10 9 8 7 6 5 4 3 2 1

Published in 2011 by BBC Books, an imprint of Ebury Publishing.
A Random House Group company.

The Random House Group Limited Reg. No. 954009

A CIP catalogue record for this book is available from the British Library.

Addresses for companies within the Random House Group can be found at www.randomhouse.co.uk

ISBN 9781846079733

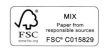

The Random House Group Limited supports The Forest Stewardship Council (FSC®), the leading international forest certification organisation. Our books carrying the FSC label are printed on FSC® certified paper. FSC is the only forest certification scheme endorsed by the leading environmental organisations, including Greenpeace. Our paper procurement policy can be found at www.randomhouse.co.uk/environment

Commissioning editor: Muna Reyal
Project editor: Joe Cottington
Designer: Charlotte Heal
Production: David Brimble

Colour origination by XY Digital Ltd
Printed and bound in Italy by Printer Trento S.r.l.

To buy books by your favourite authors and register for offers, visit: www.randomhouse.co.uk

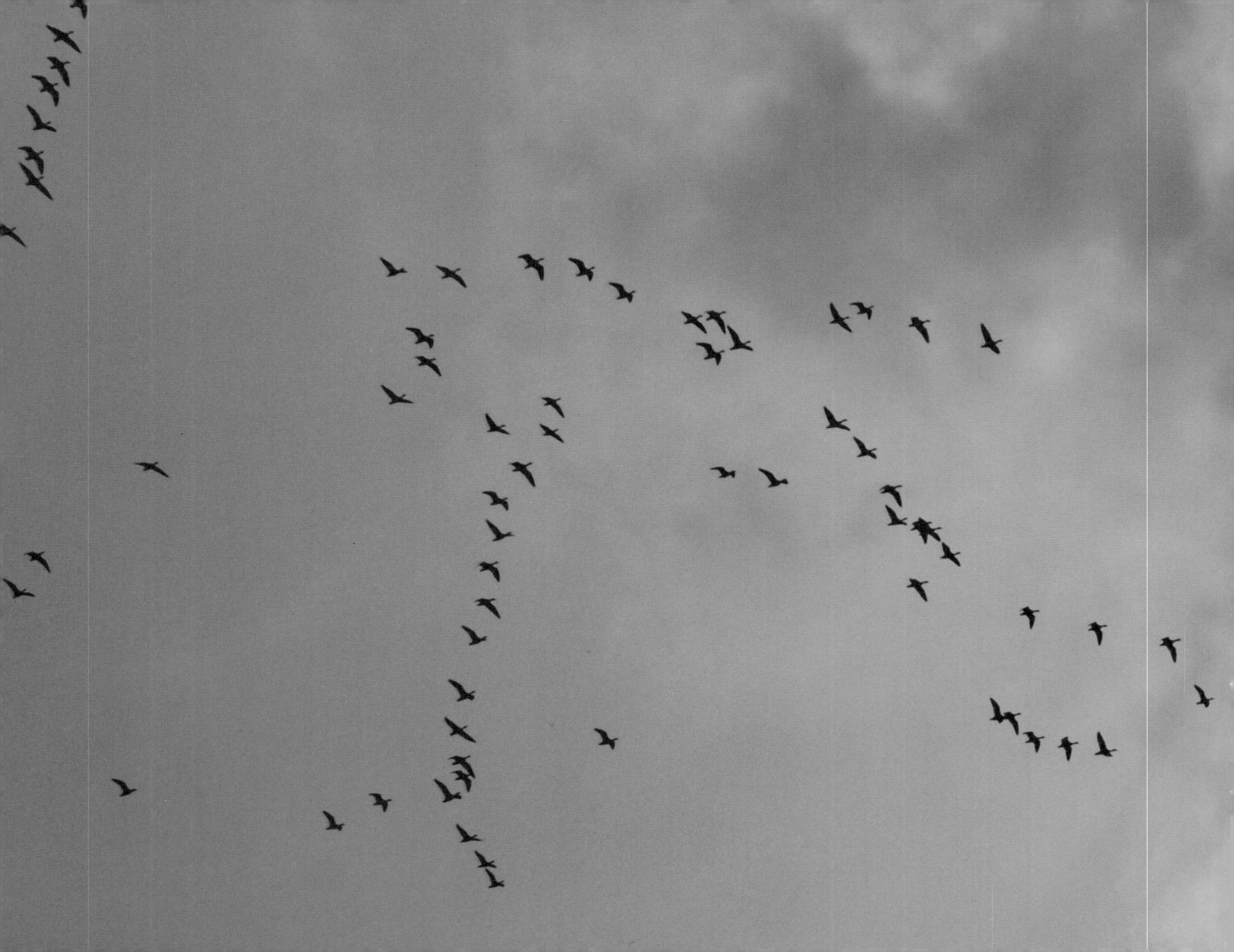